Acts of Growth

# Acts of Growth

*Development and the Politics of Abundance in Peru*

**Eric Hirsch**

Stanford University Press

Stanford, California

Stanford University Press

Stanford, California

©2022 by Eric Hirsch. All rights reserved.

Printed in the United States of America on acid-free, archival-quality paper

Library of Congress Cataloging-in-Publication Data

Names: Hirsch, Eric (Eric Michael), author.

Title: Acts of growth : development and the politics of abundance in Peru / Eric Hirsch.

Description: Stanford, California : Stanford University Press, 2022. | Includes bibliographical references and index.

Identifiers: LCCN 2021026501 (print) | LCCN 2021026502 (ebook) | ISBN 9781503630215 (cloth) | ISBN 9781503630949 (paperback) | ISBN 9781503630956 (epub)

Subjects: LCSH: Economic development—Social aspects—Peru—Caylloma (Province) | Economic development—Social aspects—Peru—Espinar (Province) | Rural development—Peru—Caylloma (Province) | Rural development—Peru—Espinar (Province) | Indians of South America—Peru—Caylloma (Province)—Economic conditions. | Indians of South America—Peru—Espinar (Province)—Economic conditions.

Classification: LCC HC228.C26 H57 2022 (print) | LCC HC228.C26 (ebook) | DDC 338.985/32—dc23

LC record available at https://lccn.loc.gov/2021026501

LC ebook record available at https://lccn.loc.gov/2021026502

Cover photo: Mural in Chivay, Peru. Eric Hirsch

Cover design: Rob Ehle

Typeset by Newgen in 11/13.5 Adobe Garamond Pro

# Contents

# Acknowledgments

This book owes its existence to a vast network of generous interlocutors, mentors, colleagues, friends, and co-conspirators. First among these is the community I have been working with in Peru over repeat visits since 2008, a time when they became all of these things. Gerardo Huaracha and Luisa Cutipa have been enthusiastic, encouraging hosts who quickly became shadow academic advisers. Their adult children, Sabino, Guzmán, María, Nestor, Maruja, and Alan, and their extended family made me feel welcome in Yanque. So did Yeny Huanaco Huerta, Dante Bayona, and their children, Renzo and Leandro, who became fast friends as we ate meals together almost every day when I lived in Yanque. Rogelio Taco, Ana Carol Condori Palma, Mercedes Mercado Gonzalez, and scores of other development project participants have stayed in touch, fielded my endless questions, and accentuated my feeling of welcome. Further thanks go to the development workers, from office directors and researchers to field agents, who took time out of their busy workdays to speak with me, orient me to their projects, and connect me with their colleagues, including Liliana Suni, Freddy Panuera, Lilia Samayani, Rafael Hanampa, Lady Sihuay, Claudia Viale, Mónica Pradel, Liliana Zamalloa, and, especially, Werner Jungbluth and Fabiola Dapino. María Benavides offered me her time and insights in Lima; I am grateful for her deep knowledge of Yanque. Mirta Casaperalta Taco facilitated research in Yanque. Thanks also to the Municipalities of Yanque and Lari in the Colca Valley for offering their permission and support for my ethnography, with institutional affiliations. During the urban portions of my research, I was sustained by conversations with Kyle Jones,

Diana Steele Jones, Emily Culver, and Kristen Heitzinger in Lima and María Ángela Deglane in Arequipa, whose introduction to the city's theater scene helped inspire some of this book's conceptual vocabulary. My research in Peru was facilitated by academic affiliations with the NGO Center for Studies and Promotion of Development (Desco) and its Arequipa division, Descosur, and I acknowledge the help of its leadership, particularly Eduardo Toche, Oscar Toro, Rodolfo Marquina, Delmy Poma, and Desco president Molvina Zeballos. I was also affiliated with the Andean Studies Program at the Pontificia Universidad Católica del Perú and thank director Marco Curatola for his energetic support.

The ideas that went into this book have been percolating since before I can remember this as a single project, but they began to come together in the anthropology department at the University of Chicago. There, Jean Comaroff, Alan Kolata, William Mazzarella, Justin Richland, Kaushik Sunder Rajan, Julie Chu, and Joe Masco helped me shape these ideas, and Anne Ch'ien was a vital force in moving this project forward. I also received feedback and advice from Hussein Agrama, Judith Farquhar, Susan Gal, and Stephan Palmié. As the project took shape as a book, Jean Comaroff and María Elena García generously read drafts of the manuscript. Florence Babb, Laura Graham, and Fabiana Li read the manuscript and then joined me for a comprehensive book manuscript workshop. I thank them for the time and effort they put into helping me develop this project. Their critical feedback and close engagement would have been significantly labor intensive even without a pandemic upending our lives. I thank the Office of the Provost at Franklin & Marshall College for supporting the workshop.

Over the years, my work has been steeped in a network of colleagues and friends who joined me in writing groups and conference audiences and at coffee shops on multiple continents. A special thanks to the following colleagues for direct feedback on the manuscript: Stephanie Bernhard, Andrea Ford, Cameron Hu, Kyle Jones, Meghan Morris, Tom Özden-Schilling, Jeremy Siegman, Jay Sosa, Yana Stainova, and Joey Weiss Leathem. I received generous advice on the publishing process from Chelsey Kivland and Canay Özden-Schilling. Thanks also to Andrew Brandel, Hannah Chazin, Jonathan DeVore, Nate Ela, Bill Feeney, Kate Goldfarb, Stefanie Graeter, Shane Hall, David Kneas, Erik Levin, Amy McLachlan, Erin Moore, Gregory Duff Morton, Jay Schutte, Samuel Shearer, Daniel Tubb, Xiao bo Yuan, and my many other fellow travelers over the years. Our engagement has been a source of both critical challenge and collegial spirit-lifting.

I have had the chance to share aspects of this book with audiences at multiple institutions, including the McGill University Anthropology Department and Institute for the Study of International Development, the Environmental Humanities Forum at Salisbury University, the Geography Department at Portland State University, and the anthropology departments at Cornell University, George Washington University, Harvard University, the University of California–Irvine, the University of Iowa, and the London School of Economics. I also presented this research in Peru to members of Desco, as part of the Andean Studies Program lecture series at the Pontificia Universidad Católica del Perú, and at that program's annual academic retreat in Pisac, Peru. Thank you to all of the faculty members, students, and conference attendees who engaged with my work. In this broader network of colleagues, I extend my thanks to Mike Cepek, Mike Chibnik, John Comaroff, Marco Curatola, Julia Elyachar, Lisa Gezon, Kevin Healy, Tracey Heatherington, Jean Jackson, Graham Jones, Katina Lilios, José Antonio Lucero, Bruce Mannheim, Bill Maurer, George Paul Meiu, Mercedes Niño-Murcia, Susan Paulson, Ted Powers, Frank Salomon, Suzana Sawyer, and Mark Schuller for their helpful and incisive feedback. This book also applies lessons from earlier wonderful teachers in the social sciences and humanities: Karen Barkey, Claudio Lomnitz, Rosalind Morris, David O'Connor, Petro Macrigiane, Evelina Zarkh, and Joan Lisecki.

This research has received vital institutional and financial support. It would not have been possible without the Postdoctoral Fellowship in Global Governance at the McGill University Institute for the Study of International Development, a fellowship supported by the Erin Jellel Collins Arsenault Trust. Special thanks to Ismael Vaccaro, who facilitated my fellowship, and to Kristin Norget, Erik Kuhonta, Iain Blair, and Sheryl Ramsahai, who made returning to McGill for a second fellowship year a seamless process. At McGill, Manuel Balán, Oliver Coomes, Eduardo Kohn, Sonia Laszlo, Catherine Lu, Ron Niezen, Colin Scott, Lisa Stevenson, and Daviken Studnicki-Gizbert conversed with me over coffee and facilitated stimulating exchanges and public talks in Montreal. Kate Bersch, Moyukh Chatterjee, S. P. Harish, and Weeda Mehran were great companions in the Peterson Hall postdoc office. Late-breaking support came from the University of Iowa's Obermann Center for Advanced Study, where a residential fellowship afforded me a much needed dose of virtual community as I finished this book. Special thanks, as well, to the University of Iowa Department of Anthropology.

I received support for fieldwork from the following generous sources: the Wenner-Gren Foundation; the Mellon Foundation Hanna Holborn Gray Fellowship; the Fulbright-Hays Fellowship; the Inter-American Foundation; a research grant from the UC Irvine Institute for Money, Technology, and Financial Inclusion; the Social Science Research Council; the University of Chicago Center for Latin American Studies and Department of Anthropology; and the Hackman Scholars Fund and the Office of College Grants at Franklin & Marshall College. My Quechua-language study at the University of Illinois at Urbana-Champaign, taught by the famed instructor Clodoaldo Soto Ruiz, was supported by a Foreign Language and Area Studies Fellowship. This book has its earliest roots in a semester abroad in Peru with the School for International Training, led by Lima-based writer Irma del Águila; I could feel my initial research questions brewing in discussions with Yonit Bousany and Maeve Cornell-Taylor.

At Franklin & Marshall's Department of Earth and Environment, I have had the pleasure of being steeped in a world of exciting interdisciplinary scholars and stellar students. Advice, conversations, and work breaks with the following colleagues were sources of intellectual sustenance as I wrote: Melissa Betrone, the late Michael Billig, Carol DeWet, Ramon Escudero, Kostis Kourelis, Giovanna Faleschini Lerner, Mary Ann Levine, Stephanie McNulty, Dorothy Merritts, Jennifer Orgill, Scott Smith, Jim Strick, Ryan Trainor, Mark Villegas, and Bob Walter. I could not ask for better environmental studies partners than Eve Bratman and Elizabeth DeSanto. Department chairs Andy DeWet and Chris Williams kindly went out of their way to help facilitate this writing. I am grateful to the five Franklin & Marshall student research assistants who joined me on my 2019 trip to Peru, where they put in significant legwork to help me conclude the fieldwork for this project: Andrea Corilloclla, Nancy Le, Katie McCarthy, Lia Tavarez, and Matthew Turetsky.

It has been a pleasure to work on this book with the capable guidance of editor Kate Wahl at Stanford University Press. I also thank production editors Jessica Ling and Charlie Clark, assistant editor Caroline McKusick, the rest of the publishing team, and two anonymous peer reviewers. Any errors or oversights in this book are my own.

The final phase of writing and revising this book took place during the COVID-19 pandemic. It is important to acknowledge the invisibilized laborers and care workers who are fundamental to the success of any sustained writing project in this historical moment. Our political energies must be devoted to correcting the injustices and vulnerabilities that these workers face.

My family has been a source of support and love from the beginning. I thank my parents, Susan and Bruce Hirsch, for their unceasing encouragement, and my brothers, Zachary and Jacob Hirsch, for being there too. My grandmother Harriet Cohen has been a source of inspiration, as has the rest of our beautifully oversized brood. I also thank the Hocks, my new chosen family. Lauren Hock has been the ideal life partner. Her relentless commitment to helping me create space for this writing, her intellectual engagement, her logistical enthusiasm for our various schemes, and her ease with a wide smile are sources of a deep and sustaining joy. This book is dedicated to the memory of Benjamin Ziegelbaum.

Acts of Growth

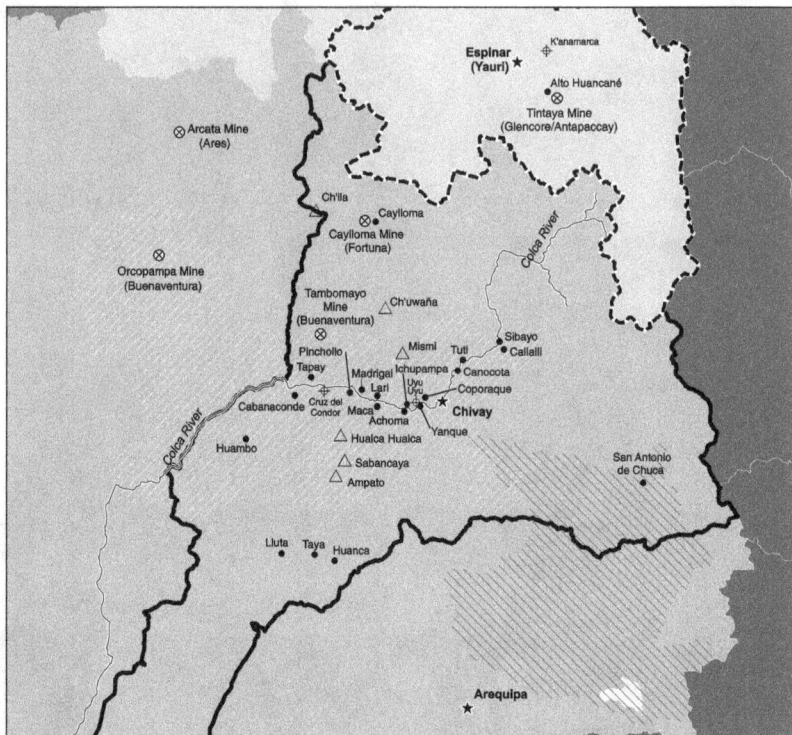

**MAP:** Caylloma and Espinar Provinces. Prepared by Angela Collins.

# Introduction

## The Richest Country in the World

**"NATURAL!" SEÑORA ELENA CALLED,** over the music of the brass band, her voice hoarse. "And typical!" Next to her, fellow villagers from Taya danced for the competition judges, flowing skirts and ponchos accentuating their movements through the open plaza of the market town of Chivay, in southern Peru. Elena continued her narration: "This is how we dance in Taya!"

I stood in the crowd gathered for that day's entrepreneurship contest, taking in the sights, sounds, and scents that made the scene about so much more than business plans. This atmosphere was engineered to overwhelm the senses. I saw Elena, microphone in hand, beside her fellow villagers, singing and narrating to make sure we in the audience felt the joy of Taya's annual Carnival celebration. She wore a yellow scarf decorated with multicolored confetti ribbons over a bright orange blouse that cut through the cool blue Andean morning.

Elena,[1] a beekeeper and Taya entrepreneurial leader, held the floor before project staff and hundreds of villagers, regional leaders, and other visitors. The three-year state-funded Sierra Sur (Southern Highlands) investment in rural entrepreneurs was drawing to a close. To celebrate, its staff held a spectacular competition, compelling participants to perform a sense of newfound plenitude. What explains Elena's tired voice? Just before leading the dance, she *also* had to give a sober technocratic presentation of the income-generating opportunities that project staff taught Taya residents to squeeze out of the "natural resources" that, as staff framed it, they did not even know surrounded them. Elena repeated the words *natural* and *typical* across her presentation, pitching Taya as a place rich in environmental and cultural assets. Here was Elena's inventory of how Taya residents were transforming newly discovered resources into income:

> Guinea pig care, beekeeping, quinoa seeding, dairy products . . . fried guinea pig (*cuy chactado*), which is Taya's typical, natural dish. So with Sierra Sur's support for raising our guinea pigs, we have improved . . . and over there [pointing to her village's booth at the edge of the plaza], we have prepared it for you to taste.

I later found Elena standing by that emblematic dish, where she asked me to take her team's picture (Figure I.1). It was part of Taya's entry into the gastronomy portion of the contest, which represented the conspicuous result of a transformation from raw material into potential profit—from "natural" and "typical" into "marketable"—in a moment of high global demand for Peruvian food. Elena was beaming over a sumptuous spread from Taya that hardly fit the table: hot orange peppers, apples, pears, juices, chewy cheeses encased in a salt-rich red skin, honey, toasted corn kernels, samples of different quinoa strains, a hulking cake covered in sweet creamy

FIGURE I.1: Señora Elena (center) and the Taya team.

frosting, and two indulgent platters of fried guinea pig that luxuriated over a bed of fried eggs.

Imagine how Taya's displays overwhelmed the senses. Now multiply this across fourteen village teams who brought bullet-point presentations, dances, fragrant delicacies, and other diverse emblems of a rural abundance. By engineering scenes that inundated the senses, scenes where economic growth could be *felt*, Sierra Sur staff members were sending a message: The rural Andes is teeming with riches. And it is Andeans' responsibility to make use of them. In project director Lilia Samayani's words, their work was to make sure that villagers "are maximizing the resource potential of their region." Given the resource potential surrounding even infrastructurally marginalized villages such as Taya, the message went, there was no reason to redistribute national wealth to aid rural Peruvians. Instead, all development agents had to do was teach villagers how to extract the riches that would unleash *their own* growth.

Looking more closely, I could see how much work this supposed unleashing actually entailed. Making use of apparently undiscovered treasure in their midst often meant engaging in exhausting physical labor. Performing a sense of growth and abundance before a public audience involved even more affective labor. Even the energetic Elena was drained as she embodied, at once, the figure of traditional dancer, capable entrepreneur, and master chef.

Development projects and state programs had been working to alleviate poverty here in the Andes' Caylloma Province since the 1970s, when rural modernization projects proliferated all over Peru under the imperative of "market penetration."[2] But in 2014 the Sierra Sur project did not see any poverty left to alleviate. According to project staff, villagers were *already* wealthy. The drought-prone southern Andes was not a site of unforgiving cold, reluctant earth, and climate change but a terrain full of potential, teeming with *future* capital capable of extending Peru's already spectacular growth.

I could not escape that same message when, during my fieldwork five years later, and right down the street from Chivay's plaza, a mining lobby representative invited me to tour a temporary exhibition on the benefits of formal mining. Open to the public, the exhibition was staged by Peru's national extractives lobby in a brand new, elegantly appointed building. Consisting of sleek infographics, videos, and ore samples, this display also told its audience that Peru was full of riches. The exhibition signaled that Caylloma was an emerging frontier of mining. Indeed, new concessions granted to Buenaventura, Peru's largest mining company, surround Chivay and extend west along the Colca River. Mining operations have just begun in the downriver village of Tapay. Espinar Province, immediately to Caylloma's north, is home to the expanding Tintaya copper mine. As they drive Peru's astronomical but uneven national growth, mining companies are aggressively exploring these terrains, approaching the southern Andes much like Sierra Sur does: as a source of latent prosperity, a "bench of gold" whose inhabitants are, inexplicably, living like paupers.[3] Carla, the staff member who guided me on my tour, walked me through displays that expressed how vital Peru's mines are for almost anyone who has used an Apple computer or a shovel or fertilizer. Other graphics conveyed just how important mining profits are for Andean jobs and municipal budgets. One display showed how mining companies' generous corporate social responsibility programs happily supported entrepreneurial activities, such as weaving, ecotourism, and gastronomy, foregrounding "typical" emblems of local ethnic identities for the market.

In both encounters, growth was *staged*. Staff on these seemingly distinct projects curated the southern Andes as a space of wealth. As they did so, they privileged a new kind of wealth extractor: the Indigenous entrepreneur, empowered to search out the "natural" resources in their midst and transform "typical" dimensions of daily life into sources of income. Any indicators I had seen that suggested high poverty or inequality in the southern Andes were, staff asserted, actually signs that wealth had not been extracted yet.[4] This insistence draws on a neoliberal logic made famous around the world by Peruvian economist (and 2021 presidential candidate) Hernando de Soto. De Soto found apparently poor countries such as his native Peru to be "teeming with entrepreneurs," but "their assets [were] dead capital,"[5] seemingly going to waste in Peru's vast informal economy. Representing the everyday world as an inexhaustible bundle of resources and painting rural dwellers of the Andes as its future extractors, these projects intertwined the extractive and productive dimensions of Peru's economy in unexpected ways.

The approach that staff at both the development contest and the mining exhibit took to staging Peruvian wealth as potent but latent reflects the influence of a national branding campaign that plays on the country's long-standing historical association with raw material. Launched in 2011 out of the high-end New York advertising firm McCann-Erickson, Marca Perú (which can be translated into English as "Peru Brand" or "Peru™")

sells the country's multicultural heritage, sensuous gastronomy, bountiful geology, and vast biodiversity to tourists, foodies, and foreign investors alike. To convey Peru's unique wealth, Marca Perú relies on emblems of Andean indigeneity, such as guinea pigs and alpaca fashion.[6] Peru is not merely a promising emerging market but rather, according to the brand, an "Empire of Hidden Treasures" and, in the words of a more recent slogan, "The Richest Country in the World."

Development in these encounters, then, was not really a way to help poor people or the means to equitably distribute a nation's bounty. It was a method for unearthing wealth that already existed. This book follows that unearthing. Scholars have critiqued sustainability projects and ethnicity-focused entrepreneurship for their narrow focus on capitalist solutions to systemic problems. Critical development researchers find that such projects often perpetuate the poverty that they are ostensibly trying to alleviate.[7] Environmental studies scholars, meanwhile, attend to the impoverishing violence of extractivism,[8] and some political scientists read mass deprivation in resource-rich countries as an inevitable result of the so-called resource curse.[9] In this book I offer a distinct approach to the structural inequalities of boom-time capitalism by moving beyond questions of poverty. How might our understanding of development, indigeneity, and capital shift when we start, instead, from the problematic of wealth?

This book is an ethnography of growth. It takes place at the expanding edges of Peru's mining economy. I followed the daily work of composing a sense that Peru is growing in a rural region where few villagers have seen their lives materially improve during a mining boom. The book is situated in a network of marginalized agricultural villages, such as Taya, in the Andean provinces of Caylloma and Espinar, a frontier of both cultural branding and mineral extraction with the dramatic Colca Valley at its center.[10] Residents of Caylloma and Espinar did not previously tend to identify as Indigenous, but between the ethnodevelopment projects and mining ventures of the 2010s, they faced calls to revitalize their pre-Inca Collagua, Cabana, and K'ana heritage as a growth-ready subjectivity, appropriating themselves as new raw material for capitalist prosperity. Locating the book here answers María Elena García's recent call for scholarship on prosperity and accumulation in Peru to look beyond Lima, the capital city where Peruvian wealth is dramatically concentrated.[11] My focus on the hunt for raw material brings me to the distributed rural networks of lopsided bounty and dispossession that characterized Peru in the booming 2010s.

Drawing on fieldwork during Peru's commodities boom and plateau between 2008 and 2019, I follow the face-to-face interactions that outsiders mobilize to transform small-scale economic development projects into capitalist growth in Peruvian mining country. I also contextualize how attachments to place and the nonhuman world in the southern Andes confront political and emotional attachments to the promises of resource extraction. The first two chapters juxtapose two local arguments about Andean wealth that are continually in tension: the colonial thesis that the Andes is a site of riches to be discovered and appropriated (Chapter 1), and the argument villagers articulated to me that Andean plenty is not a collection of resources to be found but rather a condition earned through cycles of care, labor, and obligation (Chapter 2). Situated within that space of tension over what wealth means, the following three chapters delve into specific investment projects that worked to coax growth into being by extending Peruvian prosperity beyond the mining sector to a new generation of rural entrepreneurs.

I argue that these growth projects had two broad aims. First, they reframed development work from a *redistributive effort to alleviate poverty* to the *management of resource abundance*. Second, they worked to fix indigeneity as a way of life *complementary* to Peru's mineral-driven wealth instead of as a concept to mobilize against it, in a place where the definition of "Indigenous" was contested. To development workers, a successful Indigenous-branded enterprise should not just coexist with the nearby mine. Rather, it should be the result of a parallel plunder in which every aspect of daily life might be recast as raw material for new growth. In other words, these investments positioned an idealized entrepreneurial Andean indigeneity as the cultural framework for a newly inclusive resource exploitation.

An analysis of development work that starts from wealth instead of poverty opens distinct roads into understanding economic life at the diffuse margins of extractive industry. The capitalization of nature might be one such road. The commodification of culture might be another. However, in this book I focus most directly on the overlooked question of what it means to grow. Growth is a concept that is at once literal, metaphorical, and indexical of capitalist regimes of expertise and accumulation. I want to know how villagers and development workers relate to economic growth, see it, know it, feel it, represent it, critique it, and attempt to embody it. Reading growth as an *affective* project that requires ongoing physical and emotional labor, I follow staff and villagers through the exhausting work of making an economy look and feel like it is growing. By attending to the face-to-face encounters that development projects engaged in to materially and semiotically transform daily life into a collection of extractable resources, I foreground the everyday contradictions of living at the margins of a mining boom.

## Extractive Care

Is extraction empowering? Is empowerment extractive?

In *Acts of Growth* I find resource extraction and the contemporary effort to empower rural Andeans as entrepreneurs to be fundamentally coproduced endeavors. The projects that I followed worked to extend Peru's resource wealth beyond its prolific but cloistered mines by building the *sense* that Peru was a space of abundance. In these projects, some of them funded by mines, I found development agents engaging in a repertoire of face-to-face encounters, including staged competitions, site visits, public exhibitions, and one-on-one counseling sessions. These pedagogical encounters were scenes of compassion. Agents knew their villager participants well. They would offer empowering pep talks and coach them through life choices, genuinely rooting for their success. But the underlying purpose of these validating encounters was the curation of a generation of entrepreneurs skilled in extracting profit from the immediate world around them.

I theorize this approach to development work as a project of *extractive care*: the nurturing of marginalized bodies, livelihoods, ecosystems, terrains, and worlds in a way that ultimately primes them for extractive capitalism by transforming them into resources. Extractive care entails a hold over someone or something that is at once tender and violent. It is an intimate but ultimately instrumental nurturance that furthers extractive projects. Extractive care can also describe how abundant economies are staged or *curated*, a word etymologically related to care.

In recent analyses that train scholarly attention to "matters of care,"[12] María Puig de la Bellacasa, Michelle Murphy, and other scholars show that care and extraction can be understood as complementary components of broader capitalist processes. They build on a long-standing feminist engagement with care, critiquing how capitalism puts care to work by instrumentalizing identities, feminized skills, kinship relations, environments, and many other aspects of daily life. Care, Murphy argues, "can work with and through the grain of hegemonic structures, rather than against them."[13] One of the several common definitions that Murphy offers for care is this: "to provide for, look after, protect, sustain, and be responsible for something."[14]

"Emotional labor,"[15] and other affectively embodied efforts that the "work of care" requires,[16] is frequently asymmetric and gendered and engages affect to paper over vast power asymmetries. In her reading of antipoverty development in Peru as a matter of care, Tara Cookson shows how professionals worked to curate specific outcomes and forge specific desires by drawing on the compassionate extension of advice, pedagogical tools, and nurturance.[17] Care was at the heart of the growth investments I observed in Peru, where one-on-one encounters between project staff members and the aspiring entrepreneurs they supervised could take the form of caring counseling sessions ultimately aimed at motivating villagers to scour their daily lives for extractable resources.

In the context of a multiculturalist development paradigm premised on Peru's hidden treasures, practices of extractive care positioned villagers either as inheritors of Andean wealth or as irrelevant to Peru's growth project. This framing extends capitalist resource logics into the daily lives of rural Andeans. Jennifer Wenzel defines resource logics as "ideologies and habits of mind" that position nature as disposed for human use, in a relation where "nature has always-already entered economics as 'natural resources.'"[18] The long history of labor exploitation in the southern Andes suggests that resource logics also extend to humans.[19] Along with Andean environments and geologies, human subjectivities, bodies, desires, aspirations, and daily lives can also be incorporated into capitalist projects. Anna Tsing calls this incorporation "salvage accumulation," or the generation of capitalism out of objects, relations, and feelings not *created* through capitalist processes but *found* by them.[20] My ethnography of interventions working to extend practices of salvage accumulation beyond mining sites reveals that seemingly sustainable development and extractive industrial development are not contradictory. They are complementary components of an underlying material and affective project: to expand the horizons of extractive capitalism by spreading its practices, behaviors, desires, and feelings.

Resource logics are therefore also affective claims. This has important consequences for how we imagine the entanglement of extractive and productive economies. Karl Marx, in Volume 1 of *Capital*, classically argued that capital's infinite growth imperative, driven by the perpetual pursuit of surplus value, required an endless search for raw material.[21] Peru's rural Andes is one contemporary site of such a seemingly relentless search. But as its mineral frontier expands, Andean Peru is also seeing an expansion of the very *concept* of raw material. That makes this a place where conventional understandings of extraction and production invite new ethnographic specificity. Stephen Bunker, in 1985, sought to destabilize the production centrism of development theories of his day, rooting productive economies in their "absolute dependency" on resource extraction.[22] He found that productive economies, characterized by the centralized activity of transforming raw materials into consumable goods, were inextricably reliant on the world's environmentally devastated extractive enclaves, such as the Brazilian Amazon. Such extractive economies tend to be remote and dispersed, where low levels of labor and capital are required in relation to the temporary economic gains they create. Mining in particular involves concentrated labor in open pits or underground mines in remote regions. Peru's mines provide only a limited number of permanent skilled jobs that tend to draw professionals from outside the community, along with many more temporary local labor contracts.[23] As I began to see how powerful the concept of raw material was for development work in Peru during the 2010s, it became clear to me that extraction and production were more than just materially codependent. They were also semiotically and affectively entangled through the emergent promise of Indigenous entrepreneurship. The natural resource became a sign of potentiality and a source of democratized hope as the foundation for a new generation of productive rural citizens.

Through its claims on collective affect in the southern Andes, extractivism has exceeded the mine, taking over as the key mode, metaphor, and financial underwriter of capitalist relations more broadly. Extractivism organized a "neoliberal structure of feeling" in Peruvian development in which faith in a frictionless discovery of valuable things had become the dominant affective trope for contemporary entrepreneurship.[24] In the Andes, the fantasy went, the entrepreneur of the future does not simply produce; instead, like Marcel Duchamp's artist, the Andean entrepreneur is someone who notices and salvages. They strip daily life for parts. They transform found objects into bountiful opportunities. Extending this fantasy and making it palatable required the development agent labor of extractive care.

To access these acts of care and the broader contexts where they intervened, I lived in the Colca Valley village of Yanque, population about 2,000, with a family who usually identified as *campesino* (peasant). My host father, Don Gerardo Huaracha, is an 80-year-old farmer and herder who is bilingual in Spanish and Quechua.[25] My host mother, Doña Luisa Cutipa, is 83. She speaks only Quechua and cares for the home. Both allowed me to accompany them in their daily labors when I visited them periodically between 2008 and 2019, with a sustained visit between 2013 and 2015. Gerardo and Luisa had participated in development projects but were much more engaged in communal activities beyond the reach of outsider initiatives. From 2013 to 2015 I also accompanied development agents and villager participants in their work with the state-supported Sierra Sur project and the nongovernmental organization (NGO) Desco (Center for Studies and Promotion of Development). Return visits in 2017 and 2019 gave me the chance to join professionals in Espinar employed by the private Tintaya Mine's corporate social responsibility program and to learn more about the meteoric rise of mining in southern Peru. Many staff on these projects were born in the same villages where they worked, frequently after they left the region for education in Arequipa or Lima.

The communities where I lived and worked exemplify uneven development in rural Peru. Many residents of Caylloma and Espinar Provinces work as smallholder agriculturalists, pastoralists, and market vendors. Some work in tourism or in prized hospitality jobs at one of the several luxury hotels tucked into isolated, enclosed properties in the Colca Valley's hillsides. Others leave to labor in mines near and far. And others live at least part-time in Arequipa, Peru's second city of 1 million inhabitants, four hours from Yanque by bus. There are stark disparities in income, health care, education, and services compared with Arequipa. Caylloma's communities have populations ranging from Chivay's 7,688 to Madrigal's 498. My work in Espinar Province took me to its central town, also called Espinar (or Yauri), of 33,242 residents, and the rural homes and terrains surrounding the Tintaya Mine just outside of town.[26]

## Growth as an Affective Project

One of the premises of this book is that growth is *made*. Like capitalism more broadly, growth is an ongoing project that involves affective labor and, often, tiring physical effort. Scholars have suggested that economic models and theories do not merely represent the economy but actualize it, "performing" it into being.[27] Anthropologists have built on that foundational work, showing how capitalist markets are engineered to serve asymmetric power relations.[28] Researchers pay ample attention to *the economy* as a constructed cultural form and social project. *Growth*, however, is rarely subjected to the same analytical scrutiny. Among even the most critical scholars, economic growth is all too frequently treated as an objective empirical reality, a measurable phenomenon that is either happening or not happening, uneven or egalitarian, unsustainable or sustainable. I suggest that growth is not an objective description but an aspirational composition, a public feeling rendered palpable through specific socially constituted evidence that is actively orchestrated, deliberately staged, and constantly managed.

Growth has multiple meanings. When it follows the adjective *economic*, growth in capitalist contexts usually refers to the literal enlargement of a bounded system of accumulation and exchange. It can also take on other, more figurative valences. Researchers have long studied how economists and policymakers mobilize figurative language to make sense of and enact "the national economy form."[29] They authorize and fetishize the figure of *the* economy as a system that has clear boundaries and functions according to predictable laws, drawing metaphors from fields such as physics[30] and evolutionary biology.[31] Thinkers ranging from Marx to contemporary de-growth scholars have framed economic life as a "metabolism."[32] However, although scholars have explored metaphors surrounding the economy, many overlook the figurative work of growth.

Certainly, growth references the literal increase of a statistical aggregate; it is nonmetaphorical insofar as that aggregate is real.[33] But growth also carries a positive feeling beyond the idea of simple increase. Growing is, of course, what biological beings do. The word calls forth not just augmentation but an emergent natural order coming to life. It stands for the satisfying culmination of that which is inevitable and good; the seed, germ, or embryo has already mapped out the full potential of the living being it will eventually become.[34] Similarly, maturity is the act of coming into one's own. If growth indexes a sense of happy expansion, the term can also function as what Michael Silverstein calls a second-order index.[35] Uttering the word in contexts of development indexes not just expansion but also a specialized capitalist sense of well-being rooted in resource accumulation. In the word's literal, metaphorical, and indexical resonances, growth connotes a sense of organic inevitability. In this capitalist framing, growth is perpetual. Death is not growth's ultimate end point but its opposite.

Neoliberal development discourses position growth as a condition that, under the right circumstances, is unleashed. Michelle Murphy observes how a Nike Foundation campaign frames the act of one crucial investment in an imagined impoverished girl as releasing a "cascade" of win-win outcomes. As the campaign put it, "Invest in a girl and she will do the rest."[36] By buying into this framing, Murphy suggests, philanthropists avoid concerning themselves with the hard work of dismantling systemic gender injustices. Sandro Mezzadra and Brett Neilson argue that frictionless growth is a fantasy from neoliberal boosters committed to the claim that markets are responsible for "smoothing out the world."[37] Anna Tsing suggests that the fantasy of growth is *itself* a highly mediated spectacle, a "conjuring" that is constitutive of global finance capital.[38] And, underlying such "leveling technologies of globalization," Macarena Gómez-Barris finds both the dispossessing violence of extractive capitalist and settler logics of elimination, and strategic logics of incorporation.[39] With the help of these scholars, I found that I had to unlearn my own association of growth with the positive inevitabilities it connotes in order to see growth as a specific material arrangement, a performative repertoire, and a feeling that is actively curated.

The Gens collective, a feminist scholarly collaboration led by Laura Bear, Karen Ho, Anna Tsing, and Sylvia Yanagisako, makes a similar argument for unlearning received ideas about capitalism.[40] They suggest that reading capitalism exclusively as a globally dominant, overpowering logic misses the ordinary ways it is generated in daily life through messy, intersectional, and uneven co-laboring between multiple actors, ideologies, sentiments, and nonhuman things. By tracking growth as an affective project within resource-based capitalism, I found that it too is generated in heterogeneous networks of power and activity and that it is frequently underlain and activated by unseen feminized labor. In the Sierra Sur competition, for example, Lilia, the development agent, was constantly expending emotional labor to ensure that contestants felt validated and confident in their public claims to capitalist success. Meanwhile, Elena, the contestant, engaged in the enervating labor of meeting staff expectations for a well-rounded, resource-extracting, Indigenous entrepreneurial woman. Sara Ahmed suggests that "emotions *involve* subjects and objects, but without residing positively within them."[41] Here, I ask how emotions centered on growth unevenly involve Andean villagers. In the scenes that populate this book, growth is a feeling generated in interactions staged according to the institutional fantasy that figures the market as an expanding frictionless trade in assets and resources.

Investments were essential material and rhetorical devices for stage-managing the growth projects that I followed in Peru. *Investment* is commonly defined as the act of taking on a financial stake in an asset, anticipating that its value will increase. The term is central to the contemporary global lexicon of neoliberal governance as an act that links leaders and the governed: Citizens who were once entitled to state protections or benefits are reframed as entrepreneurs that the state might choose to invest in.[42] Investment can also be read as a kind of extractive care. With its root in "clothe" (as in *vest* or *investiture*), investment means contact. It entails aligning with or placing a claim on something or someone in the hope of reaping a return. It calls for a speculative attachment. In the projects that populate this book, investments were both financial and affective. Beyond just monetary supports for promising entrepreneurs, they configured face-to-face interactions to seed promises of a vibrant economy and to extract specific behaviors and feelings. Affect smoothed over many of the frictions of financial investment, especially given that the money dispensed to villagers was usually minimal. I found that investing in the imagined figure of the growth-ready Andean entrepreneur meant pairing meager funds with elaborate "moral support" (as one project participant put it) that usually came from development staff members who were women.

If market frictionlessness is a fantasy, I found that everyday representations of that fantasy were vital to the affective labor of making growth feel real in Caylloma and Espinar Provinces. Carlos Gutierrez, a freelance development consultant based in Yanque, voiced his version of the fantasy when he told me in an interview, "I don't work with poor people. I work with entrepreneurs." He suggested that success in enterprise comes to people who want it. Other development workers I spent time with framed growth as something villagers could achieve by working against a supposedly inertial dependence on others, which they called *asistencialismo* (assistance addiction). Staff argued that aid may suit a crisis, but, like the clichéd gift of a fish, material support fails to bring about fundamental transformation.[43] Instead, small investments, they argued, provided just enough support to spur the salutary motivation for villagers to recognize their own resource wealth and build a growth-ready enterprise. In contrast to a handout, with an investment the entrepreneur would "do the rest." Staff practices of disparaging dependence as a growth inhibitor ignored the interdependence, mutual legitimation, and friction-riddled micropolitics that accompanied their actually existing growth projects.

### The Politics of Abundance
Since the European colonization of Peru in the sixteenth century, outsiders have approached the country as a site of resource abundance. The Andes, in particular, form part of a geopolitical constellation that Macarena Gómez-Barris calls the extractive zone: a region that "a successive march of colonial

and neocolonial actors" have figured as a resource-rich site of primitive accumulation,[44] instantiating South America's historical status as "an extractable
continent."[45] Scholars in a wide range of fields approach abundance as a
provocation for rethinking capitalist relations and assumptions. For Robin
Wall Kimmerer, an orientation toward abundance can subvert a consumer-
ism rooted in "unmet desires."[46] For Monica Smith, abundance is a useful
framework for rethinking material evidence in archeology.[47] For Marshall
Sahlins, starting from abundance means challenging received ideas about
life not dominated by markets.[48] For Georges Bataille, it is a destabilizing
excess.[49] I found in Peru that contingent local concepts of abundance are
essential to understanding how growth comes to work as a project of suturing capitalist practices, aspirations, attitudes, and representations to new
kinds of raw material.

Peru's recent efforts to market itself to the world as a space of untold
riches places its national identity at stake through its historically enduring
association with ancient civilizations that built Andean raw material into
impressive empires. These efforts amount to multiscalar figurations of Peru
as a space of abundance. Donna Haraway defines *figurations* as "performative
images that can be inhabited. . . . I emphasize figuration to make explicit
and inescapable the tropic quality of all material-semiotic processes."[50] The
country's self-conscious figuration as a space of resource abundance has been
the subject of heated internal debate. In his analysis of an earlier wave of
national marketing, Peruvian sociologist Victor Vich critiqued President
Alejandro Toledo's (2001–2006) portrayal of an exoticized Peru on the Discovery Channel as among "the desperate performative acts through which
Peru, as nation-state, seeks to represent itself as an attractive commodity
for the world market."[51]

In its 2011 launch of the Marca Perú campaign, Peru's state-run tourism agency PromPerú updated Toledo's message, hitching the country's
economic attractiveness and "national self-esteem"[52] to its association with
resource wealth. Peruvian sociologist Félix Lossio Chávez demonstrates
that the national brand papers over Peru's deeply engrained racism and the
frictions surrounding its uneven development. He highlights the work of
activist artists who lay bare "the historical and current fissures of a fragmented nation,"[53] in which Marca Perú evokes a proud *peruanidad* that
exists alongside chronic disdain for Quechua-speaking Andeans and other
minoritized communities.[54] For example, graphic artist Markus Ronjam
transposes the brand's logo—a spiraling P in the shape of Peru's famous

Nazca Lines—onto an open pit mine surrounded by a deadened landscape. The image features hints of a devastated small village just beyond the mine's boundaries. Ronjam conveys the argument that mining degrades Peru's mountain ecosystems without bringing promised growth to the communities in its midst. In his Master's thesis at the Pontificia Universidad Católica del Perú, Elder Cuevas Calderón argues that Marca Perú recapitulates a colonial discourse that embraces the romanticized figure of the *indio* while erasing the actual lives that might fit such a category.[55]

Peru has long been home to a tradition of elite projections of national identity and desire through the idealized figuration of the model Indigenous Andean.[56] This desire dates back to the colonial era, as I show in Chapter 1. More recently, Peru's twentieth-century *Indigenismo* movement idealized images of indigeneity, which can be seen throughout the work of painter José Sabogal, photographer Martín Chambi, writers Clorinda Matto de Turner and Luis Valcárcel, socialist intellectual José Carlos Mariátegui, and others. This was an elite movement of urban intellectuals who used their work to represent archetypical Indigenous subjects.[57] For example, Sabogal's paintings were figures, not people with names and lives. His 1923 painting of a woman working a spool of thread is simply titled *Spinner*.[58] Maria Chiara D'Argenio has explored how contemporary media in Peru, particularly the films of Claudia Llosa, update this racist "indigenista type." Llosa, like earlier indigenists, depicted not rural people with agency but voiceless "idealized subjects who were to represent the Andean culture as well as the 'authentic' roots of the nation."[59] This public cultural milieu sets the stage for how the Indigenous Andean entrepreneur is figured in Peru's contemporary economy.

Peru's abundance brand was a "disciplining force"[60] that development workers mobilized to affectively attach villagers to the promises of a national growth project. The search for precious metals, fertile land, exploitable labor, culture available for appropriation, and other raw materials is a long-standing historical trope in Peru.[61] Yet despite the persistence of frontier abundance narratives in much of the postcolonial world,[62] critical development studies has tended to overlook the ways that development often doubles as a search for treasure. Foundational critiques target the discursive strategies that development institutions engage in to perpetuate their legitimacy.[63] Recent research highlights how cultural commodification and ethnodevelopment can entrench marginalization while also cultivating new forms of affluence.[64] But many researchers leave unexamined the broad definition of their research sites as poor or critique the civilizing interventions that development imposes without accounting for their potential role in expanding the scope of capitalist accumulation. By contrast, I interrogate a paradigm that opportunistically imagines Peru as a space of wealth.

## Market Penetration: From Agricultural Land to Entrepreneurial Mind

Development began in this region as an effort to fight poverty with market penetration. In the early 1970s a group of local manual laborers, including Gerardo Huaracha, broke ground on the Majes Canal project. This was a massive international engineering project to divert water from Espinar's highland water supply to create new fertile downriver terrain to meet a growing regional demand for farmland in the wake of Peru's agrarian reforms. A deployment of state funds for new physical infrastructure, the Majes project framed the highlands of Caylloma and Espinar Provinces as development frontiers, spaces of lack in need of integration. As Gerardo said, "Before, Chivay was silence. There were no people. There wasn't much trade." In his telling, it was only with the Majes construction that "Chivay rose up" as a commercial center.

The following decade, in 1984, a group of university-educated sociologists arrived in the Colca Valley to set up a new regional office of Desco, a Lima-based NGO, after the Sendero Luminoso (Shining Path) forced its office in Huancavelica to close. They encountered a small network of agricultural villages seemingly isolated from the rest of Peru. Since then, Desco has been the region's longest serving and most consistent operator of development projects. Its work has included restoring agricultural terraces, constructing irrigation canals, establishing local banking infrastructure, and offering technical assistance in agriculture and livestock.

This infrastructural work built on Peru's broader transformations. In the 1990s President Alberto Fujimori was displaying state largesse through highly visible modernization projects.[65] By decade's end, nearly every home in the region had potable water and electricity, and every village had a school building.[66] Fujimori was also intensifying neoliberalism at the national level, implementing stringent austerity programs and, in 1995, privatizing 95% of Peru's mines.[67]

Neoliberal welfare orthodoxies around the world have for decades focused on poor peoples' willingness to embrace the discipline supposedly required to achieve social mobility. The recent global excitement with conditional cash transfers is an update of this individualist ideology, as its enthusiasts argue that the transfers are less an antipoverty aid and more "an investment in human capital."[68] Meanwhile, other investments exemplify the austerity that characterizes our current post-generosity era in global development, which came into fashion as a response to large midcentury international aid packages supporting technology transfer, agricultural improvement, and other priorities that fall into the broad category of modernization. These newer investments are focused instead on cultivating entrepreneurial subjectivities.[69] They promote a soft austerity that opportunistically allows funders to believe that restrained infusions of money will provide effective motivation for new entrepreneurs.

By the time I began my long-term fieldwork in 2013, the development professionals I met, especially in Lima, were touting Peru's new World Bank–designated status as an "upper middle-income country."[70] For many of the years since the privatization of mining, Peru's annual GDP growth rate was above 5%; before the economic slowdown brought about by the COVID-19 pandemic in 2020, Peru's GDP peaked in 2019 at $226 billion and $6,486.63 per capita. Given these aggregate indicators, the early 2010s saw international antipoverty aid to Peru start to wane.[71] Aid faded in inverse proportion to international interest in Peruvian wealth, cultural products, and tourism opportunities, and development project funding from Peru's mines rose.

During my fieldwork, two UNESCO recognitions helped set the stage for the Colca Valley's own emerging reputation as a site of wealth. The region's *Wititi* dance was added to UNESCO's global Intangible Cultural Heritage list in 2015.[72] In 2017 UNESCO declared the Colca Valley and its surrounding volcanic mountains to be a Global Geopark, which recognizes unique geological formations and calls for their conservation and sustainable development.[73] The international press release noted the region's geological and cultural riches, highlighting Colca's

> vast array of volcanic landscapes, lakes, geological faults, pre-Hispanic ruins and colonial churches. . . . Most of the inhabitants of these territories belong to rich pre-Hispanic cultures, heirs to rich customs, festivals, and dances, many of which connect them to their unique, volcanic-tectonic territory with its hot springs and highly arable soils.

This is the context in which southern Andean villagers have come to be subject to a search for wealth in recent years, a search whose results have meant little material change to the region's structurally uneven growth or to its altered climate. If Peru had become, in the aggregate, a wealthy place, development projects throughout the 2010s were encouraging communities left out of mining profits to stake claims on other forms of Peruvian abundance.

Caylloma and Espinar Provinces have recently seen a kaleidoscope of small-scale investments in programs focused on microenterprise, with the individual posited as the unit of economic improvement. Many of these programs can be traced to mining company funds. The 2010s saw Peruvian state entities and private funds parceling out investments through the framework of competition, where targeted proposals would earn small trickles of funding from large pools of donor money. Municipalities, NGOs, and other institutions, which had to compete for these investments, would then stage their own competitions for local entrepreneurs, whose winners moved on to a daily life of competition in the market. Thus the urban-led project of market penetration has migrated from the work of increasing agricultural production and connecting producers to broader trade networks, to the work of curating the seemingly organic desire to join an Indigenous entrepreneurial middle class.

### Indigeneity . . . in Peru?

In 2008, on my first visit to Yanque, Gerardo Huaracha described himself to me as *puro Inca* (pure Inca). He followed the phrase with a confident cackle. At other points he and his family members would proudly tell me that their Collagua ancestors were present in Colca even before the Incas. They referenced other ethnic groups that predated the Incas in the region, namely, the Cabanas to the west and the K'anas to the north. I quickly learned that Gerardo's occasional winking self-identification as *puro Inca* was not indicative of membership in an organized national politics that explicitly centered indigeneity. He would more regularly identify as *campesino*. Given recent histories that had diverted many Andean Peruvians from cultivating a pan-regional activism organized around indigeneity, development workers came into the region believing they had considerable power to define what an acceptable Andean indigeneity looked like. I found that in Caylloma and Espinar indigeneity took shape in direct co-production with the development work that gained intensity alongside Peru's mining boom.[74]

Scholars have identified Peru as an anomaly for its apparent absence of nationwide movements built around Indigenous politics.[75] María Elena

García argued in 2005 that, despite Peru's relatively low presence of explicitly Indigenous-identified organizations, "Indianness never disappeared from highland Peru." Rather, its social movements have taken a distinct shape. "In a long history of Indigenous resistance," she writes, "strategic action has often been mistaken for silence and absence."[76] Three defining moments help tell the story of Peru's apparent distinction: the Agrarian Reform Law of 1969, the internal armed conflict of the 1980s and 1990s, and the intensification of extractive industry after 1995.

The Agrarian Reform Law was enacted during General Juan Velasco's presidency (1968–1975). The law eliminated large private haciendas and worked to strengthen rural communities through a leftist concept of *campesino* identity.[77] Prioritizing class, Velasco eliminated the pejorative ethnoracial category of *indio*,[78] whose official use had a long history of oppressive effects on rural Andean life. As María Elena García makes clear, this did not erase indigeneity as a political option, but it did affect how it was *officially* institutionalized in Peru. For example, in the 1960s residents of Yanque's Urinsaya moiety (lower half), in Caylloma, won recognition from the state as a *comunidad indígena* (Indigenous community), which entitled them to self-governance over land tenancy and irrigation.[79] The designation became *comunidad campesina* (peasant community) after Velasco's reform.[80] That name endures today, but the state now considers groups designated as *comunidades campesinas* in the Andes to be part of the Quechua Indigenous community.[81] This makes clear that class and ethnoracial identity are not mutually exclusive means of organizing for local autonomy.

The second defining moment saw guerrilla warfare proliferate between Sendero Luminoso, the military, and thousands of civilians caught in the crossfire or actively targeted[82] across the central and southern Andes at the same time that national Indigenous movements expanded in Bolivia,[83] Ecuador,[84] and Colombia.[85] To be sure, powerful rural movements formed in Peru during the time of Sendero Luminoso, but they did not scale up to become nationwide.[86] Caylloma and Espinar were to the south of the epicenter of Sendero Luminoso violence and were mostly insulated from it. Still, a legacy of the conflict was that activist organizing became suspect, as former Desco regional director Oscar Toro told me: "Even though they were not there, in direct influence, the state saw any intention to organize within civil society as if it were directed by Sendero Luminoso."

Fujimori took credit for the defeat of Sendero Luminoso with the capture of its leader in 1992. Meanwhile, throughout Latin America top-down neoliberal multiculturalist policies by the 1990s had put new emphasis on self-determination and the celebration of "permitted" Indigenous difference, so long as it was compatible with neoliberal economic decentralization.[87] One of the 2003 Peruvian Truth and Reconciliation Commission's most striking revelations was that the conflict's casualty count was not the commonly cited 35,000 deaths, but 69,280.[88] This finding offered devastating numerical support for the argument that the violence was allowed to reach such extremes because living Quechua speakers in the rural Andes did not count as part of the Peruvian nation. As a result, a national public that had long romanticized Andean tradition but held living Andean people at arm's length found itself primed to support rural Quechua communities within the frameworks of multiculturalist sustainable development.

The intersection of privatized mining with class politics and internal armed conflict is a third reason Indigenous identification has been institutionalized distinctly in Peru. Coastal Afro-Peruvians, Amazonian communities, and other minoritized groups did gain some local autonomy and increased civil rights in the 1990s and early 2000s.[89] Peru also committed in its 1993 Constitution to offer Indigenous communities more decision-making power over extractive activities on their territory. The country ratified the 1989 International Labor Organization Convention 169 on Indigenous and Tribal Peoples and then the 2007 UN Declaration on the Rights of Indigenous Peoples, which, among other guarantees, upholds the right of Indigenous communities to free, prior, and informed consent to extractive development on their territories. In 2011 Peru implemented this right with its Prior Consultation Law, which made it illegal for a mining company to proceed with exploration on Indigenous land without engaging the local community, although it did not grant them a definitive right of refusal. But it was far from clear who the state saw as Indigenous. In Peru lowland Amazonian groups have been more commonly associated with Indigenous practices than Quechua-speaking highlanders, who long claimed rights as peasants. These slippages in what constituted "Indigenous" worked in companies' favor. When it came to territorial protections, one government official I spoke with suggested that the state "did not want to recognize Quechua populations because of mining investment." This comment resonated with a former health minister's later lament, in the context of the COVID-19 pandemic, that "the state is a subsidiary of the market."[90]

By the start of my longest stint of fieldwork in 2013, the Ministry of Culture was working toward a more rigorous state definition of indigeneity with their new publication of the expanding national Database of Indigenous or Originary Peoples. A 2015 clarification from President Ollanta Humala's administration made it explicit that Quechua groups counted as Indigenous and could file prior consultation claims. As Patricia Balbuena, Humala's vice minister of interculturalism, said, "We can no longer say that there are no Indigenous communities in the Andes. That debate is over, and I think that's a big advance."[91] Since then, several Quechua communities have successfully sued to block mining on the basis of their indigeneity.[92]

Peru's new regulatory institutionalization of indigeneity has made it imperative for mining companies to secure the social license to operate, which means convincing communities of the ways a company's extraction might benefit them. To that end, mining enterprises and their government authorizers now seek to shape Indigenous identity in a way that opens villagers to the promises of mine-friendly economic development. Through corporate social responsibility projects, mine managers work to transform Andean villagers from potential obstacles to extractive development into its accomplices. Today, they are extending the promises of mineral growth to villagers with projects that figure them as potential Indigenous entrepreneurs.

Ramón Pajuelo, a sociologist at the Institute of Peruvian Studies in Lima, suggested to me in a 2013 interview that being Indigenous "is a sociological novelty in Peru."[93] Richard Chase Smith, Lima-based director of the Common Good Institute, which aids environmentalist struggles in the Amazon, corroborated that sense of novelty. He told me that just fifteen years earlier, "Indigenous people didn't exist in Peru," but by the early 2010s, from policymaking to popular culture, indigeneity was "coming out of the closet."[94] Peruvian anthropologist Alejandro Diez Hurtado uses the term *reindigenization* to describe the new value that indigeneity has taken in Peruvian public life,[95] contrasting with its history of disavowal as a category subject to brutal racism and as something to be overcome.[96] Development workers called this *revalorization* when it was attached to a particular practice or tradition that could generate income. In my thirteen years of conversations with Gerardo Huaracha, he never once indicated that his everyday life or relationships to kin and land changed with the new attention to indigeneity in Peru. I am thus not adjudicating the "truth" of this category; I do not seek to define or judge what is or is not Indigenous. Rather, my concerns are the encounters in which Indigenous status is figured as a resource for growth in a place where development and mining projects staked a claim on the power to define the category.

## Implicit Indigeneity

Laura Graham and Glenn Penny argue that indigeneity is invoked less frequently as a primary identity than as a transnational policy category that becomes available to people who are mobilizing for specific claims.[97] In 2013 the Vice Ministry of Interculturalism in Peru's Ministry of Culture was starting to develop official criteria for determining Indigenous status for its national database project. These criteria included "historical continuity," "territorial connection," "distinct institutions," "self-determination," and "self-recognition" as Indigenous.[98] Leonor Cisneros, adviser to the vice minister during the Humala administration (2011–2016), showed me the full slide show for policymakers in an interview at her office (Figure I.2).

"When I speak about *indígenas*," Cisneros told me, "I don't just mean Amazonians. I'm speaking of Quechuas too, because we understand *indígenas* as the population that descends from those who were in this territory at the moment of the conquest." Contrasting the Andes with Amazonian groups' ready embrace of Indigenous self-identification, Cisneros noted its continued stigma in the highlands, telling me that when outsiders asked Andean villagers where Indigenous populations were, "you were told, higher up [*más arriba*]. You went *más arriba*, and you were told, *más arriba*, *más arriba*, and there's no more people!" Always higher in the mountains, indigeneity here is a deictic signifier for highland remoteness in Peru's spatial hierarchies.[99]

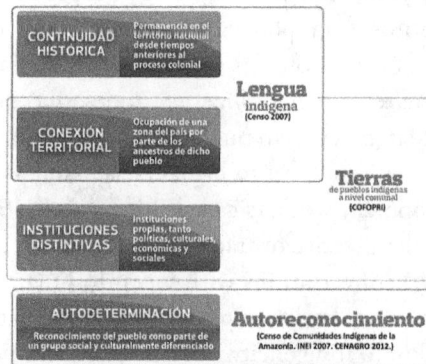

FIGURE I.2 Slide depicting the broad criteria for determining what is considered Indigenous, according to Peru's Ministry of Culture.

In the daily life of my fieldwork, especially outside of development projects, I often encountered signs of what Peruvian anthropologist Guillermo Salas Carreño calls implicit indigeneity.[100] This is an indigeneity that is not overtly acknowledged, as one might do in a territorial rights claim, but is put on display in ways that outsiders would likely associate with Indigenous status, such as the Quechua language, references to precolonial heritage and nonhuman agency, invocations of ancestors, and other practices. For example, Gerardo Huaracha sometimes called himself *puro Inca* or *puro indio*, with varying levels of irony. When he hosted tourists in his small two-room hostel, he described their interest in *nativo* (native) products, things that "are natural to the area, right, like quinoa." But he did not regularly claim Indigenous status.

This underscores an assertion widely argued by Indigenous scholars: that "Indigenous" is a relational political category.[101] Like many residents, Gerardo tends to mark his primary identity as a member of the Huaracha family and then identifies with his village *saya* (moiety or half). Each district in Caylloma is divided into an upper half (*hanansaya*) and a lower half (*urinsaya*, where Gerardo and his wife, Luisa Cutipa, live). He would then identify as a *campesino*, and a resident of Yanque. Stepping back, Gerardo might identify himself as Collagua, the predominant ethnic group in Yanque and much of Caylloma Province. He might also identify as Quechua or Quechua-speaking.[102] "Quechua" self-identification exemplifies Salas Carreño's implicit indigeneity: As Cisneros told me, "In the Andean case, they aren't self-recognizing as Indigenous, but they are now self-recognizing as Quechuas."

Like *care*, *investment*, and *growth*, *Indigenous* is a capacious term that becomes available in specific ways in Peru. In this book I do not attempt to define it comprehensively, nor do I pretend to analyze all the sociopolitical work that it does. Instead, I take the *act of defining* indigeneity as a growth-making practice in encounters between villagers and development staff. It is both imposed as a technocratic figuration and "customized," to invoke Shane Greene's term, by villagers themselves, in and beyond sites of development investment. Customization, Greene suggests, is the creative but constrained result of "the struggle to redefine one's relation to what at first appears foreign."[103] Development promoters sought to delink indigeneity from Peru's brutal racism and structural violence, instead fixing it as palatable to capital. Although they pitched indigeneity as a site of growth-bearing promise, many of the villagers I worked with found ways to move beyond the logics of identity fixing, resource wealth, and extractive care.

## An Ethnographic Agreement

I first met Gerardo Huaracha and Luisa Cutipa in an assigned homestay as part of an undergraduate semester abroad. I was the latest visitor to a family that had been host to several Peace Corps volunteers, ethnohistorians, and anthropologists from Peru, the United States, and Europe. I was thus living with a family long connected to global research networks and excited to host foreigners. They were a *campesino* family engaged mainly in cash cropping, herding, and planting. Although they did not have a high cash income, they owned several agricultural fields, had two rooms for visitor lodging, and benefited from past tourism initiatives and from a network of kin living throughout Peru.

Like the other scholars who have spent time living in the Huaracha-Cutipa home, I am urban based and university trained. As a North American white male academic, I move around the world with considerable privilege. Research with marginalized communities is all too frequently exploitative. To mitigate this as much as possible and to write in solidarity with the Andean communities I came to know without losing sight of the geopolitical power asymmetries that anthropological research perpetuates, my methodology followed an ethnographic agreement with Gerardo and Luisa. This approach was modeled on my exposure to the recent Indigenous scholarly rethinking of the power relations of research with marginalized communities[104] and the importance of forging research agreements that address local needs, concerns, and points of intellectual interest in advance of any sustained study.[105]

Most important, I began this research because Gerardo and Luisa asked me to. Upon my first departure from Peru in 2008, Gerardo asked me to "not forget" Yanque.[106] Not forgetting anchored my research methodology. On each return trip I made to Peru, the family agreed to connect me to their kin network and extended invitations to join them in the agricultural, municipal, and ritual activities that populated Yanque's calendar. To reciprocate, I would commit to a nearly annual return, which made my lodging in Yanque a periodic source of income for the family and their kin network. I made the daily practicalities of my ethnography available for uptake in my interlocutors' own projects. At my hosts' request, for example, I brought a group of five American student research assistants to Yanque in 2019; they spent part of their time teaching a free English course for the municipality. Where I can, I search out material ways that this research can benefit Yanque by budgeting for villager stipends and locally needed materials, such as digital cameras, in my research grants. I have helped several families who were working to market their homestay experiences to build their web presence. This book is the latest result of an ongoing agreement between the Huaracha family and me in which research is part of an indefinite exchange of reciprocal obligations.

I also was obligated to shape the project according to local concerns and debates. In the process of my fieldwork, I worked to center marginalized interlocutors not as "informants," positioned in a hierarchy below the anthropological "expert," but as theorists and advisers: I regularly talked through my project ideas with Gerardo and with several development project staff interlocutors. A cluster of citations in this book come from sources that Gerardo curated. Over the years, he has built an extensive museum and archive in his home. His personal collection contains ceremonial items, ancient musical instruments and ceramics, and early republican Church records. Stacked on the mirrored display cases are over four decades' worth of articles and books by ethnohistorians and archeologists who had, like me, lived in Gerardo and Luisa's house. These publications, from such scholars as Peruvian ethnohistorian María Benavides, Peruvian anthropologists Carmen Escalante and the late Ricardo Valderrama, and U.S.-based archeologist Steve Wernke, provided Gerardo with scholarly evidence of Yanque being a routine target of exploitation but also a place that outsiders could never entirely reshape according to their own imperial visions. My research was guided by this multi-decade scholarly conversation about colonialism and local well-being that Gerardo and Luisa actively mobilized to represent Yanque to officials, visitors, and tourists as a site where noncolonial, nonextractive life endures. By incorporating Gerardo's deep collection of books, articles, recordings, television documentary programs, and archival documents into my citation practices, my book explicitly signals his scholarly influence.[107]

Staying with Gerardo and Luisa on all of my visits to Yanque has meant that my view of daily life was a partial one. I do not aspire to present a complete or comprehensive understanding of growth, extractivism, and development work in this region. Indeed, one of my most fundamental arguments in this book is that growth is experienced as a partial truth.[108] It is felt distinctly by people who engage its promises or encounter its ambassadors in varied aspects of daily life. As Tanana Athabascan scholar Dian Million writes of Indigenous authors negotiating how to represent the trauma of Canada's residential schools, "Feelings are theory, important projections about what is happening in our lives."[109] This book engages Million's sense of "felt theory" in reading the economy as a felt form interpreted through the textures of everyday life. I moved between scenes of embeddedness with the Huarachas, with development project agents, and with past and present project participants. This afforded me not a God's-eye view of growth but a glimpse at some of its multiple felt perspectives.

## The Book

As its narrative arc unfolds, *Acts of Growth* traverses the conceptual terrains of extractive care to understand the labor of enacting and embodying economic growth in "The Richest Country in the World." The first two chapters address the contested nature of wealth, providing context for the growth projects I address later in the book. Chapter 1 starts from the colonial archive. Juxtaposing colonial and contemporary encounters between Yanque residents and the Spanish Crown, I argue that the growth investments that this book follows extend colonial histories of "improving" the Andes. I focus on the colonial *reducción*, a forced resettlement program meant to extract labor from Andean subjects and render their environments legible. Like today's growth projects, the *reducción* involved intimate, face-to-face moral supervision, pitched as care for subjects' salvation. I root Andean resource logics as a colonial ideology forged in the Spanish Crown's racialized acts of disciplining villagers as a means of managing imperial abundance.

In Chapter 2 my contemporary interlocutors in the Colca Valley push back against easy narratives of relentless growth, endless abundance, and human-serving nature. Beginning with their recognition of the region's long-standing water precarity, I spotlight scenes of attachment to the land, the nonhuman world, and the surrounding human community. I then detail how villagers explicitly theorize these attachments in relation to promises of resource abundance. I do not find a neat resistance to capitalist narratives or a rejection of the idea of the resource. Instead, I argue that villagers worked to maintain the messy entanglements that resource-based narratives attempt to erase by highlighting acts organized by *obligation*.

The next three chapters follow staff and participants in three growth projects—a state initiative, an NGO investment, and a mining corporate social responsibility program—through face-to-face encounters that exemplified the effort to extend capitalism during Peru's booming 2010s. Chapter 3 follows the state-based Sierra Sur project, which sought to reach Caylloma Province's most marginalized communities. In site visits and a massive development contest, growth took the form of a *celebration* of a Peruvian abundance unleashed through what was staged as spontaneous Indigenous entrepreneurship. Villagers, however, redeployed these encounters to critique the state for its otherwise chronic absence from their lives.

Chapter 4 turns to Desco's youth development project in the Colca Valley. The NGO's capacity-building sessions and one-on-one staff evaluations were central to the project's effort to teach entrepreneurial skills to a new generation of young adults, who received seed capital for proposed business plans in gastronomy, tourism, artisanship, and sustainable agriculture. Here, growth took the form of *maturity*. Staff argued that entrepreneurial growth was a function of individual psychological growth. They pitched enterprise as an index of mature citizenship. This chapter is an ethnography of financial training as an instrument of affective extraction, from an NGO project whose funding can be traced to mining company donations, and follows staff and villagers as they labored to transform daily life into a collection of resources.

Chapter 5 is a more direct engagement with Peru's mining economy. Here, I observe how mining companies curate a sense of growth in their vicinity. Growth was enacted, in its corporate iteration, as a form of *responsibility*. Starting in Espinar Province, near the Tintaya Mine, I follow a veterinary team that the mine employed to inseminate cows with Brown Swiss sperm as part of a conspicuous investment in local livelihoods. In a second encounter, a participatory feedback session, Indigenous-identifying anti-mining activists contested the mine's figuration of productive, climate-ready cattle with their own animal figure: a deformed sheep carcass that they argued was evidence of the mine's contamination and disregard for nonhuman abundance. I then return to Caylloma, where a public mining exhibition worked to seed expectations of spectacular new growth.

The Conclusion considers the stakes of starting from wealth instead of poverty in analyzing the micropolitics of development in Peru. I return to Marca Perú and reflect on the promises of its capitalist growth orthodoxies in relation to the COVID-19 pandemic, which intensified in Peru and around the world as I completed this book. If the book was written to understand how a specific growth orthodoxy works in the world, the pandemic invites us to rethink how we engage with its promises and its disappointments.

What does it mean to inhabit "The Richest Country in the World"? In this book I show how different actors and institutions enact, embody, feel, and contest growth through efforts to transform the margins of Peru's mining boom into spaces where resources abound. Subjecting growth to ethnography, I propose that we can best understand what growth means and how it feels for people who live at the margins of a booming nation by asking them.

# 1

## The Coloniality of the Resource

*Historicizing Andean Abundance*

### 1586: García Checca

On January 20, 1586, some twenty community leaders were assembled in the brand new *plaza de armas* (public square) of the recently created colonial village of Yanque in the central Colca Valley. These leaders had first been sent to Mass in the ornate Franciscan church, a structure at the village center whose doors opened onto the square. Afterward, Spanish inspector Juan de Ulloa Mogollón led them out to the square to question them as part of King Felipe II's inquiry into the resources of his realm. García Checca, one of the assembled leaders, testified about life before Spanish rule. The elderly Checca, born around 1521, was the *kuraka* (local chief) of Yanque-Urinsaya, the new district's downriver sector. Checca presented Ulloa with a history of the region's Collagua community, their agricultural and ritual labor practices, and a sense of what life was like under Inca rule, which the Spanish had ended just decades earlier in 1532.[1]

As Ulloa wrote in his 1586 "Report on the Province of the Collaguas for the Description of the Indies That Your Majesty Mandates":

> Some are called Collaguas; they call themselves this since ancient times; they have passed the name on by inheritance from parents to children, which came from a *guaca*, or ancient shrine . . . that is a snowcapped mountain [shaped] like a volcano, distinguished from the other peaks around there, which is called *Collaguata*; they say that from around or inside that mountain many people came out and descended to this province and its valley, of this river that they populated, and

conquered those that were natives and threw them out by force, while
they remained; they prove this with forts, which they call *pucaras* in
their language, which are built on some of the high peaks of the valley,
from which they descended to make war.[2]

As he captures the Collagua charter myth, Ulloa's report suggests that "Indios" first came into the Spanish gaze as the empire mapped its expansion
and inventoried its plunder. This encounter was part of the *Visita General*
(general inspection), a massive inventory of Andean colonial territory that
took place after the 1569 *Reducción General de Indios* (general resettlement
of Indians), the relocation of 1.5 million Andeans into condensed villages
under Viceroy Francisco de Toledo.[3] The resettlement that Ulloa was tracking was a violent reorganization of land, life, and subjectivity that worked
to extract wealth from and nurture the souls of people who the Spanish
opportunistically determined were spiritually and racially inferior natives.
The most important architectural manifestation of this colonial extractive
care was at once an instrument and a symbol of Christian order: a cookie-
cutter landscape of gridded villages organized around a church and a plaza
surrounded by farmland, which to this day configures daily life in the rural
Andes. Traces of Ulloa's inspection can also be felt today, as the resource
inventory has become a motif, a regular gesture that accompanies the outsider extractive gaze.

### 1999: Hilde Checca

On April 27, 1999, generations after García Checca's 1586 appearance in the
plaza, Hilde Checca, one of García's descendants and a young entrepreneur,
stood in the very same public square for another inventory. She faced not a
Spanish colonial inspector but the monarch herself: Queen Sofía of Spain.
Hilde answered similar questions about origin myths and ritual practices.
The encounter is memorialized in a photograph displayed in Hilde's home
(Figure 1.1), now the site of Casa Bella Flor, Yanque's most successful "experiential" (or homestay) cultural tourism hotel. When I visited Hilde and
her husband, Natalio Oxa (who died in 2020), one rainy afternoon in 2014,
she laughed at how young she looked in the picture. She wore her Collagua-
style embroidered vest and long skirt and a broad-brimmed Cabana-style
sombrero.[4] Queen Sofía was greeted in Yanque's plaza that April day with
ceremony: *Wititi* dances, a drink of chicha (fermented maize and barley),
gifts from local artisans, and nearly the entire village population.

FIGURE 1.1  Hilde Checca and Queen Sofía of Spain. Source: Hilde Checca.

Hilde, with a group of aspiring entrepreneurs, gave Queen Sofía a tour of the community, leading her outward from the plaza along the colonially configured grid of straight streets and evenly spaced blocks to homes recently retrofitted with adobe bricks and freshly thatched roofs. By staging Yanque as a site of rich Indigenous heritage to a fascinated political figure who had a degree in archeology, Hilde's group deployed the built environment to inaugurate a new relationship with their ancestors' colonizers: Spain would now become an investor.

The purpose of Sofía's visit was to announce funding and offer her blessing for an architectural restoration project supported by the Spanish Agency for International Development Cooperation (AECID), Spain's foreign aid

agency. Its mission was to hire local laborers to restore each Caylloma village's colonial church. Newly beautified colonial buildings, according to
Spain, would allow villages to be restored to their early modern splendor,
making them attractive as tourism gained momentum in the valley. Spain
announced its investment in the exact same space that its agents came to
inspect four centuries earlier by repeating an old idea: that the region was
a site of already existing wealth that simply had to be unearthed, restored,
and brought to light.

## An Enduring Colonial Resource Logic

In this chapter I present a selective history of uneven development in Peru's
southern Andes. I take these two encounters between members of Yanque's
Checca family and representatives of Spanish royalty, separated by more
than 400 years, as historical anchor points in the long history of treating
the southern Andes as a space of raw material. Together, they shine light
on contemporary ideologies of resource wealth in Peru's southern Andes
that are rooted in and reproduce a colonial heritage. They also demonstrate
how indigeneity has come specifically to be at stake as a resource rendered
extractable by opportunistic outsiders.

In present-day Caylloma and Espinar Provinces, both part of the former
colonial Province of Collaguas,[5] contemporary uneven development is em-
bedded in local history and local materiality as a continuation of the logic
of the colony. Contemporary efforts to unearth local wealth extend a long
history of outsiders coming to Yanque and the villages that surrounded it
in search of Andean resources and inhabitants.[6] Initially labeled *indios*, then
*campesinos*, and, later, native, autochthonous, or Indigenous, rural Andeans
have long served as what Peruvian Ministry of Culture adviser Leonor Cisneros called "an empty vessel to fill" for the colonial project. When we spoke
in her Lima office, Leonor described *Indigenous* in its colonial inception as
"a term that has no content. It's a term that defines you as lacking." Andean
residents labeled as Indigenous or one of its equivalents would repeatedly
find themselves playing central roles in an extractive choreography that positions Andean ecosystems, geologies, landscapes, nonhumans, and humans
as raw material for building a polity whose accumulated riches would never
quite find their way back to them.

The policy of *reducción* (resettlement) was essential to exploiting and
evangelizing the Andes, which was largely accomplished by reshaping public
space. I argue that one of the colonial *reducción*'s key legacies is the enduring

deployment of the Andean built environment to engage ideas of indigeneity to create an atmosphere of extractable wealth. All over the world, colonial built forms helped to lay the groundwork for extractive capitalism.[7] Today, those very same *reducción* spaces stage growth projects that put a newly "revalorized" Andean community and territory to work to expand development's extractive milieu. Thus contemporary development in the Andes is much more than a transnational neoliberal framework touching down. The relationship between what Spanish royalty found in each visit to Yanque's plaza also demonstrates "the ongoing force of the colonial encounter."[8]

The colonial built environment archives a history of extraction—of labor, of minerals, of bodies, of souls, of affects—that has not ended. Pairing the encounters from 1586 and 1999 to excavate their conspicuous continuities, I draw here on oral histories, archival documents, archeological and historical scholarship, and my time living in Yanque during the 2010s. Yanque, the historical capital of the colonial Province of Collaguas, is situated at a crossroads between what was Collagua, Cabana, and K'ana territory before Inca colonization.

This chapter is not a critical reading of foreign aid or a comprehensive historical study of Andean colonialism. Depth on those topics can be found elsewhere.[9] Rather, it is a local history of extractive care. I set the stage for understanding contemporary growth projects by weaving a selective history of the material present out of two Spanish interventions into the lived space and daily behavior of Andean villagers. I proceed with a discussion of the affective and disciplinary forces that Andean plazas exert on the communities oriented around them. Next, I turn to the local history of how new colonial built environments drew the Collaguas, Cabanas, and K'anas into Inca and Spanish extractive frameworks. Then, an ethnographic reading of more recent encounters with the Spanish Crown and Spanish foreign aid exemplifies how this history informs the ongoing material engineering of uneven development in the southern Andes.

## Affective Geographies of Andean Wealth

Yanque's plaza never looks the same when I arrive. On each visit to Yanque, the final leg of my trip ends with a public van (or *combi*) ride that drops me off in the plaza, which I have to walk across to reach Gerardo and Luisa's house. The plaza is a 4,000-square-meter rectangle. In its center is a fountain, featuring a statue of a woman in Collagua-style dress pouring a glass of chicha (Yanque is renowned for its strong brew). The central patio creates a wide staging space for public gatherings. At its corners are patches of grass and bushes trimmed into the shapes of condors and alpacas. Along one side is a series of grocery stores; along another, a shifting set of tourist cafes. On the north side is the municipality building, where Mayor Benigno Llacho would stand watch from his windowed office on the second floor. The Church of the Immaculate Conception, first built in the colonial era and rebuilt and restored over the years, lines the south side (Figure 1.2).

The plaza conveys Yanque's mood. It fills with activity for agricultural, municipal, and religious events. In the mornings it bustles with early trips to the surrounding fields and hosts the crowds arriving for the daily tourist market (Figure 1.3). Midday, the plaza is empty, as most residents are at work in the fields or outside the village. At twilight, it receives returning herds of animals and tired commuters and students who have caught the last van back from Chivay, the provincial capital about twenty minutes up the mountain. Later, as the town quiets, the plaza becomes the source of shouts from teenagers who socialize beneath its humming sodium lights.

Plazas remember. Colonial legacies endure as political and affective forces through material assemblages of built structures and reconfigured

FIGURE 1.2 The Church of the Immaculate Conception overlooking Yanque's plaza, with terraced plots in the background.

FIGURE 1.3 Yanque's plaza, viewed from the north side, during the morning tourist market.

landscapes that organize forms of care and forms of violence. Yael Navaro-Yashin foregrounds affect as a materialized form in her research in the politically contested urban terrains of Northern Cyprus. She suggests that the built environment manifests the Turkish-Cypriot de facto or "make-believe state" as "a tangibility." She reads this polity's materiality for "the affect that is discharged" from it.[10]

Plazas also forget. Using public space as a medium for shaping local subjectivity, generating affective atmospheres, and discarding things deemed excessive to outsider goals has been essential to civilizational projects meant to "improve" Andean communities for at least as long as the historical record there exists. The Spanish were not the southern Andes' first colonizers. The Incas also did major work to "develop" the valley, which was the Arequipa region's main labor tribute supplier and agricultural breadbasket,[11] by reconfiguring lived space.[12] But it was Toledo's colonists who used the built environment to forge an enduring connection between resource abundance and Indigenous subjectivity. In other words, indigeneity was special for the Spanish colonial project, whose condition of possibility was the opportunistic divide between European civilization and non-European premodernity.[13] The Spanish built spaces meant to create and regulate Indigenous difference, to frame it as the starting point of a pathway toward Christian salvation, and to put that difference to work for the realm.

Spanish colonization and contemporary development investment are historically related moments of taking things from the rural Andes. To understand this ongoing exsanguination of Latin America's "open veins,"[14] I follow the methodological framework of recent theorists who have written histories of the present against the grain of the archive of liberal progress. Lisa Lowe suggests that colonial plunder forms an invisible but indispensable infrastructure that upholds the global project of liberal modernity, "affirming liberty for modern man while subordinating the variously colonized and dispossessed peoples whose material labor and resources were the conditions of possibility for that liberty."[15] Peruvian historian Anibal Quijano maps this dynamic onto enduring racial, class, and spatial divides in Peru, describing it as the "coloniality of power."[16] Nelson Maldonado-Torres builds on Quijano's idea to propose the "coloniality of Being," which pinpoints the denial of ontological difference that subaltern subjects face around the world.[17] Both Quijano and Maldonado-Torres assert that colonial conditions persist far beyond the limits of specific colonial administrations and into the ethnoracial hierarchies that organize ostensibly "post"-colonial spaces. My own engagements with growth projects in Peru reflect the insights from these and the many other scholars who find imperial endurance in sites of resource extraction.[18] I have come to read resource logic as itself an expanding colonial project and the resource as an archetypically colonial object. By emphasizing the *coloniality of the resource* in my reading of colonially configured environments, I suggest that figuring minerals, land, plants, animals, and humans as extractable resources was the first step in what Eduardo Galeano saw as Latin America's ongoing bloodletting.

The racialized colonial machinery of improving hearts, minds, and souls out in public was part of a constant mission to expand the ambit of potential resource extraction by inculcating a behavioral discipline and affective orientation to Christian salvation. In the Spanish Andes, as in colonies throughout the so-called New World, conversion[19] and tribute collection[20] were public occasions for category making through which ethnoracial hierarchies were forged and non-Spanish Indigenous identities were fixed. Many of the "lacks" that development workers attach to rural Andeans "have their historical roots in colonial and early republican discourses on Indians."[21] Indeed, as Quijano writes, Europeans saw them as "by nature inferior and consequently *anterior*, belonging to the past in the progress of the species."[22] The hegemonic version of indigeneity here was from the beginning a mirror for outsider projects of accumulation.

Indigeneity has a long, variegated history in Peru as a political identity invoked, repressed, reshaped, and refracted through colonial resource logics. The Spanish invasion entailed "gathering under one term"—*indio*—"a great number of ethnically distinct peoples."[23] Obsessed with mineral and agricultural abundance from the beginning, the architects of colonial accumulation believed that "Indians, and not silver, were the New World's true riches."[24] To the Spanish, "Indios" were found objects, living storehouses of ecological knowledge and labor power to be used until their depletion. They were a ready army of disposable, premodern, pagan bodies that could be sent to the colony's Andean mines in Huancavelica or Potosí to find gold, silver, and copper. Or they were caretakers of a landscape that provided food and other materials to Spain's urban outposts. The institutionalized otherness imposed on them under the guise of imperial care oriented a racialized Indigenous difference that became a founding principle of domination that reverberates into the present through colonial materiality.

## Curating Difference

For both the Incas and the Spanish, the Collagua, Cabana, and K'ana communities that populated the colonial Province of Collaguas built their lives and made sense of their ecosystems in ways that came to be figured as sources of wealth. Before their colonizations, they existed near one another with relative autonomy, with boundaries marked by distinct origin narratives, settlement sites, and language.[25] Inca colonists transformed these groups into "bureaucratically equivalent tributary units,"[26] concretizing a concept of ethnospatial difference to maximize visibility for taking labor and agricultural tribute. The Spanish then redeployed these bureaucratic categories to further condense the population and extract their labor.

The inspector Ulloa reported stark distinctions between the Collaguas and the Cabanas in mythology, traditions, dress, and body and cranial modifications, "all hallmarks of ethnicity that were strictly reinforced under Inka administration."[27] According to the records of colonial *visitas*, the Collaguas of the high altitudes (in the *suni* and *puna* ranges, 3,000–4,000 meters) were herders of Andean camelids. In the middle altitudes (*quechua* range, 2,000–3,000 meters), they engaged in multi-elevation agriculture. Their subsistence crops included quinoa, fava beans, barley, and maize. Both groups adopted aspects of what John Murra called the "vertical archipelago," diversifying their agriculture by tending constellations of terrains in distant "ecological zones" that extended into the fertile reaches of the valley and the high *puna* above.[28]

Yanque resident Natalio Oxa, Hilde Checca's late husband, corroborated Ulloa's origin story for me in 2014 in an oral history of the region.

> In the Colca Valley, two ethnic groups developed, right, the Collaguas and the Cabanas. The Collaguas were people who had come from the Peruvian highlands who came in search of inter-Andean valleys, with a climate that was a bit better, right? We know that in the Peruvian highlands there is just one chance to plant with rain, and we know that there are years with rain and years when there is no rain, but here in the Colca we irrigate with water from the mountains, right? So the Collaguas came to this area. . . . My wife is Collagua, and I come from the Cabana ethnic group, from the pueblo of Pinchollo.

Here, Natalio situates the Colca Valley as historically fertile and productive. Like the Collaguas, the Cabanas have an analogous charter myth: They emerged from Hualca Hualca, a broad mountain that overlooks the western Colca Valley whose snowpack continues to supply water to the village of Cabanaconde, the historic Cabana population center. According to Ulloa, the Collaguas were Aymara speakers, whereas the Cabanas spoke Quechua. Today, Spanish and Quechua are dominant in both the valley and the highlands. Sombreros, especially those worn by women, also index distinct styles between the two groups. The Cabana sombrero is a long, colorful hat with a curved brim. The Collagua sombrero is a tall, flat-brimmed monochrome straw hat, usually with an embroidered band around it.[29] I have seen references to the "Collagua nation" and "Cabana nation" deployed on village welcome signs and at fiestas as points of local distinction. But I did not see these identities invoked to assert rights or resistance to the state.

By contrast, the K'anas to the north, in present-day Espinar, have recently mobilized a sense of indigeneity as a device for political provocation.[30] Espinar is a highland herding community long connected with Colca through trade and, today, labor migration to the Tintaya Mine. The region has recently seen an oppositional, counterhegemonic Indigenous politics emerge to contest mining expansion. In a 2017 declaration for Indigenous Peoples Day, for example, Espinar's Domingo Huarca Cruz Unified Federation of Peasants promoted its K'ana heritage by connecting colonialism to the present: "Now it is up to us to take up the challenge of reconstructing all that was destroyed by Spanish invaders and their current colonial servants."[31]

## Appropriating Andean Space: The *Ayllu*

Before the Spanish arrived, the Collaguas, like other Andean communities, organized themselves into *ayllus*. As an administrative category under Inca colonial rule, *ayllus* were bureaucratic units, groups of kin on shared terrain. But the *ayllu* as a long-standing relational principle is much deeper than an imperial category. Catherine Allen defines the *ayllu* as "a group of individuals cohering as a social body around a place, ancestor, or task that provides a unifying focus."[32] Marisol de la Cadena specifies Allen's definition to the human and earth-being relations within it. She cites Cuzco-based teacher Justo Oxa, who describes the *ayllu* as "a dynamic space where the whole community of beings that exist in the world lives; this includes humans, plants, animals, the mountains, the rivers, the rain, etc. All are related like a family. It is important to remember that this place . . . is not where we are from, it is who we are."[33]

Today, *ayllus* are no longer official administrative categories,[34] but the concept endures, as villagers I met would use the term to mark kin and place. Gerardo Huaracha theorizes the *ayllu* as the group of people with whom one says, "Let's work on this task. Let's go do this," and as the site marked by that collective task. He recounted memories from his earlier adult years, when constructing houses was a regular communal labor obligation. Upon completing their work, the group of laborers would chant a soft Quechua melody that sung the *ayllu* into being, ritually enacting the new construction, its workers, and its future residents as an *ayllu*.

> *Ay, ayllu* [oh, *ayllu*]
> *Ima sumac ayllu* [what a beautiful *ayllu*]
> *Ay, ayllu*
> *Ima sumac ayllu.*

Inca colonists institutionalized and exploited these place-based relations by way of a rotating labor draft called the *mit'a*, in which a percentage of men from every *ayllu* were forced to supply manual labor to the realm. In exchange for labor on Inca construction projects building roads, bridges, agricultural storage, and inns,[35] *ayllus* would be guaranteed protection and autonomy, even if they also came under a new imperial surveillance. *Mit'a* labor was fundamentally extractive, for "the labor time contributed produced far more than was returned by the state."[36] The Spanish extended these structures of extraction,[37] intensifying the *mit'a* labor draft to bring in as many disposable bodies as possible to work the mines of Potosí and Huancavelica. In this way, European colonization built on and intensified Inca extraction. What was new for the Spanish, however, was that indigeneity mattered: Recrafting behavior in people marked as *indios* was central to the affective projection of the new colony as a space of riches.

## Extractive Care and the Colonial Built Environment

Viceroy Toledo justified his project of mass resettlement, which entailed a complete remaking of the Andean built environment, as a benevolent means of fashioning "Indian" subjectivities.

> The principal reason for the visita general is to provide order and structure so the Indians may have competent doctrine and be better instructed in the elements of our Holy Catholic Faith and we will be able to administer them the sacraments with greater facility and advantage and they may be maintained in justice and live politically as reasoning people as the other vassals of His Majesty. In order to achieve this end it is convenient for the Indians who live dispersed and spread about to be reduced into villages with design and order, in healthy places and of good disposition.[38]

This justification marks Toledo's interest in extending both "faith" and "reason" to "the Indians." It is also affectively laden, with the dramatic condensing of the Andean population presented as an act of care that assumes that colonial rule creates good feelings and establishes health and order. Toledo's vision amounted to an intensive micromanagement of the spaces, routines, and feelings of daily life. Unwilling people were dragged out of their precolonial homes to the places designated for their resettlement, against the threat, at least in Yanque, of being burned alive. In Jeremy Mumford's gloss of the resettlement of Andean residents, "Until they were brought together in towns they could not be true Christians or, indeed, fully human."[39]

To his instructions, Toledo added in 1571 the directive "to extirpate idolatries, sorcery, and dogmatizers so that the Evangelical teaching would fall well disposed upon ground where it could bear fruit."[40] Here, Christianity—like later discourses of economic growth—was framed as something

that could sprout like a seed, given the right conditions. Idolatrous traditions had to be eliminated for the benefits of Christianity to take hold.
New homes were meant to be maximally distant from non-Catholic sacred
sites and burial grounds, an effort to enforce the forgetting of life before
Christianity.[41] Reading this arrangement more generously, Friar Paul Hagan,
a U.S. citizen who worked as a missionary in Caylloma in the 1960s and
1970s, noted that "the population centers were originally set up by the Spanish as centers of worship."[42] Tying together moral, religious, and economic
imperatives, the *reducción* was couched in a benevolent paternalism, an early
development ideology that entailed rendering subjects useful for the realm
by micromanaging how they used the built environment.

Toledo's ambition to reorganize the residential arrangements of every
colonial subject called for "social engineering on a scale previously un-
thinkable," as residents were forced to leave their ancestral *ayllus* for dense
villages, which they had to build themselves as part of their colonial labor
tribute.[43] As Cook suggests, this was Toledo's "Andean utopia":[44] a figuration
of colonial civilization that would maximize the accumulation of wealth and
Spanish control over non-Spanish bodies and souls. Life was reorganized
into neatly demarcated residential zones for disciplined living and separate
spaces for wealth accumulation. This reengineering of Andean life entailed
an almost paranoid micro-orchestration. Like later overly ambitious state
projects,[45] at least in principle it left "nothing to chance."[46] Remaking the
built environment was a civilizing project through which Spain claimed control over every square kilometer, every soul, and every minute of the empire.

The *reducción* was "one of the largest resettlement programs in history—
affecting some 1.5 million native Andeans."[47] *Reducción* was synonymous
with conversion: The 1493 papal bull *Inter caetera divinae* described Spain's
evangelical mandate to "take control of these mainlands, . . . their natives
and inhabitants, and . . . *bring them to* the Catholic faith."[48] The phrase
"bring them to" is Tom Cummins's translation of the Latin *reducere*. According to Wernke, *reducere* meant "both physical centripetal movement
and the sense of bringing about a new state or condition closer to divine
unity."[49] The term thus connotes a pathway in space and also within the self,
an internal journey toward purification of that which was deemed excessive
to Church and Crown. The centripetal gridded village diagrammed and
enacted Toledo's vision of Christian moral order. Resettlement deictically
constituted natives as a class of spatially removed persons to "bring to" the
Church.

For the Spanish, the built environment was an instrument of extractive care. The *reducción*'s remaking of living arrangements was benevolently packaged to residents as a new discipline that was for their own spiritual good and economic well-being but that primed them for labor exploitation. The gridded *reducción* space, an urban "Spanish ideal" that ironically was never fully realized in early modern Spain itself,[50] produced indigeneity contrapuntally as a state of being that required salvation through relocation. This space articulated "the intention to structure a new society based on European models."[51] *Reducción* towns were designed for space to "assert" certain encounters while "denying" others.[52] Each district's centerpiece was a large open plaza, with the church, always the tallest building, taking up one side. Coordinated with the goal of efficient tribute collection, population density was determined by a sonic discipline. Vicente Rafael describes how this worked in the parallel Spanish colonization of the Philippines, where subjects had to remain "bajo de la campana," within earshot of the church bells.[53]

Bells limited this newly claimed space for colonial subjects, configuring a Spanish and Christian temporality by reconfiguring the daily rhythms of rural Andean life, which suddenly entailed walks to the town center for Mass at the bells' command. "Before leaving for the fields each day," Friar Hagan writes in his history of Yanque's Franciscan order, "peasants would gather in the temple for prayer, directed by the catechists. Three times a week, they gathered in the patio of the convent where children sang the doctrine and the rest repeated it."[54] In this new routine, condensed groups of people regularly gathered as a population in the church and plaza, rendering them regularly visible to priests and colonial authorities. This routine rescaled kinship interactions and organized new forms of belonging and "stranger sociability."[55] Plaza gatherings positioned the central assemblage of church and square as a figurative amphitheater. It was a node of public action, a stage that demanded one's gaze while exerting a centripetal force. In this way, colonization was rooted in deploying space and remaking habits to create an atmosphere that facilitated, at once, salvation, extirpation, extraction, and selective cultural appropriation.

Priests saw evangelizing the Indigenous as a generous extension of Spanish spiritual insight. Spanish colonial evangelists imagined Christianity as a magnetic force, opportunistically viewing Catholicism's "rapid spread . . . as the inexorable manifestation of divine will pulling to itself the diverse peoples of the world," despite anxieties that "natives were incapable of—or perhaps resistant to—'sounding the depths of its mysteries.'"[56] Although conversion was forced, in Yanque the local Franciscan order permitted people to incorporate select non-Spanish traditions and symbols into their prayer practices.[57]

The *reducción*'s grids established a spacing of bodies that facilitated the relentless policing of behavior, hygiene, and appearance for those categorized as *indio*, a condescending colonial iteration of care that was not for human well-being but for a labor resource. Facing the plaza were homes of Spanish authorities and sites of municipal governance. Beyond the square, houses formed a strict grid pattern along wide, straight streets from which all family plots would be visible. "You shall lay out the Indians' houses with doors opening onto the streets," Toledo commanded, "so that no house opens into the house of another Indian, but that each have a separate house."[58] In this way, "Indians" would have limited contact with one another beyond the eyes of a colonial inspector.

This spatial arrangement endures today. Contrasting with the more dispersed precolonial housing clusters in the region that were built to accommodate the variegated mountain terrain, houses were condensed and separated by walls. Doors and windows in the new *reducción* homes pointed either to the street or to a home's internal courtyard. Villagers in Toledo's fantasy spaces were under constant supervision. The gridded church-plaza-home assemblage organized an intimate morality that entailed the remaking of subjects with renovated souls and spirits in the newly atomized household and the deep recesses of intimate life. By exposing Colcans to new "eyes on the street,"[59] this spacing was a behaviorist colonialism that disciplined the Andean populace through the perpetual possibility of surveillance.[60]

Indigeneity was a colonial resource. Spanish aspirations to utopian visibility and regulation linked moral management with the colony's extractive wealth-building imperative. The fantasy of integrating and disciplining the viceroyalty's most distant inhabitants served the project to create a total archive of every household, inhabitant, and wealth-generating resource to maximize tribute extraction. As María Benavides writes, "The thoroughness of the visitadores owes itself principally to the colonial administration's interest in learning the Indigenous productive potential and labor strength."[61] The Province of Collaguas first came into the Spanish extractive gaze as a source of laboring bodies. The late sixteenth and early seventeenth centuries saw competition for laborers between Arequipa urban elites, who depended on "Indios" to build their city and to labor in mining interests in Potosí and

Huancavelica. That competition increased after 1626, when Spanish inspectors found silver deposits near the *reducción* of Caylloma,[62] which are still being exploited today by the Canadian company Fortuna Silver Mines Inc.

The colonial figure of the *indio* also designated a category of cultural practices to appropriate. Writing of the *visitas* in Collaguas, Benavides notes that "instructions to visitors included the recommendation to investigate ancestral customs related to systems of command and social organization."[63] Colonial micromanagement did not mean total erasure. Part of this project was to recuperate what Toledo saw as useful dimensions of Inca heritage for the empire, such as irrigation practices and multiterritorial planting. Resettlement plans would also maintain spaces for feasting in *kurakas'* homes, accommodating certain local idioms of political power.[64] This enabled the Spanish to recognize and maintain *kurakas* as a class of non-Spanish local elites who would serve as colonial accomplices.

Colonial legacies reverberate in contemporary Yanque. Its population was condensed and forcibly moved across the Colca River from their agricultural fields to a high alluvial plain whose flat land better suited the church and gridiron design for the new village. Community members maintain many of those same fields, but since the *reducción*, many have had to make what can be an hour-long commute by foot to their plots, which surround the old settlement site at Uyu Uyu. The water precarity that has long characterized agricultural life in Yanque is a further legacy of resettling people away from a well-organized irrigation system.[65] Establishing *reducción* districts meant that the newly condensed population was also made to compete for limited access to water, launching regional tensions that endured long after the colonial project's official conclusion.[66]

*Indio* status activated a lasting set of reconfigured material arrangements, affective attachments, and resource logics. In making the rural Andes a site of ongoing *extractability*, Toledo's project created a historical foundation for contemporary ideologies of growth as projected through the figure of the Indigenous entrepreneur.

### From *Indio* to Peasant and Back

Since Toledo's *reducción*, the Peruvian Andes have consistently been a place to take things from: Urban and rural elites created rich lives by grabbing land and benefiting from a racial capitalism that relegated "Indios" to labor exploitation.[67] Reflecting this hardened colonial hierarchy,[68] Colca's churches, squares, and grids are still physically in place long after Spanish rule ended, although they have seen material updates and changes over the years. Until 1968 many Andean colonists' descendants still inhabited massive tracts of land and employed Indigenous peon laborers in feudal fashion: "like slaves," as Gerardo told me, recalling working for landowners along the coast in his youth (see Chapter 3).

The Velasco government's Agrarian Reform Law of 1969 outlawed the hacienda and with it the widely disparaged label of "Indian" or "native" as a policy category.[69] Doing so devolved considerable authority over territory to historically marginalized rural populations, with the state expropriating one-third of Peru's total land.[70] Although the reform was incomplete and beset by bureaucratic failures and political infighting, it was perhaps the most consequential policy intervention for the concept of Peruvian indigeneity since Toledo's *reducción*. Peruvian anthropologist Enrique Mayer suggests that the Velasco reforms were "akin to the abolition of slavery in the Americas."[71] By redistributing hacienda land into peasant cooperatives, Velasco worked to improve life for rural citizens through a technified, modernist, and nationalist reengineering of rural space and subjectivity, implementing his own form of civilizing discipline. Traditional haciendas were not present on Colca's steep terrain, but the reform was still significant there because it redistributed local power over land and provided the foundation for a new form of local autonomy by creating official *comunidades campesinas* (peasant communities). In pushing rural Andeans to adopt the vocabulary of class and to strategically self-identify as peasants, Velasco's reforms illustrate the enduring importance of collective space in mediating indigeneity. Reconfiguring landownership and recategorizing Andeans as peasants was an attempt to unmake a disparaged Indigenous underclass.

Thirty years later, the *indio* "returned" to Peru.[72] Andean public space was again put to work as a medium for selectively recuperating and extracting indigeneity. Queen Sofía's 1999 Yanque visit heralded the rise of culture-oriented development for Caylloma Province. This inaugurated an era in which publicly claiming indigeneity meant, in the eyes of these new development projects, staking a claim to legitimacy, visibility, inclusion, and newly recognized resource wealth. Sitting in Natalio and Hilde's kitchen, I listened as they described meeting the queen. I had hoped to hear from both of them. But Natalio did most of the talking, as Hilde came in and out of the room, joining our conversation when she was not needed by one of her guests. Natalio said, referring to the queen:

> She came here, to visit the house. . . . We are thinking, she is going to come like I've seen it in the books with her crown, her magic staff, and I had the idea that she could have had supernatural powers, and now I'm in charge of our hotel and I said, "What if she doesn't like the food we cook?" . . . So I was a little nervous and preoccupied, I didn't sleep at night. . . . Well, so when she came, it wasn't like I had thought, right? She was of course an elegantly dressed lady, but . . . normal, a lady.

The queen had come before cultural tourism was a widely recognized form of entrepreneurial activity in Yanque, as it is today. Because of this, Natalio and Hilde found it impossible to gauge what she was expecting. They described immense anxiety about their adequacy as cultural ambassadors, channeled through worries about their dwelling space in the days before the queen's arrival. This anxiety was an affective infrastructure of Yanque's incipient growth project. The queen's visit required significant labor and spending on their part to stage a site of living indigeneity as a new tourist attraction. Natalio and Hilde worked for days to prepare meals and complete construction on their courtyard to ensure the queen's comfort and that of her delegation. Natalio also described disciplining himself to call her "Your Majesty," which "I had to memorize for a whole day." The preparations that occupied this couple's routine for multiple days give lie to the fantasies of seamless growth, untapped markets, and entrepreneurial activation that pervade visions of ethnicity-focused development in the region.

Natalio and Hilde's experience with the queen was a dramatized version of their later encounters with tourists. There, power asymmetries and the affects of anticipation and solicitousness around them are staged through the home, the services, and the narratives they engage to provide outsiders with a sense of Collagua authenticity. After we discussed their anxious but ultimately rewarding visit from the queen, Natalio identified his and Hilde's pioneering work in cultural tourism as a result of what he had picked up as a worker at Colca Lodge, a large foreign-owned luxury hotel situated among Yanque's agricultural fields. Natalio lamented that "today we can see that the pueblo is transforming with cement. It's losing its cultural identity." He found architecture built with local materials such as straw, stone, and adobe to be much more appealing to the Colca Lodge's customers. Tourists, he realized, sought tradition. They desired an encounter with what Quijano called the *anterior*: architectural representations and human embodiments of that which came before Spanish colonization. Natalio observed how local construction workers were "recuperating" precolonial techniques in their work on the lodge after seeing its appeal: "They had to learn once again what we had lost. So this woke me up a little bit to what the tourists like." Natalio also described how tourists appreciate "the conservation of the potato, quinoa. We do it like the Incas did, their forms of conservation, right? For example, the potato has to be totally organic. . . . Hilde saves them, she conserves them like the Incas."

Despite Hilde's clear role in performing indigeneity, later in our interview Natalio lowered his voice to tell me that "one of my weaknesses was my wife, right? She didn't understand the quality of service that the tourists really wanted. So I did have another vision, but my wife didn't understand." However, Hilde had a leading role in the business. Constantly engaged in the work of hosting, Hilde was significantly more visible at the hostel; it was her family's home and lands that bound them to the emerging tourist center of Yanque; and it was she who represented the business in the local tourism consortium, called the Yanque Ayllus. Natalio erased the feminized labor vital to the routines that animated his sense of growth.

For Natalio, the objectified figure of the tourist took on an immense power to organize the dwelling and daily life of his entrepreneurial family. The tourist was Natalio's chief audience; his work was devoted to and organized by what Florence Babb has called "the tourism encounter," a phrase evocative of the face-to-face intimacy that tourism requires and whose power relations are comparable to Talal Asad's "colonial encounter" and Arturo Escobar's "development encounter."[73] In extending the neoliberal discipline of anticipating the "tourist gaze,"[74] Yanque's cultural tourism market recapitulates Spain's colonial focus on spaces and routines rerouted toward visibility, extraction, and conversion. I do not want to neglect the fact that Hilde and Natalio willingly chose to enter the tourism business and have found profit in this locally uneven market.[75] But tourism, especially of the intimate form that Hilde and Natalio practice in a place people visit to witness cultural difference, requires what Joseph Weiss calls "colonial time-discipline."[76] They had to inhabit the exhausting asymmetric affect of speculative anticipation, routing their dwelling routines toward the unpredictable tourist gaze. In-habiting this affect would become a form of entrepreneurial discipline that pervaded the region's growth projects.

## The Ongoing Force of the Colonial Encounter

The AECID initiative was inaugurated by Queen Sofía in 1999 and con-tinued through 2015. It shrunk as Spain's growth lagged behind Peru's dur-ing the global economic crisis of the early 2010s. Spain's final project in the region continued its focus on extending resource logics through the built environment. The agency worked in the Colca Valley under the aus-pices of a program called P>D Patrimonio para el Desarrollo (Heritage for Development). P>D representatives, led by a group of architects, provided the region with refurbished colonial churches, promising a future landscape of beautiful historic gems in the remotest of villages. This restored built environment sparked a new era of speculating on tourism. With restored churches marking the region's skyline, plazas in every village could become small markets, spaces for rendering local culture visible, and advertisements for the dramatic landscapes, food, and accommodations each village had to offer.

Alongside the beautification of colonial architecture, the agency pro-moted architectural revalorization by retrofitting homes in what they saw as traditional styles. Approaching the indigenization of public space as an untapped market, the agency's Rural Housing and Social Development project deployed architects to redesign homes throughout the region for those residents who saw potential profit or entrepreneurial opportunity in a retrofitted home. This fit what Leni Delgado, one of the regional coordina-tors of the Sierra Sur project (we meet her again in Chapter 3), described as development "by demand," where villagers in pursuit of investment "have to come to us." Like the colony's centripetally oriented conversions, develop-ment had become something villagers could "come to."

Spain's architecture project was a "by demand" scheme to validate local styles while creating a retrofitted landscape of traditional homes that would potentially attract tourists. Many of the project's participants had hoped to launch experiential tourism businesses, and a restored and refurbished home was enticing. A 300-page report put out by the project describes every renovated home in the region with before and after photographs and floor plans that detail each restored home's new economic "uses," with options including "household," "store," "restaurant," "hostel," "workshop,"

FIGURE 1.4 An example of a Sibayo house that underwent restoration as part of the P>D program for the Colca Valley.

and "artisan space."[77] The report also indicated the "beneficiaries" of each restoration and the traditional materials, such as adobe bricks and thatched roofs, used for each remade home (Figure 1.4).

Paralleling Spain's colonial domestic reengineering four centuries earlier, these restorations remade intimate household space as a means of orienting villagers toward the promise of entrepreneurial income. In other words, this was a project to renovate homes in a way that would create more Natalios and Hildes. Rocio Cayllahua Cayllahua, a staff member on the project who was an urban-educated architect born in the Colca Valley, described it to me when we met at her office in the Chivay headquarters of the AECID. The agency's initial investment in church restoration, she said, taught villagers new construction techniques and architectural aesthetics: "So many people worked on the church [restoration], and said, 'I can do this,' and they did it," mastering traditional architecture to retrofit their own homes.

The AECID would pay for the architectural plans and the construction labor, with the district and the villager "beneficiary" each also contributing a smaller amount of money and labor. Rocio told me that "it's really important to work with the traditional stone system." She walked me through images of restored homes on her laptop, pointing out specific features. Pointing to one image of a home with a thatched straw roof, she said, "This is another that also already existed and has just been recuperated. They painted it and they changed the rooftop, because it used to be tin, so we gave them the incentive to stop using tin." They were able, instead, to top the roof with straw, which the owner already "had in his *chakra*."[78] Consistent with other projects' approaches to already existing abundance as the extractable raw material for new enterprise, the AECID emphasized salvaging found objects and using organic materials obtainable from the regional environments where project participants were rebuilding their houses. Rocio pointed to her next image. "This one is in Callalli. In Callalli, they have *sillar* [white volcanic rock]. So, we work with *sillar*." With co-financing, Spain created traditional appearances while optimizing living spaces for tourist consumption.

This program worked to remake visible built space, speculating that an indigenized domestic aesthetic could lead to village-wide prosperity. The staff gazed on the built former *reducción* village as a resource and saw household space as a site of intervention. Reflective of the colonial project, their work also exemplifies the broader project I detail in this book: priming Andean spaces, objects, practices, desires, and people as the raw material for growth. AECID's presence was largely a welcome source of economic aid. Still, its colonial continuities through the built environment perpetuated hierarchies of power and desire between Spanish-funded, urban-educated experts and rural Andeans with home lives speculatively reconfigured for availability to the tourist gaze.

### Conclusion: Setting the Stage for Self-Plunder

The colonial project entailed a violent enclosure and dispossession with the resource at its conceptual center. Today, plazas and the colonial grids that radiate outward from them remain public stages for the mediation and management of Indigenous subjectivity. With the affective force of a capillary governmentality,[79] colonially configured public space exerts a centripetal coercion that compels villagers to desire growth and to pursue the promises of resource wealth.

Peru is intensively animated by neoliberal globalization. However, the contemporary ideology of Andean abundance also retraces material lines carved out by the racialized colonial engineering of the Andean built environment. The built environment is a crucial site for observing indigeneity as a resource in the making, reflecting that indigeneity here is far more than a simple "invention."[80] A material and affective reading of Andean colonial space reveals the local beginnings of what I describe in this book as extractive care: the gentle welcoming of Andean rural residents into extractive economic systems that are structurally violent.

Through a subtly coercive spatialized rhetoric of "coming to" (material structures, spiritual authorities, a disciplined morality, a customer-facing affect), both colonial Christianity and postcolonial development disguise the obligation to become a subject available to extractive demands as an opportunity to join the saved. Self-plunder is the current unrivaled strategy for converting villagers into entrepreneurs. Today's dominant approaches to development draw on strikingly colonial orientations to Indigenous-identified and Indigenous-identifying subalterns to shape public life. This enduring fact demonstrates how one material assemblage of built objects, the colonial *reducción* village, mediates the ways that Indigenous selves have been produced as figures of wealth in Colca's spaces of appearance. However, as much as *reducción* space staged formalized encounters, disciplined behavior, and rendered bodies and land available to extraction, these projects were always incomplete. The coming ethnographic analyses illustrate how that incompleteness rendered growth as an aspirational project that villagers were often able to contest or capture for their own distinct political projects.

# 2

## Contesting the Resource

### *Ecologies of Attachment in a Time of Water Precarity*

FROM COLONIZERS TO MINING companies to tourists and foodies, the Colca Valley village of Yanque, like Peru more broadly, has been widely identified as a place that is blessed with abundant but underexploited riches. Gerardo Huaracha told a distinct story. He suggested that Yanque was not blessed but cursed. He told me this as we walked one morning in 2019 across the Colca River and up into Yanque's agricultural fields, finally reaching a ruined settlement site called Uyu Uyu. This was the precolonial settlement where the ancestors of many current Yanque villagers lived until the Spanish forced them to relocate. After a recent archeological restoration, the site's reconstructed stone houses are now a tourist attraction, complete with an indoor interpretation center and a guard.

Here is how a placard by the Uyu Uyu site depicts the curse:

> This was a dispersed village of the Collaguas, inhabited later by the Incas, who improved its constructions with a stone finish. During the Toledan resettlements, the village was burned along with its inhabitants by Captain Lope de Suazo; from this massacre there remained one survivor, to whom an image of the Lord of the Exaltation appeared [in the stone wall]. In his efforts to bring it to Yanque, the image disappeared, leaving a curse upon the people for all time: the sacred coca plant will transform into thorns (Waqrataya), and all the water will dry up, leaving nothing but a puddle for the birds.

Gerardo read this placard to me, before adding his own interpretation: "In Quechua, this was what they called *llakillaqta*, or *pueblo de pena* [sorrowful village], right, that will not have any water. There will only be enough water for the birds. Nothing more."

At the contemporary district's colonial inception, according to this modern origin story, Yanque was cursed to be a ghost town, divinely condemned to drought and want, with the sacred becoming profane. The curse comes at the moment Spanish colonists were working hard to remake relations with the land. Ever since, villagers have been tasked with overcoming that curse by maintaining good relations despite their forced resettlement. This means negotiating the tensions between two horizons of expectation: the frontier boomtown whose exponential growth can be found in a unidirectional unearthing of resources, and the marginalized ghost town whose curse is kept at bay by working cyclically to maintain attachments to the living terrain. Here, I detail the latter and situate it in relation to the growth projects that occupy the rest of the book.

The ghost town framing presents a counternarrative to the colonial heroics of resource unearthing. The colonial narrative posits European outsiders as responsible for abundance by finding it and deploying it as the basis for civilizational projects. In contrast, the Uyu Uyu narrative reads those same outsiders as responsible for scarcity, lack, and deprivation, instantiated in the image of drought. By drawing the idea of the resource into relief, in this chapter I highlight the distinct attachments that the residents of Yanque work to strengthen and the debates, internal conflicts, anxieties, and metacommentaries that accompany those attachments. I also highlight a paradox. Communal labor and human-nonhuman interdependence are, at once, what extractive capitalism works to discipline out of existence as sites of excess and inefficiency and, when viewed up close, what it contradictorily also depends on. From the subsistence agriculture, multisited dwelling, multigenerational kinship, and care work that subsidizes migrant wage labor, to the ritual acts packaged for cultural tourists seeking Andean authenticity, daily practices of noncapitalist interdependence are essential to resource logics. Here, I lay out that contradictory field, where relations and communally entangled lives come into tension with the logics of clean and easy resource extraction that animate capitalism.

Scholars have thoroughly scrutinized ritualization and human-nonhuman connection in the Andes. My intervention in this chapter is not to retrace old steps but to read noncapitalist economic relations as part of the theoretical framework that villagers bring to bear in their own analyses of the capitalist wealth, prosperity, and growth that many institutions are now asking them to feel and embody. I ask how local acts of interdependence in the struggle against drought intersect with the story of endlessly expanding individualized growth. In other words, Yanque villagers exist within capitalism but are not overdetermined by it. The chapter follows cyclical interactions with land and ongoing interdependencies among people. It is in these sites of interdependence that I was best able to access noncapitalist narratives about wealth, the nonhuman world, and abundance as earned and based on seasonal practices. This is a realm where growth is a literal word. It refers to the biological flourishing of plants and animals. It happens in cycles. Death is not growth's opposite but its ultimate endpoint.

My aim here is not to track a neat resistance to resource logics. Instead, I argue that conflicting priorities, messy overlaps, and contradictions complicate them, "provincialize" them,[1] and draw their limits into relief. What I contest in this chapter is the *neatness* of the colonial concept of the resource. Ritualized attachments and attunements to the nonhuman world enact tacitly defiant political critiques of the limits of resource logic at the diffuse margins of extractive growth. Entrepreneurial capitalism asks people to mobilize their lives for economic gain or otherwise shed supposedly inefficient attachments. I address those attachments, showing how they are more than inefficient indulgences and indeed make up crucial dimensions of a diverse, incompletely capitalist economy as it is felt in daily life beyond the development agent's view.

In what follows, I first situate relational logics within a local political ecology that centers maintenance, cycles of abundance, and an intensive focus on negotiating water precarity but that also overlaps with capitalist markets, practices, and processes. I turn to Gerardo Huaracha's life history, which he wove through this porous political ecology. Then, I follow Gerardo and other members of his family through a tour of attachments. I describe three short scenes of giving, each of which involved strengthening and perpetuating interdependent relations with humans and nonhumans. The interdependence featured in these scenes was a frequent topic of debate, analysis, and anxiety, which I detail in the last section of the chapter. These attachments are at once vital to daily life and overlap with, interrogate, and relate ambivalently to hegemonic projects of expanding economic growth.

## From Resource to Relation

A *resource* is an object for humans to take. *Resource logic*, as I chart it in the rest of this book, frames a unidirectional relationship between a user and an object extracted from its ecosystem. But in this chapter I center practices of attachment between humans and the nonhuman world, and among humans, that follow a *relational logic*.[2] Relational logic promotes an abundance rooted in interdependent connection and obligation. Like resource logic, relational logic can be instrumental. But the affective projects and futures it underwrites are often distinct. Its care is not extractive, and its abundance does not mean economic growth. Nor does relational logic necessarily inhibit growth. Resource and relational logics can be at stake together.

Practices of attachment contest the individualizing force and extractive directionality of the resource concept. Understanding relational acts as more than simple inefficiencies, excesses to a capitalist economy, or obvious threats to an extractive order shows us evidence that capitalism is not dominating or totalizing. My intervention here is not to promote an exoticizing *pachamamismo*[3] or "Andeanism,"[4] a scholarly approach that isolates Andean ritual practices as though they were completely removed or distinct from the contemporary world. Within that framework, small-scale agriculturalists often take on the stereotypical role of the quiet anticapitalist hero allergic to cynicism or calculation. Nor am I intervening in political ontology debates on the benevolence or malevolence of sentient mountains and other nonhuman earth-beings.[5] Rather, I center a felt theory of attachment to forms of well-being and abundance that fail to articulate with the cruel promises of capitalism but that make up important aspects of life actually lived in a partial capitalist economy.[6] Relational logic calls for a political ecology of feeling: an understanding of dispersed environmental power struggles that recognizes their rootedness in particular affective orientations to the nonhuman world. The acts of attachment and the analyses about them that I detail here go beyond calculations about resource stewardship. They are also occasions for the joyful renewal of territorial attachments and the tense airing of conflicts and anxieties. Disputes in these moments are heightened by class, gender, and age inequalities that have been accentuated by uneven development in the region.

Resource logics work ironically to both erase nonresource orientations and selectively recuperate some of these practices by reappropriating them as entrepreneurial raw material. Given that, how do villagers resist, in practice, the moral and affective erasures that the coloniality of the resource calls for by separating useful nature from human nature users? How do nonresource approaches expose the deceptive neatness of neoliberal resource logics?

The politics of relationality in Yanque is perhaps most visible in its villagers' approach to water. Since the middle of the twentieth century, the

Peruvian state, through a dynamic combination of recognition, accommodation, and neglect, has allowed rural communities such as Yanque-Urinsaya substantial political space to determine their own local practices of irrigation, land tenure, labor, and ritual. The Irrigators Assembly (Junta de Regantes) for Yanque-Urinsaya was founded and granted juridical personhood from the state in 1960. In 1961 Yanque villagers also founded the Indigenous Community of the District of Yanque,[7] which was granted official status by the Ministry of Labor and Indigenous Matters in 1965.[8]

Emerging in a moment of enthusiasm for declaring legal forms of Indigenous autonomy in Yanque, the Irrigators Assembly encompassed all local agriculturalists, who banded together to collectively manage and regulate the irrigation water that they used. Resonant with widespread peasant rights mobilizations in Peru and Latin America at the time,[9] the group was formed to take local sovereignty over the limited water that came to Yanque land in the form of runoff from Mount Mismi's snowpack. With this power, the assembly could maintain collective hydrological infrastructures, dictate terms for water sharing, and prevent the illicit diversion of water in a space that, like much of the Andes, has historically required intricate and delicate irrigation techniques.[10] The updated version of the Irrigators Assembly, the Irrigators Committee (Comisión de Regantes), was founded in Yanque in August 1964.[11] Committees like these were made standard across Peru as part of President Juan Velasco's 1969 Water Law.[12] David Guillet sees the endurance of autonomous collective irrigation in the Colca Valley's "fragile and demanding environment," whose growing season is short and can easily fall victim to frost and drought, as evidence of a long-term legacy of "competent water management and well-adjusted land use" in the region.[13]

The early 2000s saw a contested state attempt to recognize formal communal water rights in Yanque-Urinsaya. Those rights would have consisted of fixed amounts of water based on models designed by urban technocrats.[14] Yanque-Urinsaya water authorities refused formalization. They argued that it did not leave room for reciprocity arrangements or account for flexible communal means of determining economic justice in the event of a dispute or a *campesino* falling on hard times. Nor did it account for dramatically fluctuating water availability as a result of climate change. Villagers have successfully held onto decision making and policing power over water rights, which could not be removed from ritualized labor into bureaucratic logics of resource management.[15]

Some Yanque-Urinsaya growers also benefit from the Majes Canal proj-ect, the ongoing, multidecade, billion dollar public-private construction project to divert water from a highland reservoir near Espinar and channel it to new farmland in the coastal desert lowlands at the eastern reaches of the province.[16] The select Colca communities, including parts of Yanque, that can access water from the canal use it to mitigate against exposure to drought, as successful harvests in recent years have required increasing volumes of irrigated water. The canal heightens regional water access dis-parities. Upstream villagers in Caylloma District and across the provincial border in Espinar have suffered extreme water loss from the project and have mounted strong protests.[17]

Although some Yanque growers' fields now fare better in terms of water access, uneven development in the region has made cash cropping a newly precarious livelihood. Most Yanque growers are part of regional cash-crop markets and also engage in some subsistence farming. By the late 2010s, because of expanding large-scale corporate farms in Peru's fertile coastal low-lands,[18] crop prices were plummeting throughout the Andes. This corporate expansion compounded the impacts of drought and unpredictable weather to make small-scale agriculture an increasingly risky market investment. Elderly Yanque peasant Juana Suico suggested that the land "is giving very few products. . . . In the past it gave well and now it doesn't." Edwin Oxa, another Yanque resident and aspiring tourism entrepreneur, speculated that agriculture would soon be "just to eat . . . no longer for business."

For farmers in cash-crop markets and subsistence farmers alike, rela-tions to land and water are an essential dimension of agricultural life. The idioms of attachment, giving, and reciprocity that accompany this region's relatively autonomous high-mountain irrigation and agricultural work ex-tend care beyond the human. Andeanist scholars have debated the meaning and purpose of this care for nonhuman earth-beings. Their interpretations range from seeing care as "mountain worship" and an instrumental means of "propitiating these spirits"[19] to an expansion of the political arena,[20] to the fearful "domestication" of mountains as "semi-social" outsiders,[21] to or-dinary relationships rooted in mutual respect.[22] I found two concepts from the Andean political ecology literature on relationality to be particularly salient in my reading of how interdependencies played out near the diffuse margins of capitalist growth. These are the ideas of *giving* and *teaching*, which frame the acts that accompanied most of the attachment practices

I witnessed. Frequent acts of *giving*, including feeding and nourishing, accompanied these practices. As Guillermo Salas Carreño writes of ritualized acts in the Cuzco region's Quyllurit'i pilgrimage, "Humans acknowledge their dependence on particular earth-beings and try to maintain good social relations with them through different ways of giving food to them."[23] The land was also described as something that can "give," as Juana Suico suggested. *Teaching* is the second concept that features in attachment practices. John Treacy mobilizes the phrase "teaching water" to describe how Colca peasants guide water's path.[24] I also saw moments of teaching beyond irrigation, orienting relations more broadly with mountains, water, soil, and land. Teaching is, at its best, not a means of domination or mastery over another but a collaborative, interdependent means of shaping specific orientations to the world. Teaching is mutual: Just as water and land were taught to work in particular ways, earth-beings also taught humans to engage in specific kinds of labor.

## Assembling Relations: Gerardo

Gerardo Huaracha (Figure 2.1), the person who brought me to the scenes of attachment that follow this section, was born on October 3, 1941. He told me that he grew up in the house just behind his current home, where we sat to talk. He identifies himself as belonging to a Quechua family that descended from Inca-era authorities: "My grandfather was the last *kuraka*[25] of Yanque, and this house, with the museum, was my grandfather's, left to me as an inheritance." Gerardo has been adding small buildings to his home over the years. In our many long interviews,[26] I would listen to his stories while beholding the increasingly lush garden he has built out of a raised stone bed in the middle of the courtyard.

Gerardo described excelling in school until age 12, after which there was no longer a local school to attend. His family owned multiple plots of land, or *chakras*,[27] and was, as he depicted it, relatively wealthy within Yanque's peasant class. Working his family's fields was a constant fact of life: "I always worked in the *chakra* [fields], helping my parents. My wife also had her *chakritas* [little fields], where we planted corn, fava beans, potatoes. So always like that, in the *chakra*, I spent my life." Gerardo's life history unfolded as a constant movement between his *chakras* and opportunities that temporarily took him away from them. "At fifteen or sixteen, I left to work in the valleys of Camaná, Majes, and Vítor, for two, three months at a time." Although he remembered the work's "slave-like" conditions, he

FIGURE 2.1 Gerardo Huaracha at a *Yarqa Haspiy* labor party. To Gerardo's right, in the background, a woman holds out a bowl of soup. This photograph is currently displayed in Gerardo's museum. Source: Gerardo Huaracha Archive.

was able to generate savings that later helped him purchase more land. The annual rice harvest at large haciendas in these lowland coastal valleys was a common destination for young male Andean labor migrants in the 1950s: "Before, we pretty much didn't have money, so we all went to the coast to work . . . with just our hands. . . . Now, no longer, the harvest is by machine."

Gerardo married Luisa Cutipa at age 22, and at 28 he was appointed district governor, the municipal representative of the Peruvian president. He spoke of the years he held that authority as a time of bountiful land and communal cooperation.

Back then the Colca was good: good climate, a lot of products, right? We planted corn, fava beans, potatoes, and we saw good harvests. But now, these days, it's not like that anymore. . . . Back then, the people in Yanque were really obedient of the [municipal] authorities, right? When I ordered that the next day we had to all work in a *faena* [communal labor party], everyone obeyed my authority.

Here, Gerardo highlights the duty that Yanque villagers felt toward one another and toward their land as an object of nostalgia, in contrast to the intensifying individualism of the present.

One of the most significant manifestations of that duty was a defining moment in 1971, when Gerardo was district governor. He recounted a deadly water conflict in which Yanque villagers were forced to physically defend the ability to irrigate their fields, affirming the *chakra* as a central theme of Gerardo's life.[28] The conflict was a direct product of colonial divide-and-conquer administration: *Reducción* district divisions and later iterations of republican governance imposed boundaries that failed to account for long-distance irrigation. The conflict took place between the Yanque-Urinsaya Peasant Community and the neighboring village of Coporaque. Fought with fists and rocks, the "Battle of Chachayllo," as it was locally known, arose over a stretch of canal that ran through a terrain called Chachayllo, in Coporaque territory, on its way to Yanque's fields. The canal's source was Mount Mismi, whose snowpack and mountain springs belonged to Yanque-Urinsaya and provided the community with most of its irrigation water. "The land of Mismi belonged to Yanque," Gerardo told me. "The water was for Yanque, right? The people from Coporaque wanted to take fifteen days of water and leave fifteen days for Yanque [each month], but we didn't let them enter. So a field war [*guerra campal*] broke out and there was one death, from Yanque, [a man] named Jesús Montalvo Suni." Gerardo's side prevailed. It is possible that losing a young man strengthened their resolve. Communal dependence on viable land was so important as to warrant the loss of a human life.

Gerardo described such strong attachments to the land as having been frayed and strengthened in later years by diverse aspects of a changing economy, which he had the chance to witness up close. The region saw broader market integration beginning with the Majes Canal project. Since then, Gerardo suggested, commitments have been altered and individualized.

Before, we planted just for consumption in the home, so fava beans, wheat, barley, potato, native potatoes, right? We brought seeds from

Cuzco . . . and now they are seeding—we are seeding for the market,
right? Potatoes—you hardly see the native potato anymore—they say
it's just for business, for the market. We plant very little for the house,
right?

Although he appeared nostalgic for the era when his community was less
fragmented and the land was more giving, Gerardo did not see new markets
as interrupting his relations with the *chakra*. He identified himself as "the
first one who began to work with tourism" in Yanque. In the late 1990s he
transformed the oldest standing structure on his small property, built in
1872, into a museum where he displays historical artifacts and archival documents. The museum is what one Arequipa-based NGO staff member called
his "brand": With the museum as his central attraction, in 2010 Gerardo
launched the Casa Museo Uyu Uyu, his experiential tourism business, where
he would host backpackers, New Age tourists, and people eager to experience
a day in the life of a Yanque *campesino*. At least several travelers a month
would stay in his house. "With tourism, Colca has improved really nicely," he
said. "All of us who work in tourism, we are all doing better. We have better
houses, educate our children, but there are other people that pretty much
have no interest in tourism, right? They say, 'What will tourism give *me*?'"

   With a subtle critique of his fellow community members, Gerardo
scrambles a neat distinction between individualizing market logics and
communal obligation, arguing that a marketized tourism could be another
shared local commitment in Yanque but that individual selfishness is an
obstacle to such a thriving market. Gerardo's story is one of multiple attachments and engagements that are consistently rooted in the *chakra* but
frequently incorporate other elements of economic life. I now follow him
through three specific arenas of attachment.

## Attachments to Cultivation Land

Singing out to the terraced fields below them and the immense valley un-
folding beyond, in call and response, Gerardo, his son Sabino, and his friend
Máximo Checca blessed the dry earth so that it would nurture the quinoa
and fava beans they had just sown. "Hai le! Hai le!" Their voices were as loud
as they could go. "Hai le! Pachamamata!" ("Hai le for the Pachamama," or
the living earth), they chanted in Quechua, illuminated by the late Andean
afternoon's tired light. "Hai le! Diuspagarapusun!" ("Hai le! May God repay
us!") Voices cracked with chicha, the drink of gently fermented barley and
maize that accompanies days spent working the fields, reverberated down

the valley. They continued: "Ima sumaqta!" ("What beauty!"). Gerardo, who owned this land, hesitated and improvised, straining to remember the other verses. "Hai le! Mama Ch'elata!" "For Mama Ch'ela," the name of this female terrain. "Hai le!"

I watched, recording with my phone, as the workers chanted. I had spent the day working the land with them. We were all exhausted; my arms were sore. I was happy to have had my phone with me that September afternoon in 2014. The first time I had heard a Hialeo song was during a preliminary research trip in 2011. I remember how surprised I was to see a group of men chanting into the valley twilight. When it ended, Gerardo turned to me with a knowing look and said, "You should have recorded that."

The complete scene that I recorded three years later shows a group of peasants singing to the land after a long day of planting, as Luisa, married to Gerardo, and Serafina, Máximo's wife, sat nearby, preparing the evening meal and filling in the lyrics that the men had forgotten. Other verses asked for continued agricultural prosperity, sought fortune and wealth (represented by the Quechua words *qori* and *qolqe*, for gold and silver), and blessed the yoke, plow, and other agricultural instruments they had used that day. Here, the *chakra* is more than a site of agricultural production measurable by yield. It is a relative, a relation, a member of the community that wanted to be sung to and that wanted to drink the laborers' chicha.

In a later conversation, Gerardo's son-in-law Miguel described feeding the *chakra* as part of a long-standing local theory of human-nonhuman relations that has animated Collagua communities since before the Incas arrived. "If you don't do a good *pago*," he suggested, "then this land is not going to give. That is to say, the land gives you a benefit, a good product, and you, what are you going to give? So, it's like an exchange." A woman leading another *pago* I attended for a newly constructed house told the group that "the Pachamama feels pain when she bears fruit, just like a mother." She can also get angry and become capriciously destructive, the ritual leader told us.[29] For that reason, the Pachamama had to share in human consumption.

The Hialeo song and nourishment are gestures that strengthen the attachments between workers and the *chakra* that are characterized by reciprocal obligations of care between sentient subjects. The workers teach the land to bear fruit. Other trips to the *chakra* involved slower ritual feedings, where Gerardo and his fellow workers would bring plastic bags filled with food for the earth that could include alpaca fat, coca leaves, dried corn cobs, wine, yogurt, Coca Cola, Caballo Viejo (an inexpensive cane liquor), and chicha.[30] These elements formed part of the *iranta* (bundle) to be burned as part of the feeding process. The bundle's baroque variety was an articulation of abundance, with many distinct items crossing the boundary from profane into sacred to enact the attachment. This act of giving emphasized that the Pachamama was both demanding and could reward abundantly.

Singing was the concluding act for a day of work that was far from simple drudgery. The work consisted of guiding two yoked bulls to create furrows in the soft dirt, for which Sabino took charge, and then dropping seeds and beans into the folds, which Serafina did. Gerardo, Máximo, and I followed her, using rakes to smooth over the furrowed soil. To plant in places that the plow could not reach, three of us, each taking a foot plow (or *chakitaklla*), would dig a small hole into a patch of ground for seeds to be dropped in. I also briefly tried directing the bulls, a difficult effort that resulted in clumsy asymmetric furrows in the soil and laughter from the group. They quickly put a stop to my attempt.

The labor was punctuated by frequent breaks, where each member of the group would drink at least one completely full tall glass of chicha, one at a time, passing the single glass to the next person once they had finished. Each drinker first had to whisper a prayer to the *chakra* and the Pachamama and offer several drops to the soil. Upon finishing, a drinker would also leave a mouthful of chicha in the glass to give to the soil again, before passing the glass to Serafina or Luisa, who poured each new serving.[31] These gently intoxicating chicha sharing sessions were at once a rest and a celebrated reward for labor. As a Yanque resident in his early 20s told me jokingly during another day of planting, "*Yanqueños* will stop for chicha for the tiniest reason," even if just to reward themselves for plowing a few feet. Villagers from Yanque were proud of their strong and flavorful brew of chicha and of their ability to consume it in immense quantities. Alcohol consumption was a frequent target of development worker concern as a gateway to dependency and delinquency. However, villagers tend to drink chicha in groups, where the act of drinking and sharing with the soil strengthens attachments with one another and with the earth. *Yanqueños* would also regularly suggest that the nutrient-rich chicha brings strength, health, and endurance to a body engaged in difficult physical labor.[32] They contrasted chicha with the stronger and more harmful alcohol processed in factories.[33]

The scene of sharing and giving in the field did not take place in isolation from the region's capitalist markets. Likely half of the fava beans and quinoa would be sold as cash crops to wholesalers in Chivay. Days in the *chakra* were just one part of Gerardo's varied economic routine, which also included tending to the occasional tourist or visitor to the museum, traveling to the national bank in Chivay to collect the state's monthly social security payment or a cash transfer from one of his urban-based children, herding alpacas in his high pastureland near Tuti, negotiating prices with an alpaca wool intermediary, and plenty of other kinds of work. Attachments to the land and to Gerardo's fellow workers were part of a more widely encompassing set of social and economic obligations that could sometimes be reinforced by financial success in capitalist spaces. Relational logic was not opposite to or mutually exclusive with those other forms of economic life; they frequently touched and influenced one another.

Songs like the Hialeo were embodied engagements with Peruvian resource logics. The song's subtexts were newly poor harvests, brutal frosts, unseasonable heat, unanticipated heavy rains, and other climatic changes that are disrupting a once predictable agricultural cycle. Drawing resource logic into relief, this act took abundance to be the hard-won result of a human-*chakra* interdependence strengthened through the caring labor of planting, nurturing, and feeding. Abundance for Gerardo and his workers, in the form of a full harvest, was earned. It was part of a relationship of exchange. Instead of a spectacular resource wealth that gushed forth only after a properly managed capitalist entrepreneurial infrastructure was put in place, abundance here meant thriving in a way that did not depend solely on market accumulation and biological growth in a way that did not perpetually increase. Abundance was the *result* of this labor and infused its entire *process* through acts of singing, feeding, drinking, and exchanging.

## Attachments to Humans

Humans were also interdependent with one another. Two acts of attachment were central for forging and strengthening these interdependencies: *ayni* and *faenas*.

*Ayni*, as Rolando "Roly" Checca explained it to me, means a chain of nonmonetary reciprocal obligations.

> You seed in your *chakra*? I come to your *chakra*. And the day that I'm seeding in my *chakra*, and you come, bringing two people, I do just the same [*igualito*]. I come early? You come early. I come midday? You come midday. I bring five people? You bring five people. But I don't pay you even a sol. Of course, you get chicha, food . . . That is *ayni*.

*Ayni* stresses a bond between humans rooted in an equivalent effort expended by each participant.[34] The food that Roly mentions as essentially a form of payment is likely to have been cooked and hauled to the field by women in the group,[35] underlining the central place of feminized labor in Roly's vision of a nonneoliberal, nonindividualist abundance. As Roly defined it, *ayni* is an indefinite mutual obligation between kin, friends, or other groups of people who know one another.

*Faenas*, or communal labor parties, are more like a tax. They are occasional obligations that encompass the entire community. *Faenas* can involve mandatory construction work, often to maintain a stretch of road, bridge, reservoir, or irrigation canal.[36] In Yanque land is privately owned but irrigation water and certain infrastructure are communal property. Labor obligations to repair, build, or maintain communal infrastructure can occupy a full day or more of work that is unpaid aside from meals and chicha. Yanque is a class-diverse community; the amount of labor that each member owes is often a function of the amount of land one owns, especially in *faenas* that are run by Yanque-Urinsaya's Irrigators Committee. *Faenas* are scenes of redistribution that make visible those Yanqueños who possess more land.

One *faena* I attended with Gerardo required all water-using community members to engage in the backbreaking labor of digging hard, mud-cracked dirt out of the bottom of a dry reservoir near the village's agricultural fields, placing it in a sack, and walking up the hill out of the reservoir to dump the heavy sediment. Another was a collective project to create new stone pools out of the natural hot springs along the shores of the Colca River. This would open a free retreat for community members and create a new income-generating tourist attraction.

Many of these work parties also began with a *pago*. But *faena* labor was clearly centered on attachments between human actors. Through this act of taking on a burden together, community members co-labored while articulating a shared will. *Faenas* were long sessions of labor for which participating could have high opportunity costs. *Faenas* today frequently fill in the gaps that neoliberal austerity leaves open. In the broader context of regional and national economies structured by capitalist extraction, *faenas* have a double role. On the one hand, they forge and build communal interdependencies. On the other, they supplement and interrupt a "porous" capitalist order,[37] subsidizing state infrastructural neglect. *Faenas* smooth out the frictions of neoliberal growth with an extractive burden that falls to rural villagers.[38]

### Attachments to Mountains

One *faena* has particular priority in Yanque, bringing together both human-human and human-nonhuman attachments: the annual canal cleaning in Yanque-Urinsaya, a ceremony known as the *Escarbo de la Sequia* in Spanish or *Yarqa Haspiy* (canal dredging) in Quechua. This labor party, run by the Irrigators Committee, is the most important four days in the community's agricultural and ritual calendar. The four-day excursion entails scraping sediment out of the entire canal that runs from the decreasingly snowy summit of Mount Mismi, a supervising earth-being, to Yanque's agricultural fields. The canal is partly built of cement and is partly an improvised path through the soil that laborers have to recreate annually to channel a stream, teaching water to run between the mountain peak and the agricultural fields.[39] This *faena* is an extended community obligation that every user of irrigation water must participate in. The alternative to laboring is sending a day laborer, a practice that the Irrigators Committee frowns on.[40] Stereotyped as rowdy, day laborers are usually young men from other villages and lower in class status than an established peasant irrigator. If users are unable to send a laborer in their stead, they must pay 80 soles per *topo* of land a laborer owns.[41] About 150 men and 30 women attended this labor party when Gerardo brought me along with him in 2015.

A crucial moment in this communal obligation is the *pago* that begins the four days of labor. In 2015 the *pago* was led by Gil Rivera, that year's water mayor, who opened the labor party's engagement with the land. This was an act meant both to ensure safe and joyous labor in the near term and to secure another year of mountain snowpack, which meant avoiding drought and keeping farmland in use in the longer term. Marking gifts to the water-providing *Apu* (or Lord) Mismi, the *pago* recognized the start of August as a moment when "the earth is alive, warm, and fertile."[42] The *pago* involved creating a bundle of fragrant plants, coca leaves, small pieces of alpaca tallow, and incense, which were offered to the canal. The *iranta* was passed to each participant, who had to blow on it in three rapid breaths before it was tossed into a small bonfire next to the canal. Taking the tray and breathing in its substance, each participant whispered prayers to Mismi and named their own *chakras*, asking for a year of fertility speculatively diagrammed by the miniatures and the bundle of gifts. People also asked for material prosperity, income for their businesses, safety for children working in the region's mines, and other wishes for their daily lives. Such ritualized reinforcements of attachment took place in an idiom distinct from that of resource logic.[43] But these attachments could closely overlap with and even reinforce efforts to attain capitalist prosperity. Every laborer present had to contribute their breath to the tray and, separately, to a trio of coca leaves (or *k'intu*). When it was my turn, Gerardo told me to whisper the name of his museum to the smoldering bundle, so that it might bring in income. Afterward, the group passed around shots of warm *almidón*, a sweet corn starch–based liquor, to drink and to offer to Mismi's thirsty soil.

The *pago* required crafting miniature figurines of mountain peaks covered in snow and thriving animal lives. Workers offered these miniature representations to Mismi by placing them in physical contact (Figure 2.2). To do this, the water mayor first had to locate a cement chamber, dug about a foot deep into the ground next to the canal. Once he found the chamber, he opened its metal door and extracted the figurines that had been living there over the previous year. They were a collection of earth-beings: three snow-covered mountains made of a miniature traditional clay pot (*q'ero*), which forms the base, and cotton on the top, representing snow at the peak. Gil, the water mayor, and a small group of helpers refreshed the snow. They glued a new puff of cotton to the spout of each clay pot with two dark corn kernels placed as eyes at the top. These figurines articulated the collective

FIGURE 2.2 Composing a tableau of figurines during the *pago a la tierra* ritual on August 1, 2015. These figurines spend the year underground in the chamber to the left.

wish for water in the coming year. Andean miniatures are often linked to desires for well-being or material wealth.[44] Here, they called for rain in an era of drought, unpredictable storms, increasingly unreliable snow, and the other destabilizing ravages of climate change.[45] By placing these figurines in a sealed box below the ground next to the canal, in contact with Mismi's soil, they would be *consubstantial* with Mismi and thus would summon snow to its peak.

Consubstantiation is the act of becoming (like) an other by consuming substances associated with that other.[46] These figurines perform consubstantiation as a speculative staging, laden with affects of hope and anxiety.[47] The mountain ground "eats" them; they stage an aspirational tableau of mountains fully covered in snow that spends a year inside a chamber touching the soil of one of those mountains. The three miniatures stand in for the surrounding mountain earth-beings whose snow supplies water to the region: Mismi, Yanque-Urinsaya's chief *Apu* near whose summit we were gathered, and the two other nearby mountains, Ch'uwaña and Ch'illa. Accompanying the mountain figurines to form a gathering of earth-beings are figurines of alpaca and corn with black seeds for eyes. There is also a mound of alpaca wax and the real head of an alpaca fetus, also decorated with seed eyes. Alan Huaracha, Gerardo's son, told me that these figures signify the rebirth of healthy animals. Anchoring the whole tableau was a waxy God figure, its head covered in a halo, standing before the animals and mountains, with hands outstretched as though addressing the assembled audience of living things and earth-beings. Once the laborer-artists finished composing these figurines, they doused the assemblage with anisette and placed the refreshed miniatures back into the chamber next to the canal.

In Figure 2.2, notice the blurred arm holding a camera in the foreground. I was far from the only person taking pictures. The younger laborers present had their digital cameras and smartphones out for much of the ceremony, attempting to capture it for their Facebook profiles, Instagram posts, WhatsApp chats, and relatives who could not attend. Peruvian anthropologist Mario Sánchez Dávila, who was present for the labor party in 2015 along with three other anthropology students visiting from Lima, finds that many young people born in Yanque are developing their connections to irrigation labor through social media. They make recordings to "audiovisually register a ritual tradition to perpetuate it, because . . . they see it as threatened."[48] Adolescents who live in Yanque and others who have moved elsewhere for education or work take seriously this practice of attachment, Sánchez Dávila suggests, even those who are not routinely engaged in agricultural labor. The enthusiastic participation of young Yanque villagers and of people born in Yanque who have spent most of their lives in urban Arequipa complicates any easy narrative of youth abandonment of rural life. Decisions to leave agricultural work or to migrate did not necessarily mean a complete departure, forgetting, or detachment from the land.

In one conversation during the work party, one of the visiting students asked Roly Checca whether it would be easier to pipe the water directly from Mismi's summit to Yanque's fields. This might, in their view, eliminate the need for annual maintenance. Roly corrected the student's misunderstanding. He told the student that the idea of "saving" labor misses the point. He distinguished between ritualized and technified uses of water, juxtaposing extractive and relational senses of abundance to defend territorial attachment as a reliable means of knowing and using Mismi's water. This did not mean a purist ban on all irrigation technology; several stretches of canal had been enhanced with cement walls and pipes to maximize water catchment. However, a comprehensive piping project would be expensive, would risk altering the local ecology, and might result in even less water, as irrigators remake the stream every year by following the water's flow. Ceasing all ritualized manual labor would also risk eroding respectful relations with the land. Failing to complete proper *pagos* could risk accidents, bad weather, and drought.

## Conflict, Critique, and Anxiety

These practices of attachment foregrounded local ideas of abundance. In speeches, debates, and other moments of explicit term setting, Gerardo, his family, and his colleagues in Yanque explicitly theorized how practices of attachment worked at the diffuse margins of extractive capitalism. Because of its heightened importance, the *Yarqa Haspiy* in particular was a space of dispute over how those practices should best be conducted. Gerardo explicitly argued for maintaining this ancestral relation-building tradition when he addressed the labor group in 2015.

> They have left us a gift, our ancestors, and it falls upon us to do the maintenance, do the cleaning. Just like the rest of my colleagues have said, if we name someone captain, then obey him; [do] what he orders you to do. Then, companions, we must work really beautifully. . . . That is my recommendation, users and brothers. We all help one another

as younger to older and older to younger. Also, all respectfully: That
canal is a gift from our ancestors, so may we all work with goodwill,
and obey our leaders. . . . Thank you very much.

Gerardo was adamant about respect for authority. The beautiful (*bonito*)
work Gerardo commands blends senses of "neat" or "even," as in bunching
up a pile of hay so that it can be carried easily, with a more ethical notion of
"proper," as in following ritual protocol. Beauty, for Gerardo, is an ethic that
orients this act of collaborative "maintenance" of a "gift," terms that locate
the practice in contrast to the expansionist imperative of capitalist growth.
Other irrigators urged the group to conduct their labor "with patience" and
to engage offerings with adequate faith, which would guarantee "that in the
rainy season we don't have any accidents."

At the labor party's daily assemblies, anxieties about the tradition's disappearance led to tense debate. During one meeting at the 2015 labor party,
irrigators disputed whether cars and trucks posed a threat to the annual
custom, voicing concerns that easy transportation could mean losing laborers. But others emphasized that transportation was essential to their
attendance; the multiplicity of jobs that men and women worked alongside
agriculture meant that some had to be able to leave in order to balance
their other economic commitments. Concerned about how the pervasive
disputes themselves might be a worrying sign of dissolution, one irrigator
protested, "Each year this is more disorganized." Some laborers challenged
Irrigators Committee president Celestino Vilcazán's ban on using donkeys
for carrying supplies up the mountain. Eventually, Celestino put a stop to
the meeting, impatiently defending the spirit of the labor party.

> No, no, no, I said it very clearly in the [earlier opening] assembly. This
> part about losing our customs? These customs continue normally. We
> have squads, we have work, we have rituals. The only change is that
> you don't use animals. . . . I certainly don't want to maintain them
> personally . . . and for tomorrow, I don't oppose [other customs like]
> the soccer game.

Celestino's indignant response rendered overt what counted as a *Yarqa
Haspiy* custom. For him, it meant not a rote repetition of certain practices
every year but the ability to continue the collective reforging of attachment
with Mismi and the water it gives.

In our 2019 life history interview, Gerardo shared his own anxieties about the labor party.

> We spend two kilometers walking the canal where the water originates. That's a beautiful custom. On [August] fourth, we return, by Uyu Uyu . . . where you and I walked . . . that's the custom. Now, this year, what will happen? Since there is nobody acting as water mayor, what's going to happen this year? . . . Will there even be musicians? What's going to happen? But according to the custom, family members, wives, kids, always have to arrive, to see the return [of the workers and the water]. We greet family members with their chicha, and they go drinking their chicha. I don't know what it will be like now. I think the custom, this year, is going to be lost.

Every year when I visited Yanque, Gerardo would forecast the labor party's demise, an anxious speculation reflecting his concerns that acts of strengthening relations to land were declining more generally. Gerardo emphasized to me that the users' faith in their exchanges with Mismi and their other *pagos* would matter for how much water would be available in the coming year and for how abundant the harvest would be. Dreading the disappearance of a custom indexed a deeper political ecology of feeling rooted in dread for the loss of sustaining relations with an altered, unpredictable landscape. I found it shocking when Gerardo suggested that although climate change was real, the newly intense droughts and poor harvests might still be the community's own fault for not conducting *pagos* with adequate faith. Roly corroborated this, telling me that the fact that such *pagos* had grown rare might have indicated a dangerous lack of commitment. "We are not like we used to be," he said. "You know, land has power. It has life. This works, you know. It's not something we joke about!"

Gerardo and Luisa often told me that *pagos* were losing their importance. In one conversation Luisa described how, in past decades, Yanque residents would conduct daily offerings, burning redolent assemblages after days of agricultural work. She could smell the burning of coal, corn, and coca from the village's gridded dirt lanes each night as dusk began to fall. For Gerardo and Luisa, a "felt theory" of loss did not just mean diminished practices or bygone economies. It meant the more intimate change of a sensory dulling.[49]

Noncapitalist practices of attachment and success in capitalist markets could be mutually reinforcing. However, in many conversations about these practices, the prospect of capitalist growth became palpable through affects of anxiety, dread, and ambivalence. One day, Epifanio Checca, Gerardo and Luisa's son-in-law, sat with Gerardo, Luisa, and me at the kitchen table. We were slowly sharing a tall glass of leftover chicha. The group expressed concern that women, who were once reliably available to take up the unpaid labor of cooking for collective labor parties, were increasingly absent from *pagos* and *faenas* because of newfound economic opportunities. In Peru and around the world, women are overdetermined targets of entrepreneurial empowerment. Scholarship on Andean women identifies them with both flexible and devalued roles in home and market spaces.[50] As Florence Babb suggests, writing about early 1990s Nicaragua, devalued and flexible women's labor positions women as "shock absorbers" for neoliberal austerity.[51] In 2010s Peru, they also absorb the shocks of climate change, price drops, and mining, which have all recently intensified the precarity of agriculture in Colca. Development experts who associate women with flexible obligations to home and family see that flexibility as a site of capitalist promise.

For example, Gerardo and Luisa's daughter Guillermina, who is married to Epifanio, had recently taken on two new jobs that occupied nearly all her time. She had a well-paid job as a chef at the Killa Wasi Lodge, a small upscale bed and breakfast in Yanque. She was also busy with her own entrepreneurial venture. She ran the Sumac Cantuta Wasi (Beautiful Cantuta House) hostel in her home,[52] and was president of the Sumac Yanque Ayllus (Beautiful Yanque Ayllus), the local business consortium of experiential tourism hotels. Guillermina's new inability to participate in extended communal obligations was consistent with the development project message that an enterprise should take priority over all other obligations. This was what Ybed Taco, an agent from the Arequipa-based NGO Grupo GEA, advised Guillermina and her consortium partners at a capacity-building workshop. Ironically, entrepreneurship for Guillermina meant a radical departure from the daily flexibility that boosters of microenterprise were so intently fixated on.

In a related irony, approaching enterprise as a disciplined de-diversification of economic life means that a paradigm of entrepreneurship that mobilizes Indigenous custom as an income-generating asset can actually disentangle villagers from those customs. Revalorizing only objects that promise to generate income, such as a home-cooked quinoa soup or a packaged farming experience for cultural tourists, has not meant recuperating everything that villagers consider worthy of maintenance. The work of this group of local tourism entrepreneurs also had to be entirely financially independent, in contrast to coexisting local emphases on a more interdependent achievement of prosperity. As Guillermina told me in a separate interview, referring to the Sumac Yanque Ayllus businesses, "We don't have even a single support of money, nor anything from our local authorities. Nobody, nobody, nobody. We just work with our own money."

That day at the kitchen table, I asked Epifanio whether it was a good thing that women in the community, such as Guillermina, were bringing in more income, even if that took them away from communal events. He was ambivalent. He acknowledged the opportunity for economic gain and told me that he was just as invested in their shared business. He also worried that when it came to relation building, "the customs keep changing." Before, he said, life was centered not so singularly on income and enterprise but instead on agricultural labor and mutual aid. "All we had was the field [el campo]. Everything was based on ayni. There isn't anybody left for ayni now."

The frequent references to loss of custom I heard in Yanque point to the ambivalences of the present moment in the region's development. Like Epifanio, Guillermina, and many other Yanque residents, Epifanio's brother Roly built his livelihood by drawing selectively from hegemonic resource logics, even as he, too, sometimes worried about their consequences. Roly owns a small hostel and an attached store where he and his wife sell snacks, fruit, and vegetables. Recently, he has also been working as a trekking guide, taking groups on multiday hiking trips to nearby mountain peaks. One of the places where this new economic success became visible was at the *Yarqa Haspiy*, which he has proudly attended every year since he was a teenager, laboring on behalf of his father, an 80-year-old agriculturalist with many landholdings. In the 2015 labor party, I saw Roly facing the cold like a tourist hiker, with a sleek winter jacket, a warm tent, and a sleeping bag. These were unusual supplies for *Yarqa Haspiy* laborers, most of whom slept in the open air on mattress pads covered by heavy alpaca blankets.

Roly spoke of a past abundance that contemporary growth could not replace. When he was a child, "we only ate natural foods," such as corn, potatoes, and quinoa, and, he emphasized, "all nat-u-ral fruits" (*todas frutas nat-u-rales*). Roly's childhood was a time of plenty in his description: of healthy food, of the will to collaborate on agricultural work, even of enjoyable labor. This ended suddenly as his family's stretched budget forced their hand. They sent him to live with his godparents in Arequipa, which he described as two years of hunger and humiliation.[53] Meanwhile, Yanque changed too, as Roly narrated, invoking Peru's president in the 1990s: "Fujimori brought electricity," which "has its advantages and disadvantages," because "before, we lived peacefully. There wasn't so much delinquency. . . . There weren't so many fiestas, like now. There were some, but they were healthy. We would seed with a little pisco, *almidón*, or chicha. Beer? There was no beer; it just appeared in the 1990s."[54]

Describing his nostalgia for a past abundance, Roly flips the moral script on the promises of market integration, as he mentions the processed food, criminality, and homogenization that markets helped expand in Yanque. He blamed the recent decline in good harvests on villagers' own failure to care for the land and engage it as a full member of the community. He also expressed concerns about climate change and other consequences of large-scale pollution.

> Before things were more beautiful, healthier. Now . . . there's no rain . . . the *chakras* don't produce like they used to, the weather is no longer like it used to be, right? The weather we'd see before, right? It's time for this fiesta. Great, it's going to rain. We already knew. That bird is singing, right? It's going to rain, and it rains. . . . We saw everything, and it all coincided. Now, we say that something's going to happen, but it doesn't work anymore. You can't talk like that anymore. The climate has changed a lot. That's how it is.

In fieldwork visits toward the end of the 2010s, I heard the refrain "it's not like it used to be" (*ya no es como antes*) repeated with uncanny consistency throughout Yanque to describe both fading practices and an erratic climate. These anxieties suggest that the village's relatively autonomous practices of water care and territorial attachment cannot be read in a vacuum. The scholars who researched irrigation practices in the Colca Valley during the 1980s and 1990s rightly appreciated the endurance of these practices through multiple colonizations and described them without overstating the valley's isolation from broader circuits of commerce. However, they were writing before climate change's accelerating time scale was widely appreciated. Some of their understandings of how intensified droughts and marginalization influence these practices require updating. For instance, Treacy's 1994 article on Colca Valley water practices features a map of water maintenance systems that refers to "permanent snowpack" on mountain summits as a consistent water source.[55] But just twenty years later, villagers would regularly comment that the mountain peaks were no longer reliably covered in snow. Roly's narratives of loss blame both the climate crisis and individuals. Others focused their environmental critiques entirely on individual responsibility; in the words of elderly *campesina* Melita Castro Cáceres, "We are polluting ourselves. Now we don't value what we used to." She lamented the overuse of chemical fertilizers, which are responsible for "seeding cancer."

Mirta Casaperalta Taco, a 30-year-old Yanque *regidora* (council member) who in her 20s had traveled to the United States to study tourism and was also a part-time farmer, couched her more direct critique of urban-centric capitalism in a similar nostalgia. "Young people," she told me, "no longer want to work in the *chakra*. They don't see a future there, or they don't see that they can have a very good livelihood dedicating themselves to agriculture." For that reason, people are leaving communities like Yanque for Arequipa and other cities; she estimated that Yanque's population was declining by 100 people per year. She was more hopeful about an economy rooted in the *chakra* than one based in the city, theorizing a sense of abundance in subsistence.

> There are many people who think that, going to the city, they are going to have a better quality of life. But it's not like that. If you migrate from here to the city, and you don't have secure work, your life is worse than here because at least here, you have land. You can cultivate potatoes or corn, but you have enough to eat. On the other hand, in the city, you have to pay. . . . Before, the high school taught us agriculture and livestock. When I studied, you had to do work in the *chakra*. They taught you to plant vegetables, right? You had knowledge, and you grew with that excitement that you can do something not just in theory, but you can also do things in the *chakra*. . . . Before, young people, I felt like, um, we were more responsible, with more activities to do. Today you don't see many of them. And it's changed a lot because again social media means that young people are tied to their phones instead of going to play or, I don't know, to the fields. That would be a waste.

Mirta's focus was the misguided dreams of urban progress that pulled young people away from Yanque. Yet like the urban life Mirta problematizes as a false promise, agriculture and cash cropping have not borne consistent fruit in the 2010s either, as prices plummet and as climate change brings unstable conditions. Her emphasis on staying in Yanque seeds a new kind of cruel optimism. However, migration rarely means complete abandonment; it can also mean the expansion of home, as Yanque families often maintain several home sites. The ability to draw on networks that cross urban and rural lines means that leaving is not necessarily irreversible.[56]

Taken together, these testimonies from Yanque residents negotiating and theorizing the intertwinement of heterogeneous dimensions of their livelihoods exemplify what Tim Choy has called "anticipatory nostalgia,"[57] a shared dread for the loss of an endangered way of life. However, as local theories of abundance through attachment have been drawn into a sharp urgency, they can *also* have the effect of provincializing and destabilizing any sense of a dominant "capitalist monolith."[58] Resources did not universally destroy relations. In some cases, as with Roly's trekking profits, market wealth enhanced experiences of participating in attachment-building practices. Other testimonies in this section draw on territorial attachments to put urban-centric extractive capitalism into perspective. Relational sensibilities can be voracious when it comes to capitalist practices.[59] As decolonial Peruvian agronomist Eduardo Grillo Fernandez writes, "We have lived and continue to live here in the Andes in our own way. . . . We have also assimilated the market by making of it one more arena for reciprocity—that is, to exercise the desire to give that is so typical of us—and for Andean interpersonal relations."[60] These ambivalences and overlaps reveal that engaging capitalism from its edges in Yanque is not a clean zero-sum prospect but a contested space where villagers agentively work out the kinds of attachments they want to build.

## Conclusion: Water's Return

The group of canal cleaners I joined in August 2015 abruptly stopped on their 12-kilometer journey back to Yanque. It was the last day of the labor party, and they had just been running down the trail from Mismi alongside the canal. The group was silent, and the air was still. On one side of us, in the direction we had just come from, was a steep rocky cliff, caked in dry dirt. On the other, we could see the reconstructed stone houses of Uyu Uyu and the yellow fields surrounding them, baking in the fading afternoon light. After a pause, three workers who had stayed higher up on the trail heard the signal from the water mayor on their walkie-talkies, telling them to open the water lock that had blocked the canal during the cleaning. The water began to trickle down the dry cliff. It gave way to a waterfall, its blast cutting through the silent awe as the renewed water reached its destination in Yanque with a deafening roar. Nearby, families and friends of the participating laborers stood ready to celebrate as the brass band played fast and loud. This moment of ecstatic celebration, the culmination of the labor party, launched the new agricultural year in Yanque on a note of hydraulic plenty. Water filled a large natural basin next to Uyu Uyu before making its way along canals into the nearby agricultural fields.

The arrival of the refreshed irrigation water happens in the exact place where villagers' ancestors were once cursed to drought. Water's return is a tableau of defiant abundance. Through "heterogeneous experiences of the transcendent" manifesting across generations, classes, and levels of community entanglement,[61] laborers reforged their connection to a terrain that would be lifeless without them and that they would be lifeless without. The *Yarqa Haspiy* teaches mountains to make water abundant, in annual defiance of the colonial curse of the *llakillaqta*.

*Pagos*, songs, and other acts of attachment to terrain meant giving (food, drink, emotion) to cement relations to nonhuman beings and other humans. As "micro-sites" for a political ecology of feeling,[62] practices affirming territorial attachments were the anxious subjects of collective speculation about disappearance. Growth, extraction, and financialization threatened to fray the social bonds at the core of such practices. But dimensions of capitalist growth ideologies could also reinforce attachments. The acts of interdependence that villagers engage in at the margins of a booming extractive capitalism suggest that resource and relational logics come to be at stake together in a tangled and often contradictory political field. Their intersection can be one of tense coexistence. It can also take the form of outright competition or close complementarity. But many Yanque-Urinsaya villagers resisted the complete erasure of the relation. Despite the expanding coloniality of resource logic, villagers insisted that certain locally organized institutions remain autonomous. They pushed back against resource logics not by insisting on a purist opposition between capitalist gain and relational community but by complicating the hegemonic narrative of a booming region in a moment of intensifying water precarity. Cultural sovereignty, in this context, takes the form of agentive and strategic decisions about how to become entangled with resource logics. Highlighting a politics of human-human and human-nonhuman *obligation* opens a space for making local meaning out of translocal economic change.

Gerardo and other villagers made clear that the maintenance of relations with the nonhuman world requires reinforcement over the course of ongoing cyclical and seasonal rhythms. The time I spent with extractive growth projects suggests that neoliberalism also needs its own constant, ritualized reinforcement. In a place where capitalism is hegemonic but patchy and lopsided, development agents worked hard to inculcate a view of the surrounding world that reduced it to a supply of resources. The rest of this book tracks that effort.

# 3

## Staging Growth

### *The Choreography of Indigenous Plenty*

Beauties of the world, loves of the soul
This is my land, pure poetry
This is my Lluta, beautiful land of mine.

—"Oh Pueblo de Lluta"

Bertha Jacobo Begazo took the stage overlooking Chivay's plaza and sang of an abundant land, accompanied by men playing guitars and *charangos*. Her home village, Lluta, in the low-lying western margin of Caylloma Province, was a place where one encounters "beauties of the world" and "pure poetry," according to the song. Bertha went on, as she faced the competition's judges, to sing of Lluta's "crystalline waters" and its "yellow barley," its "honor" and its "valor." Lyrics moved between Spanish and Quechua and between major and minor chords. I listened, noticing how they moved me, resonating with my own feelings of joy and homesickness.

This nostalgic ode is a feature of Lluta's Carnival celebration, an annual feast when those who have moved away from Lluta return. "Oh, pueblo of Lluta," the song continues, "of beautiful countryside, you are the dream of my yearnings." By repurposing the song and dance for a contest that ended a three-year Ministry of Agriculture initiative promoting rural entrepreneurs, Lluta residents recreated a celebration of their village. The reception was not entirely positive. Judges remarked on the awkward fact that the team from Taya had also just performed a Carnival dance for their entry in a contest where microcultural uniqueness was prized, even between neighbors as close as Lluta and Taya. But this is what the team had prepared. When I joined staff members on a site visit to Lluta just days earlier, participants told us that preparing for the contest was stressful. It demanded distinctive displays of "typical" practices, "original" dances and dishes, and other symbols of a thriving Indigenous heritage. Participants had to perform elaborate, colorful, sensuous spectacles of indigeneity, even though the low-budget initiative had supported only basic technical assistance and its prizes for competition winners were unimpressively low. What explains such a dramatic mismatch?

Agents of the state sought to make Peruvian growth feel real, not as the achievement of incremental technocratic improvements but as the ambient sense of spectacular potential that its minimal, austere investments would unleash. Economic growth has been undertheorized as a contingent and unstable social form in anthropological analyses of face-to-face development work.[1] In this chapter I offer an ethnographic analysis of how a state initiative staged rural Andean growth as though it were a spontaneous celebration of Indigenous difference. *Celebration* was the key motif of interaction in which state-affiliated development agents enacted growth. For the initiative staff, celebrations like the development fair were not structural interventions; these pageants of abundance did not alter the region's uneven development. Rather, their celebrations were inventories: happy displays of and routine-rupturing discourses about sources of capitalist promise beyond the boundaries of Peru's booming mining sector.

I train my focus on the Sierra Sur (Southern Highlands) Development Project, Phase II, an effort to create and support associations of agricultural entrepreneurs based in Peru's Ministry of Agriculture and Irrigation. The project, which ran from 2011 to 2014, focused on villages that had not previously received significant development aid, where residents felt "forgotten," as Elena, the district leader from Taya, would put it. Project staff incongruously punctuated basic agricultural investments with spectacular competitions that filled Caylloma's plazas with the sights, sounds, scents, tastes, textures, and affective attachments of a region conspicuously in the throes of newfound Indigenous prosperity. For a village team to have a chance at winning, or at least at gaining the nonmonetary, affective validation from initiative staff members recognizing their village as worthy of a place in the booming Peruvian economy, it was not acceptable simply to describe an improvement in alpaca fiber sales. Contestants had to *embody* that improvement. They had to put an indigeneity on opulent display that extended Marca Perú's branded celebration of difference as marketable but not destabilizing of the nation's extractive capitalist order.[2] And they had to display an independence that would contrast with staff stereotypes of chronic rural aid seeking. Paradoxically, contestants could only win prize money for independent enterprise and Indigenous empowerment by acceding to the project's baroque demands. This made participating in the apparent unleashing of growth extremely labor intensive for both villagers and development agents.

In staging growth as a spectacular celebration, the Peruvian state, embodied in the Sierra Sur staff, acted as "a hope-generating machine."[3] Yet in doing so, these celebrations also entrenched the state as "an object of psychic desire" for villagers who long felt neglected by it:[4] They read celebrations as an opening for them to forge new ties with state development projects. The promise of state presence and the promise of capitalist growth were two "cruel optimisms" that Sierra Sur's intervention seeded.[5] The project sought to demonstrate a newfound state care for underserved populations by investing in "permitted Indians."[6] But by staging growth as if it were something that would organically emerge during fixed three-year project, Sierra Sur's sensually saturated scenes also worked to transmit an optimistic attachment to surrounding resource wealth that would facilitate the state's departure. Affect and money were devices of an extractive care that devolved responsibility to grow onto villagers themselves. The project's ultimate aim was to locate new products for emerging markets of agricultural exporters, middle-class urban consumers, and foreign and domestic tourists.

Through the celebration, villagers heretofore ignored or abandoned by the state were, in the same move, cast as hopelessly dependent on state aid and offered the chance at apparent liberation from that humiliating dependence by spectacularly revitalizing their Indigenous economic lives. Sierra Sur demanded that contestants maximize their otherness to achieve inclusion in a boom economy beside a mine. To see their minimal share of Peruvian abundance, they had to reconcile the imperatives of maximal otherness and maximal market assimilation.

This was not, however, simply a villager struggle to satisfy the state's fantasy of an idealized Indigenous subject who is simultaneously independent, entrepreneurial, ready to sell the Peruvian brand, and authentic to their truest self but not so different that they destabilize that brand.[7] The state's staging of growth also opened space for villagers to recruit state representatives into their own vision of prosperity as the result of a chain of mutual obligations. Timothy Mitchell proposes reading the state as an accumulation of "mundane arrangements" that organize specific interactions that scale up to an emergent "set of structural effects," instead of seeing the state as an essentialized abstraction.[8] Mattias Borg Rasmussen describes the Andes as a site of profuse state effects, from schools to infrastructure to the governor of each district.[9] Yet Elena and the many other participants who told staff members that they had been abandoned by the state suggest that state effects may be inadequate indicators of a state's felt presence. I therefore train my focus in this chapter on *state affects*.[10] This means attending to the specific public affects that the state worked to promulgate in spectacular celebrations that were Sierra Sur's means of managing desire. It also means discerning the intimate politics of state presence as villagers articulated it when they mobilized anxieties and disappointments around its abandonment for a counterhegemonic politics of state obligation.

This chapter draws on my interactions with Sierra Sur staff and contestants. I worked as a part-time assistant with the project for over six months in 2014, spending full days in the Ichupampa office and joining staff members and participants as they prepared for the final contest. In what follows, I situate Sierra Sur within two competing understandings of what the state owes the rural Andes. Then I turn to the project, highlighting how its staff micromanaged growth into being and pinpointing how participants labored to meet staff demands while also appropriating them into their distinct political projects. I follow the Lluta, Huanca, Taya, and Tuti village teams through this labor. The chapter ends with three local appraisals of Sierra Sur's intervention.

## State as Wealth Manager

Sierra Sur relied on an image of Caylloma Province as a remote resource frontier. It is anything but. Its communities have an extensive history of long-distance exchange throughout Peru. Caylloma's villages served as bustling nodes in trans-Andean barter missions. My elderly Quechua-speaking host mother, Luisa Cutipa, described a childhood of distant trading trips—she would draw on Spanish to emphasize the words "far away" (*lejos, alla*) with a heavy glottal inflection—with her father, her brothers, and her family's many animals. With "horses, mules, lots of mules . . . I walked for four days, just on foot, with mules, to get pepper, rice, olives, hauling *chuños* [freeze-dried potatoes], just on foot, four days walking. I also traveled farther, for five weeks at a time," bartering in coastal Camaná and highland Cuzco. Despite this history of trade and the late-twentieth-century presence of infrastructure and banking, development experts even today chronically diagnose "market penetration" as the region's key challenge.[11]

For Sierra Sur, Caylloma was a frontier of both resource accumulation and an entire resource logic. Extending this frontier was vital to the broader neoliberal project of branding the nation while thinning the state. Sierra Sur staff figured Cayllominos as a population of future entrepreneurs who already had access to plentiful Andean cultures and environments. This abundance was not for the state to create but to indicate and manage by training participants to apply an extractive gaze to their daily lives. Staff members saw their job as merely *facilitating* new markets by extending the tools of start-up culture into villages where Collagua and Cabana difference was an underutilized resource. And participants, inhabiting the role of Indigenous entrepreneur in and of "The Richest Country in the World," had to perform an indigeneity that was long a target of extirpation for audiences who disparaged them for ever having lost it.

This framing of development as the venture capital–style cultivation of wealth out of an inexhaustible indigeneity is an example of what Anna Tsing calls salvage accumulation.[12] Tsing and her Gens collective co-authors argue for the need "to reveal the constructedness—the messiness and hard work involved in making, translating, suturing, converting, and linking diverse capitalist projects—that enable capitalism to appear totalizing and coherent."[13] Sierra Sur's effort to generate capitalism out of existing Indigenous wealth took on its clearest form in the work of staging. I engage the term *staging* as an ethnographically specific version of the Gens collective's concept of "generating." Staging Andean capitalism as a tableau of rural abundance means attending to performance, audience, atmosphere, production, curation, and choreography.[14] It suggests a fiction or a fabrication of something new out of existing elements. Like wealth, staging requires managers and directors. Staging does not mean a perfect enactment of stage directions; contestants pushed against the demands placed on them and improvised ways to enact their own agendas.

To stage growth as a specifically southern Andean phenomenon, the Sierra Sur project appropriated the locally common contest form. Expositions such as regional *ferias agropecuarias* (livestock and agriculture fairs) throughout Caylloma routinely feature local abundance with contests over animal girth, appearance, village gastronomy, and traditional dances. The "Munay Sipas–Miss Caylloma" beauty pageant is a beloved part of the province's anniversary celebrations. Many municipal fiestas also feature contests as central aspects of their celebrations. Sierra Sur's own pageants of resource wealth and inclusive extraction thus engaged a familiar genre of ritualized public performance.

### State as Provider

Villagers from Taya, Lluta, and other parts of Caylloma far from the provincial capital saw their territories as places where the state did not go. Emeterio Flores Jacobo, from Lluta, emphasized during a site visit that "our pueblo is always being forgotten." The feeling "of being spectators of rather than participants in development" is common to rural communities throughout Peru, given its rising GDP and their own unaltered economic lives.[15] Certainly, Lluta has a school, electricity, and residents who pay taxes. But Sierra Sur's project was the first time in recent local memory that Lluta had felt a substantive state presence beyond those ordinary state effects.

In Caylloma, development professionals frequently opposed the idealized entrepreneur to what they disparaged as an epidemic of aid addiction, or *asistencialismo*. I heard this word from at least one representative of every project I detail in this book. However, in Sierra Sur's growth projects, villagers did not simply *receive* investments. They also *provided* substantial physical and affective labor at the behest of the staff, which suggests that Sierra Sur, in practice, depended on a series of mutual obligations.[16] Participants' extensive efforts to legitimate the project by sumptuously feeding and hosting staff members during site visits, appearing in competitions that required labor-intensive spectacle, and regularly praising the project created, in villagers' view, an obligation for this state project to continue.

Sierra Sur staff members worked to cultivate an idealized independent subjectivity that articulated an argument against patronage structures while paradoxically consolidating those structures.[17] The *asistencialismo* diagnosis is rooted in technocratic anxieties about rural elite patronage. Throughout much of the twentieth century, as María Benavides writes, Caylloma's villages have been structured such that "clientelism and brokerage are built into the local stratification in which the *mistis* form a local elite of landowners, merchants and small-scale cattle ranchers," for whom peasants provide a source of inexpensive labor.[18] Patronage has long been a means of seeking economic security throughout the Andes.[19] But it is an arrangement prone to abuse.

Gerardo Huaracha, my host father, remembered a cruel cattle farmer and landowner named Manuel Rivera. Large haciendas did not exist in Colca, but powerful landowners still made their mark on the local economy. Describing his experiences of migrant labor on the coasts before the 1969 agrarian reforms, Gerardo spoke to me of "forced labor for the *patrones*" when "*hacendados*, bosses, enjoyed the people like slaves, right? They made them work, in the high part. They made them graze animals, everything, right? But when the agrarian reform arrived, the state gave everyone land. Everyone came out equal." Gerardo identified the state as the entity that accomplished this fundamental redistribution of terrain. In our conversations he would also fondly recall how President Fujimori ensured that every village had a school, potable water, and electricity. These provisions and protections were the basic obligations that Gerardo associated with the state. In his view, state support protected people from both local abuses and extreme poverty. However, even when he held posts in Yanque as vice mayor and governor, the state could feel absent to him: "The state didn't give us money. We just worked with the community's incomes. . . . The state gave a little bit . . . but it was just for a few small construction projects."

Many Sierra Sur participants described similar feelings of rural abandonment or neglect by the state. Like Gerardo, they were emotionally invested in the state as a caring entity that was obligated to provide for its citizens. Such claims of abandonment figure the state as a participant in an interpersonal relationship.[20] In contrast to Sierra Sur's visions of the state as a facilitator of growth, as merely a source of affective validation, villagers saw it as a provider whose material investments marked one act in an ongoing chain of reciprocal obligations. Forging ties of interdependence with the state was a counterhegemonic relation-building practice.

### Sierra Sur

The "Project Strengthening Markets, Diversification of Incomes and Improvement of Life Conditions in the Southern Highlands of Peru II" (or "Sierra Sur") was an initiative of Peru's Ministry of Agriculture and Irrigation, financed by a loan from the UN International Fund for Agricultural Development (IFAD), based in Rome. The loan's purpose was to work "with poor Quechua and Aymara families in the southern highlands of Peru to help improve the quality of their products, preserve their traditional knowledge and improve natural resource management to diversify their sources of income."[21] IFAD's website broadcasts two slogans that capture the philosophies echoed in development discourses throughout Caylloma: "Empowering people to lead their own development" and "Farming is a business."[22] Sierra Sur's 2011 mission statement conveyed its own argument that development is not simply about improving rural life but about "facilitating" growth for Andean "citizens, *agents of their own development*."[23]

From 2011 to 2014 Sierra Sur's Caylloma office was located in the village of Ichupampa in the central Colca Valley. It sat in the town square in rented municipal space adjacent to the municipality building and the church. The cement structure's walls were covered with a mural depicting a thriving agricultural economy with villagers of all ages working together in fertile fields surrounded by alpacas and other animals. The project's previous phase, "Sierra Sur I," took place between 2005 and 2011. During that time, the project was based in Chivay and was focused on more populous villages. "Sierra Sur II" emphasized lower-population villages that previous projects tended to overlook. The project moved its office to the village of Ichupampa so that staff members could be closer to Caylloma's most marginalized communities. However, public transportation to Ichupampa was inconsistent, making the office difficult to access. Staff members were also frequently absent, either visiting participants or at their main family homes in Arequipa, from which they would commute, staying in rented rooms in Chivay during the week.

Sierra Sur II was a massive investment in 119 villages across 33 provinces in Peru's 6 southern regions: Apurímac, Arequipa, Cuzco, Puno, Moquegua, and Tacna.[24] According to José Sialer Pasco, the project's national executive director and an agronomist by training, the budget for this second phase, which was focused on what he described as southern Peru's more "dispersed" districts, was $12 million, a cut from IFAD's initial loan of $24 million for 2005–2011. Given how many villages the investment was supporting, the $12 million loan quickly became a small trickle of material support.

I met José at his office in Quequeña, a leafy middle-class neighborhood in the city of Arequipa. On my way into the unmarked building, I was surprised to see a black Mercedes sedan parked outside, which matched the Mercedes brand merchandise that conspicuously decorated José's desk. Upon seeing his investment in luxury, I immediately thought of the wealthy patrons that the project's deliberately restrained investments were designed to fight against.

José, who was about 60, described the initiative as a frontier expansion of the previous phase. "We have arrived at the poorest districts," he told

me. "But even though the people are poor, they are engaged in preserving the environment. It's the poorest people that are most concerned with
their environment, ah? So, we need to capacitate [them] and think about
that, right?" In José's view, "poor" was not a material condition but a state
of mind. He saw existing relations between villagers and the environment
both as apparently harmonious and as a characteristic to salvage as a commodity. José described the initiative's interest in "cultural assets," suggesting
that villagers

> are very proud of their culture. Peru is a mega-[bio]diverse country but
> also a mega-cultural one. Household agriculture is a very important
> factor in this. They produce, and then they transform [their products]
> into typical dishes. Each little village [*pueblito*] has a different dish,
> an emblematic dish [*plato emblemático*]. Because of that, you get a
> great gastronomic wealth. The cultural wealth [*riqueza cultural*] of
> household production.

In José's view, biodiversity and cultural diversity form part of a single framework of Peruvian wealth. Framed alongside biodiversity, cultural diversity
was wealth to be salvaged.[25] Each *pueblito*, despite its smallness, had something to offer a broader regional, national, and international market in
culturally branded goods, services, and experiences from the Andes. This
"cultural wealth," a phrase José repeated many times during our conversation, also came in forms that were, in his impromptu inventory, "physical, architectural, cultural, linguistic, the language has been revalorized:
we express ourselves better in our own language. Before, they had shame,
but now, people are proud to speak Quechua." This statement is far from
universally true in my experience of the southern Andes, where few parents
teach Quechua to their children.[26] However, hearing this from Sierra Sur's
director makes it an *institutional* truth, fundamental to the project's rooting
of development in extractable cultural wealth and not in state provision.
Contrasting with Marisol de la Cadena's case of urban de-Indianization,[27]
this project was an imposed and aspirational "reindigenization."[28] Here,
José was representing Peru's good feelings toward rural communities that
the state had long disparaged.

Sierra Sur's investments were conferred according to a document that
project staff called the Territorial Investment Plan, a formal list of market
objectives drafted jointly between a village association formed around a

specific commodity and their Sierra Sur agent. The project invested 80–85% in newly formed associations, for which members co-invested 15–20% from the associations' budget, which generally meant from participants' own pockets. Few villagers in the valley had belonged to entrepreneurial associations before Sierra Sur's presence. Sierra Sur would fund technical assistance, guided visits to other places in Peru that had mastered the marketing of a particular product, and agronomy and tourism consultants that the association would contract. Funding amounted to less than $200 per person over three years.[29] But these investments were small by design. As Leni Delgado, the project's Arequipa regional director, indicated at the final Chivay competition, staff members were mere "facilitators" of growth whose responsibility it was to "leave seeds," in the form of "opportunities" for villagers to potentiate.

Leni elaborated Sierra Sur's approach to revalorization for me in a 2012 interview. The project's ultimate goal, she said, is to "motivate and incentivize families to rescue and revalue their culture, but at the same time, to develop products that serve to augment their incomes." Leni's "at the same time" ties an affective investment in an apparently devalued "culture" to financial investments that could yield growth by commodifying indigeneity. She continued, "We want to see how their culture *also* contributes to improving the way they live as something meaningful . . . their tradition, their history, all of that. Those are what we call 'cultural products.'" In a move that exemplifies the resource logics that organize Sierra Sur's work, here Leni reframes "the way they live," "tradition," and "history" as a bundle of "products." Note Leni's "also." She indicates with that word that "their culture" would not otherwise lead to economic improvement. It was her project's task to render culture a commodity, to bring it *both* into the public eye as something to desire and not disparage *and* into the realm of capitalist logics as an alienable resource through salvage accumulation. In this way, Leni defined how indigeneity should matter in communities that had not widely identified with the term. Certainly, income-generating cultural revival appealed to some villagers. But tasking marginalized villagers with generating their own revival was a harder sell that led some to refuse Sierra Sur's lopsided proposition.

The initiative's intervention overlooks how diverse and stratified Caylloma's districts are. *Between* villages, uneven marginalization marks distinctions. For example, Tuti has seen several prior development projects, success in organic certification, and even access to funds that supported travel for growers to present their products internationally as far as Italy and Thailand. Thus it was no surprise that Tuti would end up winning the Chivay competition. Stratification *within* villages plays out along multiple lines, including age, as older people tend to be farmers and herders and middle-aged and younger people are more likely to be engaged in entrepreneurial activities but also more likely to spend at least part of their time away from the region. Despite José's excitement for the revitalization of Quechua, the profusion of Spanish-language technical documents meant that participation in the project would be nearly impossible for anyone who spoke only Quechua, which meant most elderly women and many elderly men, limiting the project's age pool. Gender divisions also remain strong. Women leaders were prioritized in the program but also faced the "inequality problems" of a disproportionate in-home labor burden.[30] Meanwhile, men often left their villages for physically exhausting wage labor in Arequipa and the region's isolated mines.[31] This meant that villagers who were wealthier, younger, better educated, or without childcare obligations or who otherwise had more structural flexibility were those who were most likely to join Sierra Sur's intensive and time-consuming initiative.

Leni did not dispute the claim that the project might not have included every Caylloma resident. She made clear that development was no longer about aid or infrastructure. Instead, it followed a venture capital model of identifying a select class of inspiring villagers to become Indigenous entrepreneurial exemplars. She described the project as development "by demand." José reflected this almost verbatim, telling me that "NGOs, in general, are projects by supply, but [our initiatives] are projects by demand."[32] Participants, according to this framework, were not poor people in need but visionaries seeking to launch a promising entrepreneurial idea.

## Professional Investments: Lilia

The Ichupampa staff included director Lilia Samayani, promoters Rafael Hanampa and Yeny Romero Quispe, and several clerical workers. Lilia, Rafael, and Yeny were all professionals who had grown up in the province but had migrated to Arequipa to receive technical training. Lilia was heavily present during the project's most important public events. It was her interpretation of the "development by demand" philosophy that most directly shaped how Sierra Sur staged growth in Caylloma. Lilia told me that investments were targeted at export and, at the same time, at "protecting the environment, tree planting, terrace recuperation, ancestral canals" and other "activities that help them to preserve the resources they have." She encouraged participants to extract profit from every nook and cranny of their lives. At their best, Lilia said, the region's villagers "are maximizing the resource potential of their region" while "preserving" its ecologies. Lilia described her sense of Sierra Sur's priorities to me at the Ichupampa office in 2014.

> Each proposal, each territory revalorizes the cultural assets [*bienes culturales*] that they have: their dances, their gastronomy, the production that is in that place, the interest, and the value that each territory gives the emblematic product of each place. For example, you have *maíz cabanita* [Cabana corn] in Cabanaconde, quinoa in Tuti, barley in Chivay. Each place has its special characteristics, right, especially in its culture but also in its production.

The mission was to use revalorization as a source of new growth and new branding. Lilia told me that every village could distinguish itself with a specific brand that indexed a unique Indigenous heritage, a "flagship product" (*producto bandera*) that no other village could claim. This rendered indigeneity infinitely productive of potentially profitable manifestations. Lilia's vision drew on her own life story. She described her background to me.

> I come from parents who were from here, from Colca. My dad is from Sibayo and my mom is from Lari. I studied in various places, and I attended university in Arequipa, where I studied anthropology. . . . And well, I began to work, starting in my third year in university, on research in Colca, and from there I worked more in the area of consulting. . . . I worked on a project before coming here as external, or rather as a consultant on the theme of monitoring.

Lilia's relationship to villagers in the program was one of both distant authority and accessible commonality. She identified with them, shared intimate knowledge of the region, and yet clearly occupied the class position of an outsider urban technocrat. She was decidedly not a peasant. Lilia did not identify herself as Indigenous. But she did identify as a daughter of the region.

Like many other development staff members, Lilia's return to Caylloma as a professional with a degree charted a well-trodden path to class mobility. This is a route often traced by those whose parents are able to either support them financially or draw on an intraregional urban-rural network of kin, patrons, and other caretakers. This class position was inhabited by a growing sector of knowledge workers in the banks, NGOs, and government offices concentrated in Chivay. Since studying anthropology, Lilia had found a professional niche in research, consulting, and monitoring and evaluation. This particular combination of experience rendered her well suited to lead a project that involved legitimating a growth-ready indigeneity with quantification. Like the other development professionals I describe in this book, Lilia and her subordinates were selling to villagers the benefits of entrepreneurial risk while taking home a stable monthly salary. Their own financial capital was never on the line.

Four years after our 2014 interview and long after the Sierra Sur project ended, Lilia had polished her life history for the public. She was running for provincial mayor of Caylloma. She followed a course set by multiple recent elections where university-trained professionals who lived in the region tended to have more success winning than local peasant leaders. Her party was Transformation Arequipa (represented on the election ballot as a light bulb). She was unsuccessful in her race, losing to the previous provincial mayor's brother. But the way she narrated her story in a campaign advertisement posted to social media is instructive for understanding her approach to growth.

> Hi. I'm Lilia Samayani Vargas. My parents are from the District of Lari and from the District of Sibayo. In this opportunity, I'm presenting myself as a candidate for Mayor of the Province of Caylloma. I'm the only woman. The only woman. With courage. With hunger. A fighter. With management ability. A woman who has worked here in our Province of Caylloma. I did my primary schooling in the Districts of Sibayo and Callalli. Once I finished my studies, I was able to apply to the National University of St. Augustine, where I entered the Professional School of Anthropology. At the same time, that helped me a great deal with my work in everything relating to cultural identity. In our province, we've done a lot for our culture and our identity, above all, in terms of the folkloric dimensions of our tourism resources and our artisanship. My work experience [with Sierra Sur] helped me get to know our reality in our province of Caylloma. . . . We were recognized as the best office in the whole southern region in the Sierra Sur project, where we were able to access and had the opportunity to

keep working with projects here in our province, our dear terrain in the province of Caylloma. I'm a woman, a woman like you, a fighting woman, a hardworking woman, I'm a mother and I'm also a person who is very committed to the development of our pueblo. Because that's the legacy we'll leave to all of our children. So, this October 7th, I ask you to mark the light bulbs, for Transformation Arequipa. Development, with jobs and dignity, that we're going to make a reality. If you bet on us [*si apuestan por nosotros*].

Lilia's campaign video makes explicit many of the values that animated her earlier work as regional director of the Sierra Sur project. She lays out her story of successful professional growth as beneficial for the region's own growth; in her position, she was present as local businesses accessed new development funding by reframing their folklore and culture as resources. She connects her own empowered decision to be the sole woman in the race with women who want to excel throughout the province, as women in Collagua and Cabana ceremonial dress dance across the screen. And, at the end, she articulates backing her campaign as a "bet," an affective alignment that is both supportive and speculative. This was a phrase she would frequently use in her work as Sierra Sur director.

### Compositional Labor

After Sierra Sur's initial 2011 disbursements, project staff members only rarely interacted with participants. They spent most of their time "facilitating" from their Ichupampa office, which meant paperwork, verifying association expenditures and technician contracts, and planning the competitions, which occurred two or three times a year. But their face-to-face work intensified in advance of the Chivay contest, a mandatory event for all village teams that worked with the project.

A preparation session took place a week in advance of the final competition that exemplified the extractive care work of micro-orchestrating performances of abundance. Staff members asked all participating village team leaders to gather in Chivay's municipal gymnasium. The audience was mostly men, even though gender inclusion was a key pillar of the project. The gymnasium setting was fitting, for the meeting was, in part, a rally. It was also an occasion for Lilia, inhabiting the role of a coach, to spell out her stage directions. Lilia began with words of praise, telling the representatives that "even just daring to do this is really important, just participating, and if you do it well, you will be able to achieve so much."

Throughout the session, Lilia repeated the refrain "Apostamos por ustedes" (we are betting on you). This phrase broadcasts Sierra Sur's affective investments in participants' economic success. The notion of the "bet" indexes the speculation and risk inherent to financial investment. It evokes the staff's gamble that contestants will present the project in a positive light to IFAD and the Chivay public. The encouraging phrase is indicative of a strategy that microfinance scholar Anke Schwittay finds in neoliberal development initiatives around the world that entail augmenting the reach of meager financial investments by embedding them "in a moral grammar of affective sentiments and relationships."[33]

The session instantiated the project's emphasis on state transparency. It allowed Lilia to ensure that all teams were given the same information. Each was given a copy of the rubric that the judges would use to rank them. Lilia's emphasis on transparency here was, at the same time, an alibi to justify her rigorous choreography of the competition. Ensuring an equal chance at winning meant that every participant should know how best to compete, which would cumulatively produce a spectacular celebration of the sights, sounds, and scents of Collagua and Cabana abundance.

Lilia painstakingly walked her audience through the contest's protocols. Presenters were required to make a twenty-minute public pitch for their community. Each team had to bring up to the stage a large, three-dimensional papier-mâché "cultural map" of their territory detailing its economic and cultural life in the past, present, and future. They also had to prominently display a decorated binder containing physical receipts of all project-related expenses. They had to wear traditional costumes. They had to bring an emblematic dish. These material dimensions of unique micro-cultural abundance would be on display in each village's booth when they were not presenting. Last, each team had to perform a dance Indigenous to their village and distinct from every other dance. These elements, together, were meant to build a spectacular Andeanized start-up pitch competition.

Lilia's choreography extended to specific words themselves that contestants should use in their twenty-minute presentations. Her guidance was intricate and meticulous. They should "be sure to thank Sierra Sur." Men and women had to speak for equal time, a micropolitical display of inclusion across the project's sponsored villages. "I think," she continued, "that while faster is better, the more concrete, precise, and clear, the better. So for that, you have to put forward people who speak so that in just a few words, they say everything." Because time was short, representatives were told to focus the pitch on their villages' broad growth prospects.

Lilia repeatedly emphasized one specific instruction: "No matter what, the outgoing and incoming mayor need to come. No matter what. The territory for whom the outgoing and incoming mayor do not come will get fewer points. Because it's really important to commit the authorities." The competition was happening less than a month after the region's 2014 provincial and municipal elections, so most villages would soon see a leadership transition. Lilia argued that this was how to hold leaders to account: "As long as you unite as a territory, the entering mayor will always feel your strength." The mayors' presence would index development-oriented institutional memory, public evidence that Sierra Sur's seeds of growth would sprout in its absence.

Winners stood to receive a prize of 7,000 soles (about $2,380); second place would win 6,000 soles ($2,040), third, 3,000 soles ($1,020), and fourth, 2,000 soles ($680).[34] All other teams would leave with 1,000 soles ($340). Each team also received a 1,200-sol ($408) budget for travel expenses. These funds could be mobilized for shared investments or divided among team members. "Look," Lilia said, "our prizes are considerable, right?" Given that most teams had more than fifteen participants, Lilia's claim to generosity was debatable. The daylong contest and the preparation labor, site visits, and multiple preliminary meetings that the contest required were costly and took participants away from their businesses and other engagements. The contest occurred on a Thursday, market day in Chivay when the population swelled, so Lilia told participants to consider it a chance to test their entrepreneurial capacity: "You have to bring products to sell too." Even for teams that did not win, the contest would be an opportunity for publicity; teams should see it as both a start-up-style competition and a trade show.

In what would come to be a frequent motif in participant critiques of the program, one audience member asked Lilia about Sierra Sur's future after 2014. Lilia was vague. She genuinely did not know whether another state project would follow. Her uncertain response was an evasion that simultaneously articulated the project's affective investment in its participants: "I'll come visit you whether or not I have a job!" This evoked warm laughter but did not allay concerns about state abandonment. Anxieties about future state project presence saturated our site visits and many of the contest presentations.

Returning from the affect of a stage manager to that of a coach, Lilia closed the session with an impromptu cheer: "What are you going to do?" Several replied, weakly, "Win."

> *Lilia*: Louder! What's that?
> *Group*: Win!
> *Lilia*: Like men! What?
> *Group*: Win!
> *Lilia*: Loud! One, two, three, what?
> *Group*: Win!

This session was one of the many occasions in which staff members engaged in significant compositional labor to stage growth as the seemingly spontaneous capture of local abundance. Rallying the group's enthusiasm, Lilia rendered development a factor of individual motivation and masculine energy. This affective labor continued through a round of site visits.

## The Site Visit

After the gymnasium session, I joined Lilia, Rafael, and Yeny on their site visits to evaluate entrepreneurial associations in action and to remind teams of their obligation to attend the final Chivay contest. The contest date, initially scheduled for late September, was repeatedly postponed for weeks, ultimately to October 30, because of the varying schedules of the many visiting officials. Despite this postponement, site visits were scheduled at the last minute, often after frantic mobile phone calls and, in several districts, without any notice at all. In many cases, these visits were the first contact participants had had with the staff since the previous competition in February. Site visits were notable exceptions to the staff's typical office-bound routine. Staff labor during these visits consisted of "work[ing] hard to maintain representations" of project success.[35] Site visits were exemplary of the deliberate labor required to compose a growing market. They were not, as I had expected, rigorous evaluations but mostly continuations of Lilia's coaching session. Although several visits were little more than brief conversations between staff members and the one participant they could find, others were elaborate affairs.

We sat with families, listened to stories of progress, and heard from residents in community meetings. I found that in these longer visits, villagers tended to pitch their potential for growth with the specific purpose not of gaining staff favor for the upcoming competition but of making the case for ongoing state presence in a place that has long felt abandoned. Rasmussen sees such guilt-inducing claims of abandonment as a tactical move visible throughout the Andes that scales state-community interactions down to a matter of interpersonal reciprocity.[36] In contrast to neoliberal ideologies in the 2010s that posited "the state as a barrier to prosperity,"[37] villagers worked to recruit state-based development workers into an ongoing relationship.

The site visits I participated in captured the range of ways it is possible to be marginalized in Caylloma. San Antonio de Chuca was a sparsely populated community in the highlands between Arequipa and the Colca Valley. Residents were devoted to herding and trout fishing. Sierra Sur had helped them develop two trout fisheries. One fisher described to me how his association, Vinco Fish, envisioned exporting trout to the United States but had started with "the local market first, until we have produced a good amount, because the international market is going to ask for a good amount. So that's to say, we're starting out small." The fisher called forth a logic of growth in which scaling up was an inevitable outcome of Sierra Sur's initial investment.

Our walk through this highland landscape reminded me of what Carol Farbotko has called the "litany of smallness" in exoticizing Western depictions of island nations.[38] Smallness is an epistemic framework that renders communities and economics comprehensible, digestible, and uncomplicated while creating distance from them. Director José Sialer, in our Arequipa interview, called the places receiving investment *pueblitos*, little villages. Rafael described the community as its own small "nation." In the most striking invocation of smallness I heard, Lilia referred to "their little heads" (*cabezitas*), implying the limited worldview of someone living so distant from the region's population centers. We were guided on a walk through a peasant home, past alpaca meat drying on a wire and into the kitchen. As Lilia posed for a photograph next to pots piled around a blackened hearth, she suggested to me that "in their minds, the theme of modernity doesn't exist." Here in this space of smallness, revalorization from an urban-trained anthropologist had the practical effect of consolidating the coloniality of the resource, as her work of finding and extracting cultural resources reproduced the racialized binary logic of civilization and premodernity.[39]

At the other end of the province, marginalization took on a distinct appearance. Four days before the final contest, I joined Sierra Sur promoters Yeny and Rafael on a visit to the warm, low-elevation community of Huanca. Huanca sits in the balmy Ampato Valley, about a three-hour drive northwest from Arequipa. The Huanca visit was a joyful occasion. Staff members and I were treated as honored guests. The first visit of the four we were meant to make that day, this was a celebration of abundance, with entrepreneurs dressed in traditional outfits and ready with tart *aguaymanto* (goldenberry) cocktails and a filling lunch of fried guinea pig. We quickly found ourselves uncomfortably stuffed, viscerally experiencing Huanca's wealth. This physical effect on the staff's bodies was essential to the performance of local abundance. It was also an unremunerated expense that association members had to incur themselves. I see this act of extravagant feeding as a means of placing an affective pressure on the staff, creating the obligation for them to remember and return as an act of reciprocity.[40] Huanca escalated the project's concept of an abundance that a state investment could potentiate to an abundance that was the result of ongoing reciprocal affective and material support between village and state.

One of the male leaders of Huanca's cattle farmer association welcomed us with an optimistic speech about the village's prospects for growth. With Sierra Sur's help, he said, they have learned how to "improve, little by little. We have arrived at the point of being able to show you that Huanca, even though it's hidden, has riches, in dairy cattle, in beef cattle, in genetic material, and that the people are determined. They have courage to say, I can do more." Rafael encouraged the group: "You have had this opportunity. Don't let it slip by." He cited, as a counterexample, his birthplace of Madrigal, a rural community in the central Colca Valley that, after devastation by a nearby mine (see Chapter 5), was nearly abandoned, with "only six or seven old people [*viejitos*] left." Rafael then speculated about Sierra Sur's future.

> If next year we have the opportunity for Sierra Sur to return, and if they hire me again, if I have the luck, I already know where I will head. I know. I already know you. I will seek you out [in Huanca] . . . or perhaps another program will return, or [as he turned to me, the visiting American, to the group's laughter], Obama might fund something for us.

Acknowledging Huanca's need for more external help, Rafael's words, encouraging demeanor, and joking reference, through my presence, to a potentially generous U.S. government deepened the state initiative's affective investment in this marginalized village by seeding promises of future aid.

The visit to Lluta later that day was more subdued, largely because we arrived at night, many hours after our scheduled meeting. We had been delayed because of a flat tire on our Toyota Hilux truck.[41] The Lluta representatives invited us into their municipality building by the plaza, where they had been waiting all afternoon. At first, the reception was cold, given our lateness. It was after dark and the representatives appeared exhausted. Despite the long wait, Rafael mentioned that this had to be a brief meeting, because we had another visit and time was running short. He prioritized the staff's time while being dismissive of that of the participants.

Yeny, who was Lluta's staff point person, elaborated on the expectations for the contest and echoed Lilia's coaching: "I want my territories to win because I have worked with you." With her possessive "my," Yeny cemented her affective connection to Lluta. When they began to discuss their advances in tourism, Yeny urged the community to pitch something unique, because "Huanca also has tourism." She said that they had to print and pack a large banner for each association they were promoting, along with their wares, like Lluta's locally made breads and yogurts. They also needed to bring their cultural map, the three-dimensional diorama that would highlight all of Lluta's economic assets in as large and detailed a fashion as possible. At this command, Emeterio Flores bristled: "Well, now that is going to make us uncomfortable. It will be a little bit hard to bring a model from here. How are we going to take it?"

This was how critique of the project emerged during site visits. Participants grappled with its burdensome expectations and its last-minute demands on their time. Yeny's response was to spin their concern as a positive sign for Lluta's growth. "So, you have many riches to bring!"

Bertha Jacobo then presented Lluta's successes in tourism.

> Our objective is, as I tell you, to recuperate, revalue, and execute through a business plan, more than what we have obtained up to now, with the goal of installing a touristic restaurant that can attend to the tourist, in addition to live-in tourism. . . . We have developed from zero with the capacity, with the help of technical assistance from Sierra Sur's economic support. We have developed our management of artisanship, hand-weaving, textiles, embroidery, different special-

ties, right? . . . Even though we're small, we've had the intention of attending to local tourists. Tourists from the region, from Peru, and the world could all come to Lluta because it's good.

After inventorying advances in different aspects of the economy targeted to tourist consumption, Bertha closed by saying, "We have made some mistakes," yet "we have overcome them because we see the importance of tourism. Now we just need to put it into practice." She received generous applause. Yeny responded, "You should feel proud of yourselves."

Then Emeterio took the floor. He inventoried his progress with Lluta's trout fisheries association, before noting, "I'm not discontented. No, . . . I'm, I thank you . . . that you are an entity of the state" coming to this community. "Lluta has been abandoned by provincial mayors, regional leaders, by everyone." This abandonment, he argued, meant that local residents failed to appreciate Lluta's existing wealth and profound economic potential, which is "now, indeed, tremendous." The encounter demonstrates a dual effort: On one hand, presenting advances attributed to Sierra Sur performed the idea that growth had come to Lluta. On the other, their constant attention to abandonment was a ploy to engage long-term state presence in Lluta.

As we prepared to depart, Bertha called out, "Un ratito"—"just a moment"—as the whir of a blender echoed into the meeting room. We were offered pisco sour cocktails flavored with goldenberry, to go with the cornbread and salty cheese they handed out. They would not permit us to leave until we had tasted a range of Lluta delicacies. Huanca and Lluta both overwhelmed us with food and gifts in what I found to be a "hidden transcript" that engineered a continued chain of giving, receiving, and reciprocating with the state.[42] By prolonging the visit despite the mountain chill filling the municipal meeting room, the late hour, and Rafael's urgency to reach our next appointment in Ccasao, the Lluta participants tacitly articulated the critique that Sierra Sur's intervention was too brief.

Several moments of more explicit discontentment emerged during these hastily scheduled visits. In our visit to Cabanaconde three days before the contest, we met Saida Mendoza, president of the growers association devoted to the long white *maíz cabanita*, the locality's ethnically branded flagship product. Referring to the competition, she told Rafael, "Nobody notified me of anything. You only communicate with me when you need me." She indicated that the project had not engaged with her association for many months and remarked on the incessant rescheduling of the final contest date and Rafael's unapologetically short notice.

Saida's exasperation demonstrates that there existed a mutual dependence between Sierra Sur and its participants. Although Saida benefited from the project's investment in technical consultants, she also provided the project with legitimacy. The massive competition events were spectacular validations of project success that required enthusiastic participation to be an adequate display of local abundance before the national directors, IFAD guests, and political leaders. This meant that participants had to demonstrate their own affective investment in their village's growth alongside considerable artistic effort while investing the intellectual labor of displaying traditional expertise and the emotional labor of their enthusiasm.

With program staff absent and unreliable, in Saida's view, the requirement to perform her association's advances appeared as an unjustly asymmetric obligation. Reframing project requirements in the affective register of obligation is a tactical move that resists the state's on-paper austerity. Saida suggested that there was an opportunity cost to attending the event, especially at the last minute. Many other participants were hesitant about the effort and expenses beyond what Sierra Sur budgeted for preparations. Yeny repeatedly told them to "think of this as an investment." Saida's complaint highlighted the extractive mismatch between the entrepreneurial discipline and independence that participants were asked to embody and the humiliating obligation to show the patronlike staff a complete availability.

## The Contest

Peru is a beggar sitting on a bench of gold.
—Attributed to Antonio Raimondi, Italian-Peruvian naturalist (1824–1890)

Peru is seated on a bench of gold.
—Representative of the Huambo village team

On the morning of October 30, 2014, the Tuti village entrepreneurs made their grand entrance into the Chivay plaza. I watched, facing the stage, from the all-male judges' table, where Lilia generously designated me an honorary competition judge. Wearing Collagua straw hats and vests with polychrome hummingbird and flower motifs, the Tuti team presented a colorful caravan of business plan displays and short speeches. Then they left the stage in a line accompanied by two live costumed cows, papier-mâché maps, banners highlighting each association, quinoa cakes, and an embroidered binder that documented their expenditures. The dance portion of their presentation was a skit that humorously acted out a village wedding celebration.

The Huanca team's turn came later, at dusk, with its dance following a village team that had used the space to conduct a *pago a la tierra* (offering to the earth), whose burnt incense filled the plaza with sweet smoke. Their *q'amile* dance, pairs of red vests moving to the sounds of obscured bass drums and trumpet bursts, cut through the fragrant haze.

These groups, and twelve other village teams following a similar routine, assembled for Sierra Sur's final regional business pitch competition before a crowd of hundreds of Caylloma residents, IFAD administrators, Ministry of Agriculture staff, visitors, tourists, members of the press, and regional officials. The judges' panel included provincial mayor-elect Rómulo Tinta, folklorist and mapmaker Zacarías Ocsa, and Porfirio Pillco, the agricultural extension agent.

Sierra Sur's 2013 annual report describes its contests, officially called INTERCONs (Intercambios de Experiencias y Valoración de Conocimientos Locales), or Exchanges of Experiences and Valuation of Local Knowledges, as "scenes of learning."[43] As a pedagogical device, the contest conveys to spectators that every Caylloma resident is a potential Indigenous entrepreneur. Such language engages the brief technocratic temporality of exchanges, which take place in specific moments of learning, a contrast with what participants saw as *obligations*, which are long term and indefinite.

Four key dimensions of the contest illuminate how project staff enacted economic growth as a scene of celebrated difference: the *rubric*, the *booth*, the *pitch*, and the *critique*.

### The Rubric

The competition rubric was an essential artifact of Sierra Sur's technocratic mediation of and accounting for Andean abundance (Figure 3.1). This document's intricate requirements for each competing village team demonstrate the project's tangle of priorities. José Sialer described the project to me as a three-year effort to reach Caylloma's most "dispersed" communities that had not seen recent development projects from the state. However, the rubric relied heavily on education, technical literacy, public speaking

ORGANIZATION TIP: _____

| ORGANIZATION NRMP 1 | |
| --- | --- |
| ORGANIZATION NRMP 2 | |
| ORGANIZATION BP 1 | |
| ORGANIZATION BP 2 | |
| ORGANIZATION BP n | |

| Criteria | Point Range | Points Determined |
| --- | --- | --- |
| TERRITORIAL INVESTMENT PLAN – CULTURAL MAPS | | |
| Presentation of TIP: level of knowledge of the territory through Cultural Maps (past, present, and future) and relevance of the execution of Rural Initiatives, participation of women and youth | 01 to 04 points | |
| Presentation of the Booth: Cultural Maps, photographic panels, cultural elements, relevant information, binder with documentation, other | 01 to 04 points | |
| NATURAL RESOURCES MANAGEMENT PLAN | | |
| Presentation of the results obtained by the NRMP: command of relevant information (CIF, guided visit, % of participating families, other), photographic panels, display of products, benefits that the implemented themes bring | 01 to 04 points | |
| Public speaking ability, clarity, coherence, participation of women, youth, time management | 01 to 04 points | |
| Evidence presented for the organization about management activities developed that permit the continuity of initiatives related to natural resources (Coordinations, agreements, leverage of resources, other) | 01 to 02 points | |
| Relevant documentation, updated and organized that evidences the execution of the NRMP | 01 to 02 points | |
| BUSINESS PLAN | | |
| Presentation of results obtained by the BP: changes achieved in their product or service upon accessing the services of technical assistance, benefits of the guided visit and of participation in expositions, level of knowledge about prices, costs, market articulation (sales), photographic panels, display of products | 01 to 04 points | |
| Public speaking ability, clarity, coherence, participation of women, youth, time management | 01 to 04 points | |
| Evidence presented for the organization about management activities developed that permit the continuity of BP (Coordinations, agreements, leverage of resources, other) | 01 to 02 points | |
| Relevant documentation, updated and organized that evidences the execution of the BP | 01 to 02 points | |
| CULTURAL MANIFESTATIONS – DANCES | | |
| Choreography, deployment of participants onstage, time management | 01 to 06 points | |
| Originality of the dance, written reference about the dance's significance, dress | 01 to 04 points | |
| CULTURAL MANIFESTATIONS – GASTRONOMY | | |
| Quality of the dish(es) and presentation, public speaking capacity of the participants, use of local ingredients, command of the preparation | 01 to 05 points | |
| Written reference about the origins of the typical cuisine, local ingredients, and form of preparation, participant dress, time management established | 01 to 03 points | |
| TOTAL | 50 POINTS | |

| Observations | |
| --- | --- |
| Name of Judge | |
| National Identity Number | |
| Signature | |

**FIGURE 3.1** The fifty-point rubric for the Sierra Sur contest in Chivay, October 30, 2014. LO, Local Office; TIP, Territorial Investment Plan; NRMP, Natural Resources Management Plan; BP, Business Plan. Source: Sierra Sur (2014b) (my translation).

ability, Spanish fluency, and proper comportment before an audience. This suggests that those actors best positioned to win the prize money—and thus those who most clearly embody the region's growth—are people already acquainted with the kind of skilled subjectivity that entrepreneurial development projects demand.

Like the many other documents that filled the binders of Sierra Sur's audit-heavy project, this rubric engages a specific technocratic aesthetic of simplicity, transparency, and objectivity. Through the quantitative authority it purports to convey, the rubric transmits a state affect of confidence in and certainty about the specific technical interventions that lead to growth. It diagrams the project's argument that specific inputs, in the form of material investment and occasional staff supervision, result in the specific output of growth. The rubric structures a judge who is capable of evaluating growth and growth worthiness in the language of points. In a grid that represents clean, discernable qualities indicating that growth has occurred, Sierra Sur's rubric represents, in James Scott's term, an archetypical state "seeing," which reduces messy realities and ongoing struggles to an uncomplicated reality captured by an objective, ostensibly apolitical technocrat.[44] The rubric reflects a relentless bureaucratic emphasis on graphics that follows the imperative from multinational entities such as IFAD to index a Western and urban form of knowledge registry and accountability. Lilia's training in anthropology and her previous work in monitoring and evaluation rendered her well suited to bringing the rubric to life on stage.

As the template organizing what looked like a simple celebration of already existing Indigenous abundance, the rubric exposes Sierra Sur's performative economic showcasing as an elaborate technical mechanism for *producing* a sense of growth. The largest sources of potential points were the dance and gastronomy presentations. Each dance, according to the rubric, had to be distinct: The more "original" and "typical" of a local tradition that a team's dance was, with its significance verifiable by written reference in the historical record, the more it would earn.

The rubric also essentializes the bureaucratic category of the bounded population center, despite local histories of cultural linkages, diffuse boundaries, and multisited living. Such essentialism evokes Bourdieu's sense of distinction as a boundary-making scheme that, here, was an index of capitalist potential through extractable cultural uniqueness.[45] The rubric's imposition of sharp distinctions between closely connected villages was manifested in the judges' surprise that Lluta and Taya featured the same dance, even though Taya is a neighboring municipal annex of Lluta. The rubric framed a hyperlocalized identity meaningful principally *as* difference.

### The Booth

Village teams each had to host a booth where they inventoried and displayed their hyperlocal cultural capital in colorful posters, artistic maps, flowcharts, and dioramas. A village's cooks assembled in each booth, preparing their most important ceremonial dish for the gastronomy competition. The signature dish, along with the flagship product, further marked each village as a bounded site of distinct heritage. Dishes included variations on fried guinea pig, quinoa soups, cheeses and dairy products, and desserts and cocktails made out of locally grown fruit, such as the tart *aguaymanto* (goldenberry) and the sour *sancayo* (cactus fruit).

The most labor-intensive assignment was the cultural map, an elaborate diorama of each village's local economy that demonstrated how Sierra Sur's investment enabled it to grow. These dioramas were created collaboratively by each entrepreneurial association, occupying much of their preparation time in the days before the contest. They were created specifically for the competition; they highlighted natural and cultural resources that accumulated as a result of Sierra Sur. Some maps loosely interpreted a village's entire terrain; others were more symbolic, showing the distinct economic sectors of each village. These maps were infantilizing assignments that certainly did not convey an equal exchange of knowledge between adults.

Maps diagrammed a linear relationship between past, present, and future centered on Sierra Sur's influence. As the "before," "now," and "after" scenarios of one team's cultural map depict (Figures 3.2, 3.3, 3.4, and 3.5), the maps expressed a past of harmoniously thriving engagement with the surrounding ecology. Contrasting with the idyllic "before" of subsistence agriculture and peasant community, the "now" scenario represents villages in a state of underdevelopment and deprivation, where the beauty of "before" has been lost. The "after" map projects a thriving economy with indexes of both Andean tradition (terraced farming, clothing) and Andean growth. Crucial to the contest's striking visual economy of abundance, these colorful maps enacted the project's fundamental argument that growth was happening because of Sierra Sur. They added to the baroque variety of the contest as a whole.

FIGURE 3.2 "Before" map illustrating an idyllic agrarian past.

FIGURE 3.3 "Before" map, zoomed in to highlight the diorama's meticulous detail and labor-intensive composition.

FIGURE 3.4 "Now" map showing brown, dry land, abandoned agricultural terraces, and inefficient resource use, along with initial improvements such as the "Sierra Sur Nursery" (lower right).

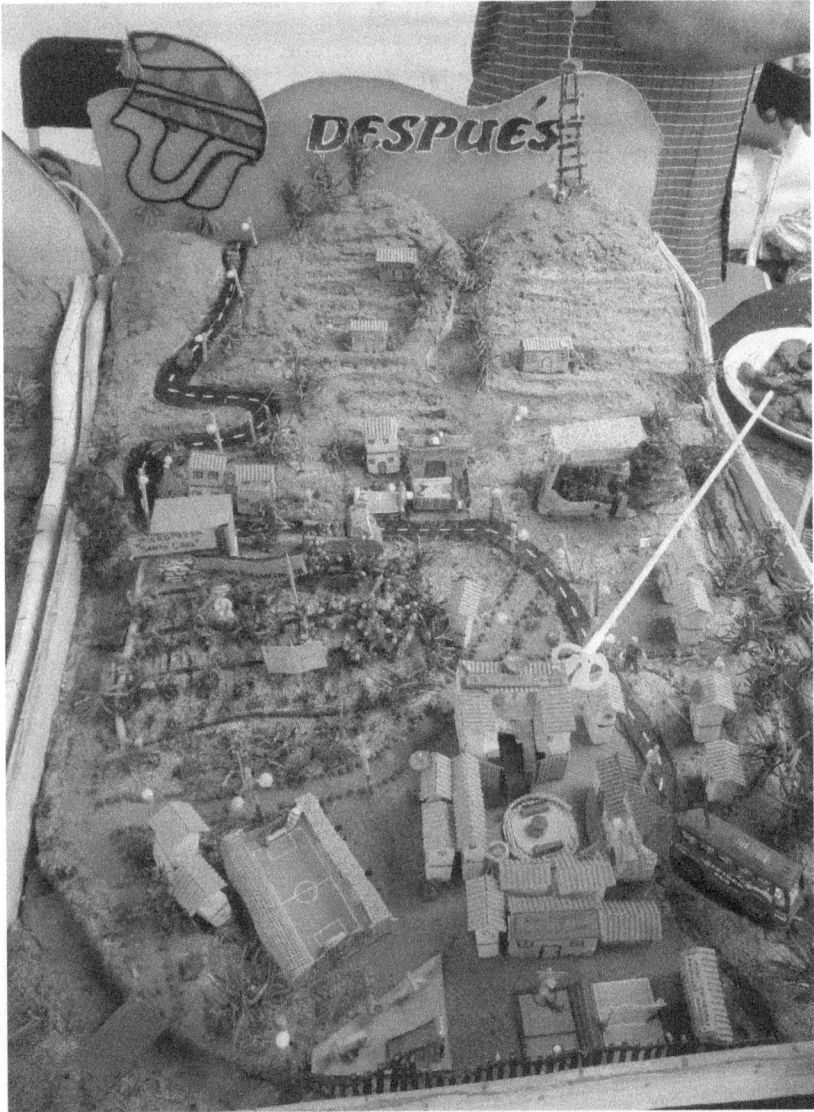

FIGURE 3.5 "After" map indicating high levels of connectivity, effective land use, a commitment to agriculture and small business, and a bustling economy.

### The Pitch

Each team's presentation was an effort to demonstrate explicitly that a village entrepreneurial team was embodying Sierra Sur's image of Indigenous actors who make economies grow.

One presenter from Tuti was a woman representing the association for "Genetic Improvement, Transformation, and Commercialization of Alpaca Fiber and Meat." For her pitch, she wore a shawl woven from Tuti alpaca wool, as the woman next to her stood weaving.

> We have managed to transform artisanal threads as they are in diverse colors and have come to transform by giving value added [*valor agregado*] to scarves, the poncho I have displayed here, shawls, hats, and gloves with this value added. We have given to our wool a high value added, for example, this poncho here, which we are selling for 100 soles [$34]. . . . Apart from giving a value added, we have given laborers jobs in our locality since the artisans of our district are creating and elaborating them.

This presenter's almost obsessive repetition of the phrase "value added" demonstrates her effort to perform technical competence, which she expertly balanced next to her association partner's active weaving to enact a tableau of Tuti indigeneity. Lluta's presenters made their own indigeneity explicit, listing "the recuperation of the autochthonous music of Lluta" as among the ways Sierra Sur helped them unearth resources for growth. Villagers uttered the word *autochthonous* (*autóctono/a*) frequently during the day's presentations.

Statements of thanks to Sierra Sur were profuse. For example, a representative from Huambo told the crowd that "we have learned with Sierra Sur II something really important that should be made really clear: Growth and development, but with identity, is really important, brothers and sisters. Customs and traditions go hand-in-hand with economic development of our pueblos." Here, he sang the praises not only of Sierra Sur but of its "development with identity" paradigm.[46] A second speaker on the team incorporated that idea into an explicit resource logic.

> With the support of all of the authorities, we will make these dreams a reality, always looking for a good future for the pueblo. It is in this line of work that we proceed. As Ricardo Palma [*sic*] said, "Peru is

seated on a bench of gold." Yes, folks. We should reflect on that sentence. All of us have the opportunity to become entrepreneurs, to be innovators, to be competitive with whatever product our province of Caylloma produces.

In voicing half of a geopolitical cliché about Peru's apparently unrecognized wealth while leaving out the rest of the observation that its people are paradoxically impoverished, this speaker indicates that Sierra Sur's work helped Huambo realize its own resource abundance.

As contestants pitched their ventures (Figure 3.6) and performed their songs and dances, Lilia conveyed her support, smiling, clapping, and occasionally even dancing with contestants (Figure 3.7), embodying Sierra Sur's affective investment in its participants. She would sometimes interject by praising a particular presenter or offering context on a community's progress overcoming obstacles.

Judges marked time with rhythmic sighs of disappointment, murmured critiques, and approving nods. They debated time management,

FIGURE 3.6 A Huambo representative describing the implementation of technical assistance for guinea pig farming.

FIGURE 3.7 Lilia Samayani, onstage, smiles and claps as villagers from San Antonio de Chuca perform their dance.

choreography, and the extent to which each team captured the project's commitment to inclusion in their presentation. They were poised to root out any apparent misuse of the invested funds. They were extremely faithful to the rubric in their questioning. I found some of their questions and commentaries to be harsh statements of their own technocratic superiority. For example, one judge told the Tuti team, "You have spoken to us about organic certification, but you have not told us of what product, what is the advantage, and how you will realize organic certification." Another judge, the agricultural extension agent, later questioned what he saw as Lluta's overly optimistic projections for a booming tourism economy. In their shrewd response, Lluta representatives attributed their presentation's shortcomings to Sierra Sur's own incompleteness as an initiative whose presence was far too brief to offer adequate training.

Following Lilia's demand, incoming and outgoing mayors were present for nearly all the pitches. These elected officials' mandatory role in the contest illustrates Sierra Sur's patronlike power. When each presentation ended, Lilia had the new mayor formally commit to supporting entrepreneurship after Sierra Sur left. In one instance, Lilia pointed at a news camera filming the competition and smiled as she said to an incoming mayor, "I am asking publicly for your commitment, which is being recorded on television!" The commitment to sustainable development that she required of mayors enacted a devolution of care from a state entity to local leaders at the symbolic finale of the state's intervention. It marked the completion of Sierra Sur's offloading of responsibility for creating the conditions for growth from state to village and civil society, reflecting Peru's ongoing national decentralization project.[47] In practice, this ostensibly empowering handoff of responsibility from state to village manifested itself as the supplication of a village leader to a state development project before an audience of hundreds.

Lilia kept time rigorously. After the Madrigal team finished, she said, "Good, please, band, play the typical music of Madrigal so that they can make their exit." Still, the contest continued eight hours past its planned 2 pm finish. At the end, Lilia reprised her role as coach: Building suspense before the dwindled late-night audience, she announced Tuti as the winning team. The champions stormed the plaza. They danced and passed around shots of warm *almidón*, a liquor made of corn starch, as their brass band's notes reverberated through the plaza.

### The Critique

Nearly every team publicly lamented Sierra Sur's impending departure, a tactical move that enabled them to heap praise on the project, critique the state for leaving, and attempt to obligate it to stay. A small sample of this narrative charge demonstrates the ubiquitous sense that Sierra Sur's presence was insufficiently brief in Caylloma's most marginalized communities.

Elena, from Taya, indicated that "we still have more to do. We would like, and request, that Sierra Sur continue supporting us, and thanks to them, our economy is much better."

A representative from Pinchollo said, "Now comes the challenge: that the authorities don't allow Sierra Sur to stop there, Sierra Sur II shouldn't stop there, folks. Sierra Sur II should continue, continue as Sierra Sur III or continue as II, or other institutions should continue here. That's the challenge for you, my friend and brother, [provincial mayor-elect] Rómulo."

Lluta's mayor lamented that "unfortunately, we are forgotten. This is the first time that state organizations and social programs have arrived at our district . . . to a place where they never arrived before. I think it's mandatory to complain, to say that this area has never been included."

From Huambo, a representative said, "Authorities, Mr. Mayor-elect Don Rómulo Tinta, don't forget about the low part. We are always being forgotten, and like our brothers from Lluta, Huanca, Taya, we have been forgotten. Just now these institutions have reached Huambo."

Even Rómulo Tinta, the provincial mayor-elect, echoed the desire for this state development institution to stay. "We request that Sierra Sur definitely amplify or bring in another project so that, in this way, we can continue to work together."

Here, participants and local authorities alike drew on the affective idiom of abandonment to compel an ongoing state presence in the region. In this subtle way, they pushed beyond the boundaries of the rubric document.[48] Their parting words suggest that Sierra Sur's impending departure would violate the expectation of ongoing mutual obligation. But in the end, the program's rigid structure articulated its asymmetric power and its own external financial pressures. Staff terminated the project according to the timeline of an IFAD loan whose terms were created in a space far removed from the needs that Caylloma residents expressed.

## The Exemplary Subject: Reynaldo

Tuti's brass band blared once again a month later as association president Reynaldo Churro led his massive village team in another march. This time, they were in the city of Arequipa, the site of Sierra Sur's headquarters. Having won the Chivay contest, the group competed once more with winners from all the participating provinces. Leading Tuti's team, Reynaldo held a 5-foot-tall Paschal candle in one hand and his farmer's fedora in the other. He wore a golden sash and a ceremonial shawl that carried a bundle of wheat and was tied around his torso, simulating his status as the host of an abundant feast. They marched in the Characato neighborhood plaza. Masked figures behind Reynaldo danced *El Turko*, a UNESCO-recognized dance that draws on an exoticized imagery of suns and moons to act out tensions between Spain and the Islamic East as an allegory for Spain's failure to subdue the Incas and their Collagua and Cabana subjects.

Reynaldo's Tuti team won the project-wide contest in Arequipa. They celebrated in the plaza once more, breaking out into a spontaneous *El Turko* reprise after hearing the results.

Reynaldo, a 27-year-old cattle farmer, came to exemplify the Indigenous entrepreneurial subject in which Sierra Sur was financially and affectively invested. He has traveled to cattle expos and trade shows throughout southern

Peru. He was also a participant in the Desco project I describe in the next chapter. Building on his success in securing development funding, he laid the groundwork for a 2018 run for Tuti mayor (he was ultimately unsuccessful). Reynaldo enthusiastically endorsed the contest genre as a means of staging growth in public.

> It's really interesting. Because through a contest, through an evaluation, only the best plans are evaluated, those that are viable. . . . If it weren't like that, everybody would be doing whatever. You would have funds without a purpose, funds without a purpose, but through a contest, you only have the best getting funded in the first place.

Simply giving out money would be a waste, he maintained. Contests prevented that. However, Reynaldo's endorsement of Sierra Sur's results for Tuti came with a tactical nuance that illustrated how Sierra Sur consolidated the imperatives of patronage even as it publicly disavowed them. After the project ended, Reynaldo was determined to find the next pool of investment, revealing that embodying an idealized entrepreneurial subjectivity also means acknowledging the micropolitical realities of patronage: "We will work with more projects. You have to capitalize. We will search them out. You have to search, no? If we go and nothing comes, we will work anyway. . . . The most important thing is to work." In taking this stance, Reynaldo blurred the line between an expertly entrepreneurial search for new investors and an effort to secure new patrons. He illustrated that what looked like an exemplary performance of entrepreneurial independence could mask the "other concurrent objectives" that Laura Graham notes can characterize strategic performances of indigeneity.[49]

Although certainly aware of his individual strength as a self-possessed entrepreneurial subject, Reynaldo situated his team's victories as a product of his community's recent history. Tuti is one of Caylloma's smaller villages. Tuti had 775 total residents in 2014.[50] Far fewer live in Tuti year-round. Residents' main occupations are herding and livestock care. However, given Tuti's position within an hour of Chivay, its inhabitants have had access to development projects and Peace Corps volunteers since the early 2000s. When I lived in the region, they were working to project a new brand. A sign on the road leading into Tuti read, "Constructing an ecological village." Taking up this "construction" was a group of young entrepreneurial growers, some of whom have engaged Sierra Sur's network of experts to secure funds for international travel, including multiple trips to Turin, Italy, for the Slow Food organization's Terra Madre forum.[51] Just days before the competition, a group of producers from Tuti showcased their products in Thailand. Tuti producers have also been featured at the Mistura culinary festival in Lima.[52]

Reynaldo credits the town's dry law with the entrepreneurial motivation he sees among Tuteños of his generation. In the mid-1980s a municipal ordinance banned the sale of alcohol aside from the festivals of Santa Cruz in May and the Virgin of the Immaculate Conception in December. In Reynaldo's telling, this dry law remade village life, virtually eliminating a once chronic alcoholism and its corollary abuses. People no longer neglect their work, he said. The growing presence of Evangelical and other non-Catholic churches likely bolstered support for the law. Informally, Tuti's restraint, manifested in the dry law, is part of its ecological brand as a healthy, wholesome rural community. Tuti has since improved its economic situation: By 2017 Tuti's mayor announced that its extreme poverty rate had decreased from 50% to 22.9%.[53]

I asked Reynaldo whether he would consider Tuti poor today. "Poor? No. No, I wouldn't say that. Poor in knowledge, yes. We have more work to do. Strengthening capacities is the idea." Reynaldo's response posits Tuti as a place that perfectly exemplifies the neoliberal use of resources that are already abundant and already at villagers' disposal. Through a narration to me that validated Sierra Sur's results, he embodied the ethos that the project idealized. For Sierra Sur, Reynaldo was a role model, his individual successes furthering the sense that Caylloma Province was a space of abundance.

### From Investment to Abandonment: Mercedes

In contrast to Reynaldo, Mercedes Mercado Gonzales demonstrates the stakes of Sierra Sur's failure to intervene more structurally in the province's uneven development. Mercedes was the middle-aged president of the Huanca Beekeepers' Association and its Experiential Tourism Association. In 2014 she praised Sierra Sur's work and invested a great deal of hope in Huanca's potential. Her team placed second in Chivay and was invited to host a booth in the subsequent Arequipa competition. I spent time with her and several other women leaders from Huanca as they gathered in their booth by their display of tourism brochures, Huanca honey, and other emblems of their lives. Mercedes' description of Huanca to me as a site of undiscovered plenitude reflected Sierra Sur's resource logics: Huanca "is beautiful, extremely beautiful [*es hermoso, es hermosisimo*]. It has so much potential. It has livestock, dairy, everything."

A second leader at the booth chimed in, expressing skepticism about Sierra Sur's overreliance on technical assistance. Staff members, she said, helped Huanca leaders contract an agronomist who failed to understand their needs. "He just 'organizes' us and disappears. That's it. How are we going to move forward with the orientation [to the market]?" But Mercedes appeared to buy into Sierra Sur's promises that Huanca could become a thriving tourist district.

> At least, they have given us a start, acquainting us with what we are really losing in Huanca, right: experiential tourism, livestock, *aguaymanto*—that we didn't know that, really, that little plant generated so much medicine, so much, right? . . . We also have this Young Agriculturalists [association], a little bit of everything, so I mean, really Sierra Sur has adopted us in every way. . . . We are thrilled with them, so much that we want them to continue, right, for them not to abandon us, right? That's the idea.

Mercedes references the wealth that Huanca already has in an idiom of frontier salvage: Multiple kinds of abundance, she suggests, stood to be "lost" without Sierra Sur's help. The *aguaymanto* stands out as an example of that abundance. Other representatives at the booth emphasized this point, repeating toward my voice recorder "Nativa, nativa" at the mention of *aguaymantos*. Salvaging more than they thought possible out of an Indigenous berry, the tart fruit could be repackaged as a source of growth in multiple profitable ways, according to this logic. In our visit to Huanca, staff members and I were offered *aguaymanto* jam, sauce, smoothies, and cocktails, exemplifying their ability to squeeze juice and capital out of a previously unappreciated product. Mercedes' invocation of an adoptive relationship with Sierra Sur reveals her sense of its affective investments in her. She lamented that the adoption would be temporary, anticipating the project's departure without realizing that she would not hear a word from them after that day.

Huanca was marginal to most of Caylloma. It was a three-hour bus trip from Arequipa on a route that was largely unpaved and filled with dangerous switchbacks and unprotected steep drops. It saw only rare bus service.

**FIGURE 3.8** Mercedes Mercado Gonzales and her Barbie doll at Huanca's Sierra Sur booth in Arequipa.

The low-elevation village boasted a more verdant landscape than many frequently visited tourist stops. Given its archeological sites, hiking trails, and its terrains' fertility, Mercedes argued that Huanca held a competitive edge in tourism and other markets over the more well-trodden Colca Valley: "Colca is afraid of us," Mercedes said.

At her booth, Mercedes was dressed in Huanca fiesta apparel. She also held an identically dressed Barbie doll (Figure 3.8), embodying a figure of growth as a typical representative of her village. Here, as anthropologist Blenda Femenias notes, the Barbie doll helped to "signify the condensation of ethnicity within gender."[54] Identically dressed in clothing fit for a celebration and sitting among images, brochures, and binders that were evidence of Huanca's immense economic potential, Mercedes was a figuration of idealized Indigenous entrepreneurial growth.

Five years after Sierra Sur closed, in 2019, my five U.S.-based student research assistants and I traveled to Huanca to interview its former participants. Given the large enthusiastic crowd that greeted the Sierra Sur staff and me for our elaborately stage-managed site visit in October 2014, I was surprised to encounter a place that felt utterly desolate. "The town is basically a ghost town," Mercedes told us once we settled in, conveying that the emptiness we found in Huanca was deeper than the effect of seasonal migration or the absence of a development agency visit. "There's nobody left." Villagers, especially younger ones, had been unceasingly migrating to Arequipa. The population was down to about 1,500 from nearly 2,000 in 2014.

I first asked the group to tell me more about Huanca's contemporary economic situation. Perhaps because my students and I were foreigners, they immediately turned to tourism. Terencia Huaracha Llukra, a beekeeper and livestock herder, told me that "what we need is for tourism to arrive." She said, "We have lots of water. We have lots of farmland, terrains, but what we don't have is a market, and tourism, right, for us to give work to everybody." Yony Vilca Olivares, a nurse who runs the local health post, suggested that "if we had tourism, we would have more mobility. There is no mobility." I asked whether they considered any alternatives, in the event that tourism never came. They refused to entertain the possibility.

Then, I asked the group to describe Sierra Sur's long-term legacy now that five years had passed with tourists yet to arrive. To my surprise, Mercedes maintained her praise.

> They impacted us quite a bit. They helped us a lot. At least to get to know our touristic sites, because before we lived by our animals, our crops, but we didn't know that we had these beautiful touristic sites. To begin with, Sierra Sur meant getting to know all of those sites, right, and I have seen that we have great potential to get ahead. It would be a real help if [similar projects] would come from other countries, that would help us.

Mercedes also found hope in the project's push to cultivate and sell organic products, where she argued there existed a potentially lucrative international market. The promise of the "organic" designation was a site of immense hope, but in practice it would be impossible to achieve without additional support, given the expense and expertise required to attain it.

> All of those organic products have a little bit more value. But we need a lot of help. Who will help us to, um, to organize, plant the organic products, and where do we take them? Right? And like they're saying, tourism is really necessary here in our district because we have many

sites, tourist attractions, right? We have so many, and it's still something we need to work on. There isn't good access. We still have a ways to go. So we are pretty much all ready to begin.

I was surprised to hear Mercedes mention that Huanca was "ready to begin" after working with Sierra Sur for years. For the project, meaningful knowledge transfer was the tradeoff of minimal monetary investments.[55] But what help did knowledge serve in a place that uneven capital accumulation had left poorly connected and marginalized? Huanca's leaders recognized the riches in their surroundings and imagined using them for new sources of income, but they could not build better roads, create markets, or spark demand for their products while their village was losing inhabitants. "It was sad" when Sierra Sur left, Terencia told us. "It all fell apart."

Sierra Sur departed Huanca with little more than an inventory of riches. Staff members pointed out archeological ruins and hiking trails that might be exciting for adventure tourists and expressed excitement for Huanca's beekeeping, all-natural honey products, and *aguaymanto* cocktails. Despite the staff's emphasis on the need to hand off responsibility for development to local leaders and entrepreneurs, Sierra Sur's absence left this group asking for more aid. The state's effort to facilitate economic autonomy by extending resource logics failed: It overlooked both the affective register of mutual obligation between project staff and villagers and the material fact of uneven development that left Huanca out of the region's patchwork prosperity.

### Entrepreneurship and Patronage: Feliciano

Feliciano Llallacachi Catasi, a vendor of ice cream, cocktails, and other products based on the locally grown *sancayo* (cactus fruit), refused to join his community's Sierra Sur team. Instead, he sent me to the Sierra Sur office with a request: Would they support his enterprise with 1,000 soles ($340) for a generator? We discussed his plans at his booth at the 2014 Holy Week Fair, which also took place in Chivay's plaza, where he was selling *sancayo* ice cream products. Without a generator to power his freezer, he was limited to the sale of the few samples he had brought in a cooler. The sun began to warm the stone plaza as the frosty highland morning gave way to scorching midday heat. Our conversation was punctuated by customers who wanted to buy one of his *sancayo* slushies, and Feliciano's frustrated response: "Ya no hay." There are no more left.

Feliciano was skeptical about how independent Sierra Sur really wanted its participants to be. Like many Caylloma villagers, Feliciano had multiple sources of income. He tended to crops and livestock on several small plots of land; he operated a store with his wife; and he transported people on his motorcycle, a vital service in a part of the valley without consistent transportation. "I have eight children!" he said, smiling. "I will have to work until I'm really old." He has also held *cargos*, rotating civic roles, within his community. He was once a member of the Sierra Sur–supported Pinchollo Sancayo Association. In his telling, economic diversification was an obstacle to working with Sierra Sur. "The problem is, I don't have time," he told me, describing his inability to participate in such activities as the group's daylong wine-making workshop. His resistance demonstrates that Sierra Sur's ideal subject of development, an entrepreneur who can commit totally to a single enterprise, is inconsistent with the diversity of most rural economic lives in Caylloma. The institutional imaginary of such a figure suggests that staff members did not see participants as people with busy lives.

Feliciano's *sancayo* products clearly lent themselves to marketability as Indigenous and recognizably Colcan. *Sancayo* is the defining addition to the pisco, egg white, and bitters that make up the Colca sour, the regional take on Peru's national cocktail, the pisco sour. Feliciano described the *sancayo* as an example of previously unrecognized wealth, much in the same way that Mercedes glossed the *aguaymanto*'s newly appreciated benefits.

> Before, nobody gave [*sancayo*] importance; nobody ate it. Just the animals, when the fruits fell, they ate it. Now, people are giving it value, and now, I have an investigation from the National University of San Marcos in Lima . . . showing that the *sancayo* is one of the fruits that has the most potassium, so, it's really good, right?

He suggested that *sancayo* could be lucrative, similar to quinoa in its promise of market success.

In other ways, too, Feliciano's testimony indexed the subjectivity that Sierra Sur sought. He strongly identified with Cabana culture. His home village of Pinchollo has a welcome archway identifying it as part of the "Cabana Nation." He told me that his clothing was "clearly Cabana" and described Cabana inflections in his Quechua. He had hoped to extend his business selling *sancayo* products to a stall at the Cruz del Condor, a popular tourist site at the end of a well-traveled tourism circuit that meanders along the Colca River's high left bank. A small cash infusion for a new generator for his freezer would activate his profit, Feliciano believed, and seemed to fit these institutions' interest in cultivating independent Indigenous entrepreneurs with minimal aid: "They don't sell *sancayo* ice cream at the Cruz del Condor. I already have my *moto*, so transportation is not a problem. Why join an association? What I need is a generator. A good brand, Honda, isn't more than 1,000 soles [$340]."

He did not need any of the affective dimensions of the investment. In seeking support, and by asking me to make the request on his behalf, Feliciano was circumventing the need to join an association or take out a loan by tapping into the model of patronage that has been customary in the region. This was Feliciano's own enactment of capitalist growth. When I took the request to Rafael Hanampa, the reply was an abrupt no, as though it should have been obvious: Sierra Sur does not give out "gifts." Feliciano expressed frustration that a project based on cultivating entrepreneurs was averse to making a single modest investment he knew would bring a return.

## Conclusion: Rethinking the Handout

Sierra Sur II was a short-term program that worked, through financial and affective investments, to inculcate entrepreneurship as a means of finding and extracting wealth. Its contests were the culmination of the effort to enact growth as a celebration of Indigenous plenty unearthed because of Sierra Sur's indispensable but purposely brief help. For teams that, like Huanca, failed to maintain a local sense of prosperity in the years since the program's end, participants faced the humiliating fiction that failure was their fault alone.

The project's effort to channel state affects of validation, pride, and hope through promises of Indigenous entrepreneurial growth came into tension with a distinct set of emotional attachments to the promises of state provision. The goal of this extractive care, in a nation as high in aggregate wealth as Peru, was to facilitate the state's retreat by extending the field of capitalist practice and capitalist affirmation. Yet almost universally, participants disputed the utility of brief and minimal investments whose elusive initiative staff left the region after a mere three years. They asked for more material benefit and more presence from the state. What development agents saw as *asistencialismo*—a handout—villagers interpreted as the latest turn in a chain of obligations, to which they had given much. They were burdened with the labor of performing in Sierra Sur's theater of growth and believed that they were owed more. By shifting the costs and labor of economic empowerment onto the people who sought it, Sierra Sur consolidated and likely heightened already existing inequalities in the region.

This was, in part, by design: Sierra Sur's contests, like the investments I turn to in the next chapter, worked not to create an egalitarian prosperity but to highlight neoliberal exemplars. In this particular case, the project rewarded excellence, in the form of role model communities such as Tuti that could put their indigeneity on display and unearth the resource wealth in their midst. By abruptly ending the uneven obligations through which it staged spectacles of growth, Sierra Sur consolidated the humiliations of asymmetric power in an unprecedentedly unequal Peru. Feelings of abundance evoked through the contest's saturated sensorium did not inevitably translate to local feelings of growth. In the eyes of Caylloma's marginalized villagers, extractive entrepreneurial capitalism had a certain appeal, but many also saw it as a practice that required a long-term state presence. Few villagers could feel growth in a state of abandonment.

# 4

## Economies of Empowerment

### *Making Mature Subjects*

ON A RAINY MORNING IN MARCH 2014, I traveled with two development
workers to the Colca Valley village of Lari to meet with Rogelio Taco, who
had recently started a guinea pig farm. Rogelio was a participant in a project
to create a new generation of young entrepreneurs throughout the valley
who were building businesses that incorporated a sense of local and Indigenous rootedness into their branding. The project was run by the Center
for Studies and Promotion of Development (Desco), a Peruvian NGO. We
arrived in Lari as the late morning sun emerged. A three-month drought
had just given way to an erratic rainy season, with unusually fierce rains
and hail ensuring another poor harvest.

At 21 years old, Rogelio was one of Desco's success stories. He began his
time with the NGO in early 2013 as one of twenty winners of seed capital
out of more than 300 who competed for the investment. He shrugged off
the project's early benchmarks. His prospects appeared grim. Then, in late
2013, Rogelio's attitude seemed to transform overnight. With the help of
a loan, he built a massive barn and was already filling it with guinea pigs.
He had also, at around the same time, completed his conversion from
life as a "libertine" (as he described it) to a member of Lari's Evangelical
church, forsaking alcohol and the multiday Catholic fiestas that populated
the agricultural calendar. By March, Rogelio was quickly becoming one
of the province's most productive guinea pig breeders. Guinea pig studs,
he realized, are excellent investments: They reproduce abundantly, require
minimal overhead, and are central to Peru's gastronomy boom as an icon
of pan-Andean indigeneity.[1]

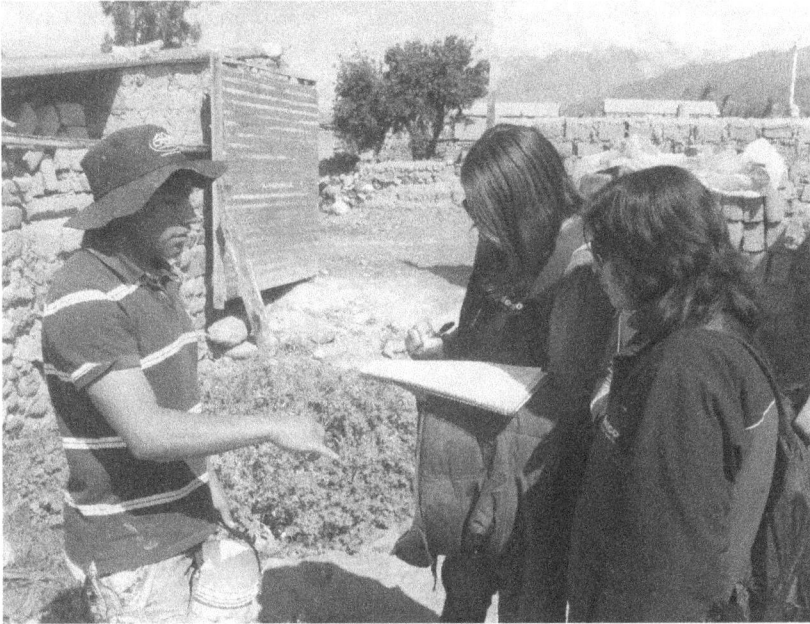

FIGURE 4.1 Fabiola Dapino and Luz Marina Rosas auditing Rogelio Taco's books near his guinea pig barn.

I stood quietly next to Desco staff members Fabiola Dapino and Luz Marina Rosas as they audited Rogelio's books (Figure 4.1). Once their perusal was complete, they began the part of the site visit that I came to recognize as the development catechism.

"Okay," Fabiola said. "You are making profit. Great. So the next step is? In—?" She awaited the rest of the word, to no avail. She finished for him: "—vestment!" Here we see a pedagogical quizzing to train Rogelio to be a financially adept small-business owner for whom entrepreneurial discipline should come naturally. Beginning the word for Rogelio—"In?"—renders him childlike next to the asymmetrically authoritative agent. According to the agents' script, economic growth was a function of personal maturity. It was only by growing into a mature, independent financial actor that Rogelio could launch a growing business.

Several days later, Luz Marina addressed residents of Yanque gathered in the municipal hall's assembly room for International Women's Day. Various speakers described the progress women had made in the province, along with their ongoing challenges. Coming from Desco, the province's oldest and most influential NGO, Luz Marina offered a presentation on the benefits of independently managing household savings and taking out credit. She identified credit as so unequivocally empowering for rural women that everyone present should apply for a microloan.

Luz Marina framed credit as a gendered human right[2] while speaking as the representative of a group of women NGO workers who were members of an urban-educated, feminized, "pink-collar" sector in the rural Colca Valley.[3] The financial empowerment that credit promises is a familiar argument from the globalized field of gender and development work.[4] Luz Marina's presentation enacted what Michelle Murphy has called "the girling of human capital,"[5] or the figuration of entrepreneurial women and girls whose empowerment is a solution to global poverty. It also concealed the fact that small loans could be lucrative opportunities for credit-granting agencies. Colca's microcredit economy was booming, which meant to Desco staff that every woman would be able to augment her self-determination with this tool. Potential clients could shop among microcredit banks with such optimistic names as Caja Nuestra Gente (Our People's Bank) and Caja Los Andes: Banca de Inclusión Social (Andes Chest: Bank of Social Inclusion).

The notion that investment and credit should be automatic impulses, inevitable moves for any villager interested in increasing their prosperity, animates Desco's deeper effort to tie economic growth to personal growth. In contrast to the Sierra Sur project, which staged growth as a public *celebration* of Indigenous difference, Desco's enactment of growth was much more intimate. For Desco, growth meant individual *maturity*. Maturity frames a personal realization that associates adulthood with specific activities, such as taking out credit, budgeting, forging financial autonomy even within a household, committing to a specific life project, and other signs of an economically reinforced independence. Desco naturalized economic growth as the result of an intimate life-course intervention. According to Liliana Suni, a third staff member who was trained as a clinical psychologist, the project supported "development, as much personal development as economic development."

Desco has its origins in Lima. Its national president, Molvina Zeballos, describes its founding as rooted in 1960s Catholic liberation theology. Desco launched its Colca Valley office in the 1980s, in what founding staff saw as a frontier of market penetration. They established Desco as the region's longest serving NGO with projects aimed at orienting peasants to new market opportunities. Today, however, given distinct donor priorities,

Desco has embraced neoliberal narratives of individualized triumph through entrepreneurship that Ananya Roy calls "millennial development."[6] This is affectively forwarded by an expanding network of Evangelical, Latter-Day Saints, Pentecostal, and other Protestant churches that call on villagers to adopt a self-disciplined individualism.

Growth in neoliberalism is frequently glossed as something that is unleashed, a "free" market "flowing" without obstacle or friction. However, across distinct kinds of growth projects in Peru, I repeatedly found that growth is deliberately and painstakingly composed. In this chapter I follow staff members as they led Desco's 2013–2014 entrepreneurship initiative and I also track several of its participants. I focus here on the parallel affective labor of making an economy appear to be growing and the affective labor of becoming an entrepreneur on Desco's terms.

Writing on real estate speculation in India, Llerena Searle argues that "capital does not expand to produce new landscapes of its own accord. . . . It is not an agent. Rather, *capitalists* circulate, invest, and accumulate capital."[7] It takes particular agents, acts, and labor to make capitalism function and to construct its expansion into new terrains. Similarly, Donald MacKenzie, extending the notion that economic theories do not simply measure "the economy" but in fact perform it, frames the financial model as "An Engine, Not a Camera"; instead of *capturing* facts about financial markets, models and theories *produce* them.[8] Desco worked to implement its own localized models for microenterprise financing and theories of capitalist growth in the financial training it offered to aspiring entrepreneurs. I thus work here to extend a recent trajectory of research that has drawn the anthropology of finance out of urban trading floors[9] and corporate boardrooms[10] and into communities in the global South[11] and dispossessed regions of the global North,[12] where financial promises work to reconfigure local economic priorities. I describe how growth is *made* and *felt* as a fact of daily life in the context of an NGO project that pairs financial learning with individual self-realization.

Since the 1990s, NGOs in Peru have frequently stepped in to carry out those priorities. This is consistent with the global rise in NGOs as neoliberal states have worked to decentralize, privatize, and diminish their presence. I had the chance to observe Desco in action from its national headquarters in Lima and its regional headquarters in Arequipa and through the youth entrepreneurship project, which was run out of its Chivay office. In the time I spent across this institution during my fieldwork, I began to discern a specific NGO style of growth making that was distinct from this book's other Peruvian growth institutions. Desco's approach was to build a new kind of *neoliberal citizenship*. This might seem to be a contradiction.[13] But I read their work as a sincere mission to curate civic agency within neoliberal limits by working to improve decentralized institutions and selectively extend market life to the marginalized.[14]

Scholars have documented how NGOs attempt to fill gaps in state support for overlooked or abandoned communities,[15] building what Mark Schuller calls a "civic infrastructure."[16] As intermediaries between national or international funders and the communities where they work, NGOs are connective institutions. In Schuller's memorable phrase, NGOs are often tasked with the work of "gluing globalization," patching together supply chains, market exchanges, and local economies.[17] Affect theory also engages a memorable metaphor of adhesion. Sara Ahmed conceptualizes affect as "sticky"; it connects, orients, and assembles.[18] Although the study of development NGOs is well-trodden scholarly ground, here I articulate how one NGO mobilizes affect to attach young people to resource logics. Affect, as NGOs engage it, fills gaps in financial support. It connects people separated by hierarchy. As Desco's staff members labor to enact inclusive growth beyond the mining sector through the medium of investment, the NGO acts as an "affective intermediary."[19] It is responsible for translating a country's resource-driven growth into a set of ideals that new generations desire. To the Desco staff, the Indigenous entrepreneur embodied those ideals as a figure of civic participation, citizenly cultivation, and individual self-realization.

In this chapter I follow the feminized labor of crafting individuals in a way that makes the free market look like it is working. The *capacity-building session* and the *one-on-one staff evaluation* were the principal encounters where this labor was visible. I argue that transforming young villagers into mature Indigenous entrepreneurs and their daily lives and ordinary feelings into raw material for new businesses worked to create a sense of ambient growth that complemented the benefits of Peru's mining boom. This made sense, given that mining companies figured prominently among the project's donors. A behavioral extractivism characterized by face-to-face moments of affective empowerment at the micropolitical level and the assumed presence of ubiquitous but underutilized resources at the macropolitical level allowed the project to overlook the structural inequalities of boom-time capitalism.

Desco staff members worked not to eliminate hardship but to create what Fabiola called paradigms, rare individual examples of thriving entrepreneurship. These role models would enable the project to claim success even if few participants generated income. Working with Desco as a research assistant, I spent substantial time with the staff and likely came to be aligned with them in participants' eyes. I also independently interviewed many participants, who varied in how openly critical of the project they were willing to be with me. In the next section I introduce finance as a device for shaping affective attachments. After that, I turn to my ethnography of the project's growth-making encounters by following Liliana and Fabiola and several participants through the three stages of Desco's investment: *credit*, *audit*, and *debt*.

### Financial Figurations

Finance is a tool of speculative attachment in time and space. The specific intervals, moments, and arenas that Andean financialized development organizes are crucial for understanding how villagers who use financial tools are tasked with fashioning themselves and their attachments to a region and nation branded for its resource abundance. As a micropolitical tool, finance works to configure specific subjectivities, aspirations, attachments, and orientations to the interior self and the exterior world. Social theorists have long been drawn to questions of money, exchange, and finance in frontier spaces. This has been the case at least since Marcel Mauss's *The Gift* deployed ethnographic reports from the Pacific Northwest and Melanesia to argue that indebtedness is not always a negative, undesirable, and powerless position in which to find oneself but can be a condition constitutive of social life and a means of attaining social mobility.[20]

With the same etymological root (*fin*) as the word *end* (like the words *finish* and *fine*), *finance* is a term that first referred to the process of settling a debt. Its contemporary connotations of capital transfer and the promise of future returns encapsulate the management of value at many scales.[21] Greta Krippner defines *financial* as a term indicating "the provision (or transfer) of capital in expectation of future interest, dividends, or capital gains."[22] Finance takes place in time: It is fundamentally about incompleteness, imbalance, and becoming within an unsteady state of tension between present instability and the promise of a settled future, mediated by deferral.[23] Finance is a tool for framing temporal trajectories. It configures specific aspirations by way of an incompleteness that it promises to resolve in time.

If finance is rooted in the promise, an anticipated exchange of obligations over *time*, its work is also *spatially* encompassing. It draws boundaries, articulates sites of aspiration, and creates lines of inclusion and exclusion.[24] Desco's financialized project worked to unleash the promises of Indigenous entrepreneurship by linking a micropolitics of routinized risk taking, investment, and the daily labor of generating capitalism to a macropolitics of resource wealth. At the same time, reigning ideas about enterprising attitudes and Indigenous futures *unleash finance.* Converging conceptions of indigeneity and entrepreneurship have framed the Colca Valley as a region ripe for the microfinance industry to flourish: In the 2010s, Chivay became a bustling local banking center. Although the Desco staff did not overtly work toward this end, the financial skills they taught had the effect of entrenching and expanding the local credit economy.

## The Project

The Desco project was officially titled Development of Youth Entrepreneurship and Generation of Self-Employment in the Province of Caylloma, Arequipa Region. It was funded by a competitive grant from Fondoempleo (National Fund for Labor Capacity Building and the Promotion of Employment), a Peruvian nonprofit organization that supports job creation. Fondoempleo's funds are composed of donations from a cross-section of Peru's largest companies and some of the world's most profitable multinational corporations. Its donor list for 2012, the year the project was funded, is dominated by Peruvian mining companies.[25] It also includes oil firms, energy providers, and telecommunications giants.[26] The importance of mining among these donors demonstrates the intimate material, semiotic, and affective connection that Desco's project to cultivate small-scale entrepreneurial growth in rural Caylloma has to the rest of Peru's extractive economy.

To secure the relatively modest investment of private donor money from this massive nonprofit, Desco leadership had to compete with NGOs throughout Peru in Fondoempleo's annual call for proposals. The total project budget, including staff pay, was 795,000 soles ($270,300), of which 700,000 ($238,000) were secured from Fondoempleo, with the remaining funds contributed by Desco, the provincial government, and the municipality of Cabanaconde.[27]

According to Desco's successful proposal to Fondoempleo, the project focused on young adults as a particularly precarious generation. Although children and elderly people could count on certain government benefits and although many middle-aged villagers engaged in wage labor or at least a bare minimum of regular subsistence agriculture, young adults faced a "lack of opportunities,"[28] with few state programs oriented to their needs and goals. They were also a generation whose presence as economic agents and members of kinship networks in the rural province had high stakes for local well-being: They were potential caretakers of families, fields, and markets. Desco's concern with youth was about more than generating income. It also had a moral component. As the proposal reads, the tendency among youth to migrate to Arequipa and Peru's other cities "creates an unfavorable environment for the personal and professional development of the young person, exposing him to informality, vices, and illegality, instead of pursuing incomes to sustain himself and his family."[29] Setting the stakes of precarity this way, Desco saw itself as saving young people from the city's "vices" that its own urban-educated staff had happened to avoid.

The project as initially proposed was solely focused on tourism. When implemented, it expanded to multiple sectors of the economy, incorporating gastronomy, artisanship, museum curation, and construction. Its authors positioned the project to "generate favorable local conditions" for youth enterprise and self-employment.[30] Desco also hoped to extend credit to young people, a population it framed as a frontier of finance, a group that had yet to populate Chivay's microfinance institutions. Its target population was recent graduates of the region's high schools and technical institutes, people most likely to leave the region.

Like Sierra Sur, Desco's project was not meant to be a structural intervention. Eligible candidates had to have at least 500 soles in initial capital, whether in available funds or in assets. They also had to be available for a full year of capacity building and entrepreneurial advising. The staff assigned to the project were Fabiola, a specialist in microenterprise, Luz Marina, who had previously worked as a teacher, and Liliana, a psychologist. Delmy Poma, the Chivay office director at the time, supervised the project but only rarely made the rounds of the region with the three-woman team. Several independent consultants in branding, hospitality, textile work, and other specialties were contracted on a rotating basis to lead capacity-building sessions.

### Professional Investments: Fabiola

Fabiola Dapino Picardo was born in Tacna, a coastal city near Peru's border with Chile. Her upbringing was urban and middle class. In a life history we conducted in early 2014, she described attending a private Catholic high school, which gave her an early sense of the importance of helping the less fortunate: "For me, when I got the chance to do community service [*labor social*], it was the best thing ever." This sense of joy in service was heightened in relief when, in her depiction, out of her youthful ignorance she chose to attend university for business engineering, ideal for someone hoping to work at a bank. She quickly learned that she had chosen the wrong field. Her time at the Private University of Tacna was formative, though, because it coincided with President Fujimori's intensifying authoritarianism. Fabiola became involved in local pro-democracy activism, where she engaged in anti-Fujimori marches, sit-ins, and other resistance activities with a network of Tacna-based activists. She delayed her bachelor's degree when Fujimori won a third consecutive term in 2000. Her activism was cushioned by parental support, a class privilege she was explicit about: "Thankfully, my parents gifted me the year."

After Fujimori resigned, Fabiola's career took shape in the forge of anti-authoritarianism.

> What is the breeding ground for a dictatorship? People who are in poverty and who are always extending their hand. *Asistencialismo*. What's *asistencialismo*? It makes it so that people for their whole lives have to submit to another for a plate of food. . . . It became really clear to me that this was really about social development. So if you don't have a country with social development, you have nothing. This was really, really clear to me. And obviously for my career, I had to figure out how to locate myself. And I was clear that I didn't want to go work for a bank.

Fabiola saw an urgent need for social development, a term she defined as a combination of citizenly and economic responsibility at the individual level that scaled up to a society of people able to think for and support themselves. This sense of urgency led her to seek successive positions in small foundations and NGOs that had her working in marginalized urban and rural communities throughout the country. Delmy Poma hired Fabiola for the Desco youth entrepreneurship project after she had worked on several similar youth-focused initiatives.

Fabiola's coastal identity was particularly pronounced when she would lament the cold of high-elevation Chivay, where she rented a room in a hostel and commuted ten hours back home to Tacna every other weekend.

Although her job with Desco was to train young people in business skills, she had a nuanced view of the limits of entrepreneurship. Her critique of standards set in a foundation's Lima boardroom was consistent with her earlier realization that development should emphasize independence and local agency. She did not seem convinced by Fondoempleo's faith that entrepreneurship would be universally helpful. "The truth is that the young people who respond best to the entrepreneurial thing are those whose parents are entrepreneurs. That's what's typical, pretty much as a rule, though some, sure, might have just been born with the bug, you know?" Fabiola found that across development jobs she held, she usually ended up working with local middle classes, people who had enough economic and social cushioning to take the risks that enterprise required. I asked whether she saw her work in the Colca Valley as work with the region's middle class.

> I think so, because when you look at incomes or quantity of—or like, if you, the lifestyle here, maybe it's not what one thinks would fit "middle class," but when you see the goods or the assets that they have, it's a lot, right, that you don't see at first. . . . Frankly, I haven't seen much poverty here.

Most of the development projects Fabiola worked with, before and after Desco, involved youth. "Young people," she said, "want to try everything." She complained about young people as overconfident, unserious, and "easily bored." They could be notoriously hard to pin down. Yet her frustration gave way to an affect of tenderness as she took out her phone and showed me photographs of people she had worked with in previous years, recounting stories of their triumphs against the odds. In later conversations, after the Desco project concluded, Fabiola expressed her ambivalence about overly narrow interpretations of entrepreneurship. She was adamant that entrepreneurship was not a generic, modular form that could be transported anywhere in the country. It needed to be shaped specifically according to the place where it was meant to exert its impacts. "Why not create a methodology based in traditions of the region that can propel development?" This rhetorical question oriented her work with the Desco project.

### Professional Investments: Liliana

Liliana Suni Condori's personal story differs significantly from Fabiola's. Liliana was born in Yanque to a large peasant family. She did not explicitly identify as Indigenous but described growing up in a Quechua-speaking family with deep roots in Yanque. One of eight siblings in an overwhelmed household, her parents shifted her to other guardians when she was 10. She first lived with a teacher in Yanque. When the teacher was reassigned to Arequipa, Liliana moved with her and afterward lived with relatives in Lima. There, she felt "like another daughter, more in emotional terms but not in economic terms. Economically, they gave lots of support to their son but not to me." Throughout this time, Liliana had to support herself. She was perpetually on the hunt for ways to make money. A life-defining moment came in secondary school, in Callao, the port city adjacent to Lima. She took me to midmorning break time in the schoolyard.

> We had just one kiosk [snack stand]. Imagine that: all of us, from each class . . . we were a ton of people. So getting to the kiosk to buy something was an *odyssey*, right, for just a fifteen-minute break, to actually get something. And I don't know, it occurred to me that I could sell during the break. I could sell sweets, cookies, and I remember, I began with a box of Sublime [chocolate bars], a little box. . . . Little by little, I grew. I remember that when I did this in secondary school, soon almost half the class owed me money! I sold them everything: chocolate, candies, cookies. I carried a backpack that was totally full of sweets in front, and on my back, my other backpack with my notebooks. . . . And I made a lot of capital. That money served me a great deal, for example, to pay the costs of applying to university and to pay the initial enrollment fees.

From there, Liliana was able to win a university scholarship, and as she framed it, she built on her early momentum to continue growing, both in terms of her education and as a person constantly looking for new ways to earn money. Liliana was perpetually searching for entrepreneurial opportunity. At university, she sold mail-order cosmetics and jewelry. She studied psychology and trained as a school psychologist at an underserved high school in Lima. There, she realized that she was working with students who were the same age as her own younger siblings, whom she did not know well, and she felt the pull to return to Yanque. Once she moved back, she put her training as a psychologist to work in several local development projects and for a term in Yanque as an elected *regidora* (town council member).

Liliana has remained entrepreneurial. When I first met her, she and her husband Freddy (see Chapter 5) were constructing a hotel on their property that by the end of the decade would count among Yanque's most successful budget tourism hotels. Perhaps even more than Fabiola, Liliana sincerely believed in the project of entrepreneurship as a means of self-realization. What these two staff members shared was education and formative years spent in cities, which in Peru, can be vital to class mobility. Liliana's personal experience as an entrepreneur born in Yanque placed her at the intellectual center of the Desco project in two specific respects: its focus on indigeneity as an asset and its emphasis on economic growth as a form of personal growth.

### Indigeneity as Raw Material

Before Desco hired her, Liliana played an influential policy role in forging local scenes of indigeneity in Yanque. In 2004, soon after moving back to Yanque, Liliana was elected as a *regidora*. She quickly noted Yanque's unmet potential as a tourist center, given its place along the route to the Cruz del Condor overlook, where every morning, masses of tourists gathered to photograph condors circling above the Colca Canyon. In the early 2000s, the Spanish Agency for International Development Cooperation was also refurbishing all the region's churches and plazas to help spur tourism interest. However, most of the new tourism profits found their way to Arequipa-based corporate touring companies and foreign-owned luxury hotels, such as the Colca Lodge. Liliana sought to extend the benefits of tourism to Yanque residents. "We need to find something," she recalled telling fellow district leaders in 2004. "What characterizes Yanque? What does Yanque have?"

Much has been written about cultural tourism's role in efforts to build inclusive development, in Peru and beyond.[31] But with her questions, Liliana's language suggested something locally new for Yanque about tourism as a specific intervention: that it activates growth as an extractive project. "We could take advantage of the fact that there are people who come from outside who profit from what's ours, who take advantage of that, but in the end don't leave us even one drop." To transform this tourist presence into a resource that Yanque residents themselves could tap, Liliana proposed setting up a new market in Yanque's plaza where tourists could stop, marvel at the village, and purchase goods made by local artisans. She recalled standing out along the main highway that leads from Chivay to the Cruz del Condor, waving down tourist buses as they sped toward the overlook and inviting them to divert their route and turn into Yanque's plaza. This gesture to physically connect new entrepreneurs with potential customers was an act of making growth. It demonstrates the importance of contingent, embodied interactions for how new markets are materially and semiotically constructed.

In the plaza, Liliana invited women weavers to sell alpaca wool sweaters, blankets, and handbags. Other women would charge tourists to pose for pictures with live alpacas, llamas, and condors. Liliana soon built the plaza market into a full-scale spectacle, inviting local students to dance the *Wititi*, Yanque's UNESCO-recognized dance that dramatizes the surreptitious coupling of a young woman and a man dressed in a traditional woman's fiesta outfit. Student dancers would seek tips from tourists, which they would save for an end-of-term trip each year. Since 2005 the *Wititiazo* has been on display from 6 to 8 o'clock every morning, aligning with the daily tour bus schedule. The event was named after the daily *Cañonazo*, or cannon firing, ceremony in Havana, Cuba, a tourist attraction that then-mayor Ramon Cayllahua witnessed as part of a cultural exchange trip he took during his administration. Liliana shared what she saw as the effect of Yanque's own daily performance.

> It's not only to help them raise money, but also to help them begin to value what is theirs: their clothing that they are beginning to value, their cultural identity, their roots. . . . Currently, this identity is being reborn anew, right? It's becoming their own once again. . . . They are now valuing what before they didn't give any value. Nobody had received a cent for having [typical] clothing. Nobody would receive a cent for showing a dance, nor would anybody receive a cent for showing an archeological or architectural site.

Liliana, speaking for young villagers, is using her authority to determine what "they" value. Like Sierra Sur's regional director, she equates "value" with income. Not every villager agreed with this equation. Marcos,[32] a participant in the Desco project, critiqued such performances of indigeneity not as an expression of what local people value but as a cynical imposition: "I think they see it as a business. Everything, up to the dances, always comes with the objective of promoting tourism here. It's not like it used to be. . . . It's much less authentic."

Liliana's early work to search out new culturally inflected sources of already existing wealth provided an extractive model for the Desco project. Her approach from 2005 continued eight years later: Just as she asked her fellow municipal leaders, "What does Yanque have?" she would ask participants, What do you have? How can you generate income out of your daily life?

## Economic Growth as Personal Growth

"The only way out of this poverty," consultant Antonio Rojas told participants gathered at a Desco capacity-building session, "is independent work, starting a business." Antonio's use of the deictic *this* highlights a characteristic young people were supposed to know they shared. Although it was not Desco's main focus, "poverty" was still part of its vocabulary, especially in a hierarchical interaction in which a facilitator sought to establish his expertise. Entrepreneurship may have struck the group as a highly particular solution to poverty, far from "the only way out" to which there existed (in Margaret Thatcher's words) "no alternative." But Antonio's urging captures a formula in which entrepreneurship solves three related problems at once: economic hardship, local marginalization, and personal confusion about what one wants that inhibits individuals from becoming agents of their own livelihood. Investing time, money, energy, and, crucially, attitude in a business is for Antonio the most practical way to realize economic growth. This follows widespread assumptions about the inherently entrepreneurial nature of "poor" people.[33] Competing for seed capital, taking out credit, and learning resource logic put individual self-worth at stake in a way that rendered villagers either engines of economic growth or "personally responsible for market failure."[34]

When I first became acquainted with the Desco project, I was surprised to encounter a clinical psychologist as part of the team. But Liliana's presence made clear to me that for Desco, to be an Indigenous entrepreneur was essentially part of a life-course intervention. It meant coming into one's own as an adult, a citizen, and an agent of one's own destiny who could mine daily life for business assets. Liliana critiqued the chronic obsession with infrastructure projects among local politicians, but she argued that "infrastructure doesn't do anything for you if you don't have training or build capacity, or if you don't generate, right, develop more capacities." The region's problem, in her view, was that its young people lacked goals and motivation.

> Part of the development of emotional equilibrium is the motivation factor. It's really important in how we plan for a life project. In the

majority of people I see, well, at least here in the region, they don't have a life project, a clear and concrete idea of what they want to do. And part of this is that here there have been so many NGOs that they have made people really, really dependent on them.

Liliana blames previous development projects for inculcating dependence, because NGOs, in her view, would hand out aid without working to transform residents' lives more fundamentally. Fitting the definition of what Fabiola described as *asistencialismo*, villagers would engage in projects that offered what Liliana called "extrinsic" benefits, but, in the absence of any incentives for fundamental transformations, they were not "intrinsically" motivated. Liliana described Desco as distinct in its effort to create independent entrepreneurs. She also offered scientific backing for the psychological impacts of inculcating dependence.

Throughout the project, Liliana's psychology training became an undisputed source of objective knowledge about young Colca villagers. One of the ways she mobilized her training was by compiling a psychological profile of the project's participants, based on a group survey she administered (Figure 4.2). The report proposes a psychological answer to the following question: Why do young people suffer from poverty in the midst of plenty? It pathologizes the group, situating successful entrepreneurship as the result of a personality intervention that Desco must carry out. This invasive biopolitical artifact rests on four assumptions: that psychological difficulties can be accurately diagnosed without long-term therapy; that they

**Psychological Profile of entrepreneurs in Caylloma Province**

- **Self-esteem**, 48% of entrepreneurs have an oscillating and intermittent self-esteem between positive and negative, making it difficult to arrive at emotional equilibrium, [inhibiting] their facility with intra-and interpersonal interaction, limiting the possibility of adequate decision making, and additionally giving them a low tolerance for frustration.
- **Social skills**, 34% come to have a below normal level of development, which means that the majority of entrepreneurs require a strengthening of social skills that they must allow to develop.
- **Assertiveness**, 37% arrive to a level of development of low-level, with a smaller group of 9% that arrive to a normal-high level, translating into low capacity for expressing thoughts and feelings.
- **Personality**, 54% of the entrepreneurs are introverts, characterized basically by being spectators, reserved, not used to taking risks on the contrary they are used to planning things with much anticipation.
- **Emotional aspect**, 19% have a tendency toward emotional instability, with 11% of the entrepreneurs who are highly unstable at the emotional level.

FIGURE 4.2 Psychological report generated by Liliana Suni in August 2013. In my translation I have tried to preserve the report's tone and bureaucratic redundance.

originate in the home; that they are unique to the participant age range; and that they could be a barrier to entrepreneurship if not properly rerouted through Desco's intervention.

The psychological survey renders young aspiring entrepreneurs as in need of a technical fix.[35] Their lack of capacity justifies Desco's capacity-building program. For Liliana, the lack of self-esteem or motivation that she found in participants did not form part of a broader story of deprioritized rural service provision, substandard schooling, or a host of other signs of regional marginalization. Nor does the aversion to risk taking noted here reflect a deeper sense of economic or familial precarity. These analyses patholo-gize rural youth in a way that evacuates their conditions from a political economy of uneven development. Barbara Cruikshank sees self-esteem as a concept rooted in mid-twentieth-century feminism but appropriated by neoliberalism in post-welfare contexts, in which "the political has been re-constituted at the level of the self. . . . There is little that is personal about self-esteem."[36] Here, self-esteem depoliticizes long histories of racism and antirural spatial prejudice.

Fabiola shared Liliana's interest in personal independence. Fabiola told me how she would anger participants with the demands she put on them, but "sometimes when people treat you really well, you also suffer, or rather, you get used to it, and take advantage." The project was not about mak-ing sure participants learned every last entrepreneurial tool, Fabiola said, "but you can open their minds." She posited entrepreneurship as a total individual fact,[37] a commitment that encompasses every aspect of daily life, where "you are going to have to wake up every day at six in the morning, perhaps go to bed at ten at night, twelve at night, for your business." This totalizing selfhood would appear during a showcase of the project at the tourist-heavy Holy Week Fair in 2014, when participants wore shirts with the Desco and Fondoempleo logos on one side and, where a name tag might go, the declaration "I'm an entrepreneur" (Figure 4.3).

Fabiola had no illusions about how few businesses would ultimately be successful. She was aware of existing critiques of the promises of unequivo-cal uplift ubiquitous in microenterprise programs. Still, she said, it was not "necessary to despair because in the end, there may be only a few that succeed or there may be many, but the few that remain are like paradigms. They remain as examples, and . . . they are going to make others want to be like them." Those paradigms, in Fabiola's view, promised to render growth as an ambient feeling.

FIGURE 4.3 Ludgardo Suni (left) and a colleague during Colca's Holy Week celebrations. Behind them a banner displays logos for each Desco-supported enterprise.

However, paradigms did not simply emerge. They had to be brought into being. Staff members accomplished this by working intensively to curate their participants' entrepreneurial mind-set and by offering attentive support as participants endured dramatic changes to their lives, highlighting both the violent and tender aspects of extractive care. If Desco staff members saw economic and personal growth as one and the same, in practice, participant personal growth was often the product of uncompensated staff affective labor. The permanent staff performed affective labor that mediated the frictions between the project's ideals and the realities of setting up a business in the Colca Valley. Staff members would frequently find themselves lending an ear to stories of abuse, marital distress, mental health problems, and intimate partner violence—often issues as personal as they were structural and political. Fabiola described comforting participants as they sat in her office in tears. Beyond their capacity-building sessions and site visits, Fabiola and Liliana also performed the labor of social workers, therapists, legal advocates, educators, financial advisers, accountants, and even absent parental figures. As Delmy told me, there was no room in Desco's budget for the "social element." But affective investment was unpaid labor. Staff affective labor thus constituted another neoliberal extraction, a sanctioned exploitation of women field agents in the NGO. Although they were engaged in affective extraction with their participants, Fabiola and Liliana were also on the bottom rungs of an exploitative institutional structure.

## Credit

The first phase of the project was a time of responsible dreaming. During this phase, Desco staff members selected seed capital winners, held capacity-building sessions and training in taking out credit, and tutored participants in how to embrace the mature labor of envisioning an enterprise.

### Responsible Dreaming: Launching the Project

The project began with a contest. Rogelio heard the announcement from the loudspeaker perched on the roof of the Lari municipality building. More than 300 other aspiring participants from throughout the valley's 19 villages heard the same announcement: a call for participants in one of two competitions happening in January 2013 in Chivay for residents of villages on the eastern side of the valley or in Cabanaconde for residents who lived at the western end.

Behind closed doors, aspiring participants gave short presentations on their business idea and fielded questions from Desco staff, a rotating cast of technocrats, and a representative from the local financial sector. They selected fifty finalists. Then, a second competition took place, where the top twenty contestants were selected for seed capital investments. Structurally, most winners came from positions of relative privilege, given the demand that they come to the project with secondary education and at least 500 soles in cash or assets. Most pitched an idea that explicitly or implicitly marketed a sense of Andean indigeneity.[38] All fifty finalists received training, advice, and ongoing audits for their incipient enterprises. In return, they submitted to the obligation to participate, which meant consistent work on their enterprises, attendance at capacity-building sessions, and open-ended availability for one-on-one evaluations.

The seed capital investment amounted to 3,650 soles ($1,147) in material assets (e.g., ovens, bricks, rent). This modest sum was conferred as a prize that did not have to be repaid. As Fabiola noted in our interview, "I don't think this is too much help." It was, in her view, just enough to spur action but sufficiently austere to avoid inculcating dependence on the project. As Antonio put it to the participants, "That's why we call it seed *capital* and not a seed *gift*!" The other thirty participants had to take out credit from

Fondesurco (Southern Regional Fund), the microcredit NGO that an earlier generation of Desco staff members had helped to launch in the region in 1994. However, nearly all fifty finalists ended up taking out additional credit, following the staff's aggressive advice to do so. As the result of an interinstitutional agreement, Fondesurco offered credit to participants with discounted preferential interest rates between 1% and 1.5%. This alliance shows one of the many ways that the Desco staff worked to compose economic growth out of contingent connections by engaging low-cost Fondesurco loans for project participants as a kind of subsidized financial training, with the idea that they would later become regular Fondesurco customers. Desco gave participants the chance to practice taking out credit but maintained a secret emergency fund in case a participant defaulted on a loan.

### Creating "Credit Culture"

In Desco's project proposal, staff members framed young Caylloma residents as a frontier of credit. They posited "low demand for credit on the part of young people" as an urgent development challenge that entrenches the unquestioned value of credit and debt.[39] Fondesurco, the microcredit NGO, was an ally in this frontier mission. According to a post on its website titled "Fondesurco: First in Financial Inclusion," Fondesurco sees itself as heroically "taking microcredit to those areas where before, nobody would dare go"; pitching itself as a pioneer, Fondesurco repeatedly refers to its role in opening Peru's "most obscure places" to the national economy.[40] Fondesurco credit counselors whom I spoke with described Caylloma as one of Peru's "last corners" (*últimas esquinas*). Brochures would advertise with the slogan, "Farmers, we are betting on you" (*apostamos por ustedes*), highlighting, as Sierra Sur staff did, the financial, speculative, and affective dimensions of investment.

I met Plinio Trelles Mamani, Fondesurco's branch director, in his office on Chivay's bustling Twentieth Century Avenue, where microfinance institutions, bank branches, NGOs, and hotels with increasingly sleek façades line the town's dusty main thoroughfare. Plinio told me how, aligned in their framing of the psychologically transformative potential of credit, Desco and Fondesurco worked together "to form a credit culture [*cultura crediticia*] in the population."

Plinio's use of "culture," here, is a judgment of collective maturity. One of the definitions of *cultura* in the *Real Academia Española* is the "set of knowledge that permits one to develop critical judgment."[41] The concept is a matter of behavior, class propriety, and education; the term would often be used in Colca in paternalistic commands, such as "culture begins at home" and "demonstrate your culture." Creditworthiness is a sign that an individual embodies culture, as Plinio sees it. For a Fondesurco loan, creditworthiness depends on the credit seekers' maturity, their relationships, and the reputation of their family, along with any business experience they may have. "We evaluate their income, the experience that they have in their business area," Plinio described, "from whom they buy their materials," but also "what they are like in their community," whether they "are responsible or have bad habits. . . . Perhaps they owe their neighbors and don't pay their debts." Repayment is a measure of the correct use of capital, which in turn indexes an effective self-actualization. The future is always at stake in a credit-debt relationship. As Plinio continued, "The client always has to keep the future in mind. If a client can't repay his or her credit, all institutions close their doors."

### The Capacity-Building Session

The credit phase of Desco's project involved training participants in this credit culture. Lessons that disciplined them to be properly primed for growth in this context were transmitted through capacity-building sessions. As Paige West has written, capacity building highlights "the long-articulated colonial notion of Indigenous peoples and colonized peoples having an inherent lack" of capacity to accomplish a certain end, which must be "built" by an expert.[42] It also individualizes that supposed incapacity, rendering an individual at fault for what often prove to be structural constraints. The sense among Desco staff that villagers were somehow poor in the midst of a cornucopia of natural, cultural, and financial resources enhanced a sense of *individualized* waste: Why else would young people have difficulty finding work, given the profusion of tourists and consumers of Colca Valley goods?

Through training sessions to transform villagers into wealth prospectors and their daily lives into extractable resources, capacity builders coaxed growth into being by showing participants how it should look and feel. The first session I attended began late. It was a January afternoon in 2014. We were in the windowless conference room in Desco's Chivay office. After opening by announcing that entrepreneurship was "the only way out" of poverty, Antonio Rojas, an independent consultant in small-business promotion, taped six large pieces of paper to the wall. They had the following headings: "Attitude," "Marketing Strategies," "Costs," "Registers of Sales,"

"Merchandising" (in English), and "Formalization." These were the six fundamental elements of running an enterprise. Antonio invited the fifteen participants in attendance to create and share their own personal plan for each. The meeting ran about two hours; its first half-hour was punctured by attendees entering late. One woman held her baby in her lap for the entire two-hour session. Every attendee had a mobile phone either in their hand or sitting on the conference table in front of them. The baby cooed as phones beeped and buzzed.

Most of the session was a group discussion about how each of these priorities helped to form a successful business. Antonio guided the group to see that "Attitude" was about "self-confidence," "support networks," the ability to "search out information," "goal setting," and as he posed to the group, "persis—?" an unfinished word the attendees were meant to finish but which met silence: "—tence!" Despite this paternalistic quizzing, he then added, "You have to be mature. You are adults." Optimism was essential: "You have to believe that tourism is going to *double* this year," he told the group, many of whose business plans depended either directly or indirectly on the tourist market. Participants had to "know your clients" and be prepared to continually promote the business: "Promotion cannot stop." Antonio constantly brought the conversation back to attitude as the fundamental driver of entrepreneurial success.

The session was a scene of ethical crafting. Entrepreneurship was not simply an activity but an orientation to the world. Participants were aggressively encouraged to be bold, despite the fact that for many, boldness could mean risking potentially irreversible debts, the inability to contribute to care obligations, and even the emotional toll of becoming more visible in public market spaces. Several participants were timid about their prospects. One mentioned high rent as a barrier. At this, Antonio chided the participant for failing to maintain a positive attitude.

Throughout the workshop Antonio talked of the "promises" and "commitments" that participants had to make for their enterprises, simultaneously to themselves and to project staff. Fabiola joined to tell the group that "we can't do anything more for you if you don't help us help you." She made it clear that, although "you are the chosen ones," as winners of the pitch competition, seed capital and access to Desco's expertise would be given to somebody else if a winner failed to put these resources to felicitous use. This happened when Rubén, a seed capital winner who enthusiastically opened a sandwich shop in Chivay, abandoned his business and moved to

Arequipa. Fabiola suggested that Rubén left because of his youthful indecisiveness and his eagerness for the dynamic life of a city. To the Desco staff, his departure reflected the problematic inability of many young people to commit to a single goal.

Other capacity-building workshops were geared toward specific specialties and included sessions on baking, customer service, dairy product commercialization, and textile work. All participants had to attend the workshop on branding with Sergio Calderon, which resulted in each coming up with a distinct logo for their enterprise, visible on the banner in Figure 4.3.

Reflecting on these workshops, Rogelio told me, "I like them a lot because they give us—they open your mind. A workshop that gives us more vision is the most important thing." Capacity-building sessions conveyed how to embody growth through a mature entrepreneurial posture toward daily life. A fundamentally affective project, growth emerged as attitude, maturity, and commitment that would organize acts of financial risk taking, business formalization, and self-plunder. Growth was staged as attainable when participants behaved in a certain way, followed a specific procedure, and stayed positive. Here, a psychology of motivation to exploiting the resources of one's life was a misdirection from the region's structural inequalities. This was, after all, a place where massive multinational corporations were reaping disproportionate benefit from the region's mines, agriculture, alpaca fiber, and luxury hotels. Part coaching and part self-help, Desco's capacity-building sessions instructed participants to become entrepreneurs through introspective work on the self. Capitalism could expand as entrepreneurs became confident engines of prosperity. Participants devoted considerable labor to attending the sessions. Empowerment was not a simple matter of absorption. The personal growth required to create a business was supposed to be hard, from the project staff's point of view. But they did not account for the labor time of waiting for transportation, the opportunity costs of suspending other work, or childcare obligations that raised the stakes of their effort to render entrepreneurship all-encompassing.

### Behavioral Interventions as Salvage Accumulation

Capacity-building sessions situated entrepreneurial microdevelopment as a local extension of the broader extractive logics driving Peru's aggregate growth. Liliana frequently conveyed the message to participants that "you have so much at your fingertips. Use it." As Antonio said, "None of you are alone." This reflected not that Desco would always be there but that personal networks and kin connections could become resources. Desco staff members instructed participants to count social ties as entrepreneurial raw material.

In a distinct pedagogical environment from the Sierra Sur project, this behavioral training amounted to lessons in salvage accumulation. "Accumulation is the amassment of wealth under capitalism," Anna Tsing writes. "Salvage here refers to the conversion of stuff with other histories of social relations (human and not human) into capitalist wealth."[43] Tsing engages this concept to describe how workers in contemporary capitalism are compelled to recruit diverse "noneconomic factors" of their lives into their labor. In Desco's work, kinship, expertise, talents, celebrated Indigenous difference, feminized and masculinized forms of dignity, relations to nonhumans, and people able to vouch for one's good standing in a credit application were all noneconomic factors that could be transformed into entrepreneurial assets. Desco staff were not after novice entrepreneurs but people who had proven themselves as potential business owners—individuals who were, in a sense, already wealthy. Ana Carol "Anacé" Condori made this clear when I asked how she won her seed capital.

> They told us that it would be worth more points if we already owned a business. And I already had the artisan shop. And I was the only one who competed who was running an artisan shop. . . . The problem is that the rent there [in a previous location] was really high. I ended up doing well, but it took a lot of sacrifice. I had to work a lot to pay the rent, but then, this is my in-laws' house, my husband's parents, so all we had to do here was clean it up and that's it.

We were conversing in Anacé's new restaurant, which she set up behind her tourist gift shop. This was an expansion on her original business idea. A customer could experience both gastronomy and artisanship that tapped into the region's Collagua and Cabana styles. Here, she illustrated that Desco saw its work as the mere activation of Anacé's ability to exploit the world around her. She also listed a second noneconomic factor: her motivation to avoid dependence on her husband, who did not approve of her enterprise. "I want to feel developed as a woman also," she told me, "and I want to work, because I like it and I want to contribute to our income, but my husband doesn't like that idea." Certainly, Anacé benefited from his kin network, but it was important to her to be able to generate her own income and be her own boss.[44]

A further example of salvage accumulation came from Lari. That village's Desco participants, led by Rogelio, established a district entrepreneurial association that would rely on *ayni*.[45] Rogelio proposed to Fabiola that the group could engage this Andean practice as a strategy to save them money while giving one another the seemingly inexhaustible resource of their labor time. *Ayni* is not practiced widely in Colca today. Recruiting *ayni* into the project was, in part, a salvage accumulation that foisted the costs of empowerment onto laborers themselves. Rogelio's proposal fit the ideology that development was about managing already existing abundance. It was also, in part, a means by which he and his colleagues recruited Desco support *into their own economic projects*. Fabiola was happy to resuscitate this index of a legible indigeneity that could help bring about an imagined future where entrepreneurship and tradition could together build a self-sustaining rural Andes. Rogelio was felicitously maximizing noneconomic factors that could build his village's enterprises and uphold their responsible dreams, a motivation that made him one of Desco's exemplary participants.

## Audit

In the next phase, Desco staff members expended their labor time auditing participants. The key face-to-face encounter for this phase was the visit, where surveillance became a strategy of financial tutelage. Participants had to begin demonstrating that they were deserving of their probationary financial inclusion.

### The One-on-One Visit

Audits by Desco staff usually occurred as surprise visits (*visitas inopinadas*). *Visita* was the same term used for Spain's colonial inspections; these visits channeled power hierarchies through which the colonial encounter still reverberates.[46] Invasive inspection is a price of entry for benefiting from Desco's project. Seed capital, credit, and the institutional and emotional support that came with it meant that everything in a participant's economic life was open to policing in the name of a perpetual test of entrepreneurship.

This surveillance—and staff frustration at failing to find participants in their business sites—underlined the project's de-diversifying expectation that an enterprise ought to be an aspiring entrepreneur's sole commitment. Surprise visiting was a common practice that echoed financial institution supervision: Just like Desco, Fondesurco's analysts liked to catch their clients in the act of entrepreneurship. Plinio told me that "analysts are always visiting" their clients to keep them accountable, describing a much more intimate, irregular mode of structuring time than a conventional schedule of credit and repayment. Desco staff members sought a similar disciplinary command over participants' time. Their efforts were often in vain.

Desco staff would spend many full workdays traversing the valley from village to village. These commutes could take anywhere from fifteen minutes to two hours. Staff sometimes had use of the NGO's Toyota Hilux pickup truck, but its budgets were tight and the staff was dispersed, so workers often relied on public vans (*combis*) that shuttled the region's residents between Chivay and smaller villages. This hub-and-spoke transportation could be uneven and unreliable. Much of their daily labor consisted of the "work of waiting"[47] for transportation and traveling in *combis*. Staff members routinely described how frustrating it was to expend so much effort traveling when they could not find participants. "This is the last time I work with young people," Fabiola told me and the team over lunch one afternoon in Chivay—a promise she would later abandon—as staff commented on the mercurial nature of the 18–29 age group.

Locating participants was difficult precisely because Desco had purposely selected well-connected, often politically engaged young people whose economic lives were highly diversified. Opportunistically maintaining simultaneous activities was a feature of keeping households afloat in the Colca Valley and could be glossed as a vernacular conception of Andean entrepreneurship.[48] Obligations ranged from childcare to municipal and church duties, to schooling, to household and agricultural labor, and to engagements in potential business opportunities. Liliana and Fabiola were not oblivious to these multiple commitments. However, they felt compelled to uphold the ideology of all-consuming entrepreneurship by the pressures of the Lima-based Fondoempleo, whose own audits of the project required meticulous documentation of participant advances. When Fabiola did locate her elusive participants, they often greeted her with the fear of a student who has not done their homework. Visits were an effort to produce a Foucauldian discipline, as the evaluator could arrive at any moment. Marcos described the hair on his neck standing up at the sight of a Desco vest, telling me, "The evaluations were constant."

In one visit I witnessed in Lari, Fabiola and Liliana were searching for Raquel, whose business was a small hog farm; Raquel was also a parent, about to be married, and involved in Lari's Evangelical church and in village politics as a council member. Unable to find her, they grew exasperated.

After attempting to call her mobile phone and waiting at her farm, they left, only to find her running breathlessly, apologetically saying, "I don't have time. My mother just died." The staff were sympathetic in their interactions with Raquel, who appeared to be in shock. But they still asked about the notebook, which Raquel did not have; after the encounter, staff members still registered Raquel's failure to meet entrepreneurial commitments.

Staff annoyance appeared to flare up more with women participants than with men. The overcommitment of men like Rogelio was seen as exemplary of the mature attitude required of entrepreneurship. Given gendered structural constraints and the disproportionate obligation for women in the region to be primary caregivers for children, elderly parents, and the household, it was significantly easier for men to display independence and maturity.

When staff did connect with an entrepreneur, the surprise audit centered on the incomes and expenditures notebook that all fifty participants were required to keep. A review of the books served as the point of departure for every visit. Staff evaluated the progress of each enterprise and then, continuing the pedagogical intervention, assigned what they called homework (*tarea*) that should be completed by the next visit. Having to share information about one's incomes and assets could be invasive and humiliating in a community where money tends to be a private matter. In addition, filling out the double-entry incomes and expenditures notebook was not intuitive. Most participants had their own written budgeting systems. Adopting Desco's vision of growth meant, in practice, adapting to its modular bureaucratic requirements.

As perpetually possible tests for "hidden entrepreneurial qualities,"[49] *visitas* were exemplary moments of extractive care that played out in distinct ways, as the scenes I witnessed with Rogelio, Silvia, Ludgardo, and Pati demonstrate. A site of invasive behavioral training, the audit is at once about teaching participants how to put together a business and about evaluating those participants' progress toward entrepreneurial subjectivity.

### Attitude: Rogelio

On our March visit to Lari, Rogelio triumphantly told the staff that he had to take out a loan to expand his nursery; his new pen was the size of a small gymnasium. I later asked him how he found staff visits. He expressed effusive appreciation and suggested that he had internalized the emphasis on entrepreneurship as his sole focus: "It teaches you that you constantly have to be there with the project and constantly with your business. It's not that you can hide."

The way he narrated his own progress elegantly fit Desco's vision. Before the project, what Rogelio "did not know to harvest is optimism and perseverance." He learned to shift his attitude: "Before I didn't have so much responsibility. And with Desco I'm here now, and I have already been a mini-entrepreneur, micro-entrepreneur, and I have to be responsible in all areas, in sales, in everything." Visits and capacity building opened his mind to resource logics. Reflecting on his Desco-sponsored trip to Cuzco, for example, he noted:

> They do not have good terrain. They have yellow earth, and even with that, they make their farms, and there it's colder than here, where it's warmer. There it's higher up, and they care for guinea pigs, and many of them in [significant] quantities, so [I noted] how they do it there, because here I have everything.

The idea that he had everything in the Colca Valley individualizes the project's positioning of participants in a context of ubiquitous extractable wealth. Unlike some of the other participants, Rogelio also had a keen eye for self-promotion, internalizing the fact that his own personal appeal could be a resource. Most participants I encountered while accompanying Desco staff were wary of my presence and nervously tried to ignore me. But Rogelio brought me into his network of urban and foreign visitors. During the most important audit of the program, the day of the visit from Fondoempleo supervisor Fernando Gonzalo, Rogelio strategically staged the grand opening of his enterprise, named El Aposento de Don Cututo (The Chamber of Sir Stud). I followed the team through the day's visits when both entrepreneurs and staff members came under scrutiny. Fernando, Desco staff, Rogelio's father, a group of fellow Lari residents, and I watched Rogelio ritually declare the barn open for business as he stood in its doorway on his parents' property. Marking the occasion, Fabiola cracked open a bottle of sparkling wine hanging from the barn's lintel. Rogelio gave an eloquent speech narrating his progress from a "libertine" who "took this as a joke" to a serious entrepreneur and a youth leader in Lari's Evangelical church.

Steeped in the growing Evangelical movement in the Colca Valley and the Andes more broadly, Rogelio's conspicuously post-libertine work ethic reflects what James Huff has called "pentecostalized development."[50] Huff notes that emerging Christian publics throughout Latin America apply ethics of disciplined restraint and individualized hard work cultivated in church to secular economic aims. In Rogelio's case, membership in the Evangelical church was one more fact from his daily life that Desco helped him salvage as an entrepreneurial resource. After the celebration, Rogelio and the other Lari-based participants invited Fernando, the Desco staff, and me to a feast of fried guinea pig from Rogelio's barn. This was a move similar to how Huanca's entrepreneurs fed the visiting Sierra Sur staff. The Lari participants offered a taste of their locally cultivated abundance, legitimating the development staff's work before their supervisor and opening the potential for future engagements with Desco.

### Maturity: Silvia

Another participant was Silvia Mamani, age 22, who was from Lari and received seed capital to launch a bakery in Chivay. Silvia was one of several participants who discussed their projects on Desco's YouTube channel (Figure 4.4), where she expressed her personal definition of economic growth: "Going forward, to sell, I think, cakes now in [larger] quantities, not just here to the population, but, maybe, to take orders from other districts, from outside of the region."[51] In the video Silvia exhibits an attitude of confident

Promoción de emprendimientos en Lari
80 views • Mar 10, 2014

FIGURE 4.4 Silvia Mamani describing her bakery for Desco's YouTube channel.

expansion that was markedly distinct from the interaction I witnessed during Fabiola's audit of her shop. I accompanied Fabiola to the new bakery, a rented storefront on the busy dirt road lining Chivay's outdoor market. Silvia's shop was well situated for foot traffic from commuters and tourists. Yet she found herself waiting long periods without any customers. It was Fabiola's task to help Silvia overcome this apparent paradox of plenty.

Fabiola and Silvia greeted each other, Fabiola introduced me, and then she handed me her clipboard that held a survey of entrepreneurial progress for each participant. Fabiola had me begin the audit by taking part in the development catechism. My presence likely added anxiety to this already tense encounter, as Silvia now had to explain her progress to two outsiders. However, Silvia appeared to be significantly more nervous about how Fabiola would react to her answers. I read through Silvia's homework as Fabiola had outlined it, asking whether she was using "standard recipes" as she agreed to do on Fabiola's previous visit. Silvia stammered her answer directly to Fabiola, who quickly took over.

> *Silvia*: Well, a few, a few Señorita—
> *Fabiola*: [slightly raising her voice] WHY? Now, in the workshops [they told you that] you have to use standard recipes.
> *Silvia*: It's that I have used other recipes, Señorita. I'm coming out with more.
> *Fabiola*: Right, but are you using the spreadsheet?
> *Silvia*: It's just a notebook, that's all. I don't have a computer.

Fabiola maintained her professional and supportive demeanor but did not attempt to contain her frustration at Silvia's failure to complete what she had "committed" to do at her baking capacity-building session. Although Silvia lacked computer access, it still seemed to me that Fabiola interpreted not having a computer as just one more excuse. Fabiola ordered several pieces of cake for us to try in a small gesture of support for Silvia's new business. Silvia then described her anxiety about the shop's location.

> The majority of my customers, the ones I see continuously, tell me that I should go to the center by the plaza, over there by the plaza where it's more expensive. Why not go? So I don't know. I don't know how to do it. I was thinking I could do only custom orders. I don't know, sometimes I, alone here, I . . . I . . . I make things complicated,

Señorita. Why am I doing poorly? It's that I get desperate, because everyone tells me, you're in a bad location.

Exemplifying the tough love approach Fabiola had previously described to me, she brusquely glossed Silvia's anxiety as an excuse: "You're lying. It's not location." Instead, she argued, the problem was Silvia's lack of direction, a sign of immaturity manifesting as the failure to put sustained effort into advertising. Fabiola began listing Silvia's problems, echoing Liliana's psychological profile.

> *Fabiola*: So let's see. In terms of location. Look at what you are more or
> less telling me. Location of store. Product preparation. Instability
> about making decisions, which is what I'm seeing right now. And lack
> of a clear promotion plan. What do you think is the main problem?
> *Silvia*: [after a long silence] Promotion, maybe? Business cards—
> *Fabiola*: To me it appears that this is, or rather, like, you don't have
> a clear promotion plan, so you feel insecure and you let yourself
> be swayed by what people who come by here tell you, because of
> course, obviously you have to keep in mind what people say, but to
> help you to get ahead, search out alternatives. [Instead] it makes you
> struggle. It's making you depressed, and you're not getting out of
> that, it seems. I ought to send you to the psychologist, eh? And also
> you, or it's like you don't have a clear promotion plan or you feel
> that the location is a problem, but, look, right now you've seen a ton
> of people pass by.
> *Silvia*: Right, but they don't enter.
> *Fabiola*: They don't enter. Why don't they enter?
> *Silvia*: Because they won't enter.
> *Fabiola*: Do you know why? Because you have to advertise! Remember.
> We have always talked about this. Advertise. . . . Where are your
> deals?
> *Silvia*: It's that I have another problem. I can't keep up with the pro-
> duction and with the sales, and sometimes I have orders coming
> continuously, right, and they're not even full cakes . . .
> *Fabiola*: So we have done nothing about promotion for this, right? And
> what are the results of these weaknesses?
> *Silvia*: [silent]
> *Fabiola*: Decrease in sales, Silvita. Your business doesn't take off.

Fabiola lays out a chain of activities that begins in an attitude, continues with promotion, and ends in growth, captured by the idea of taking off. For Silvia, Fabiola suggests, growth could mean hiring a second baker to make her workload manageable. Growth is an interactional project to frame plans with the proper entrepreneurial affects, manifested here as decisiveness. Fabiola engages the psychological category of indecisiveness, previously established as a technical problem in Liliana's profile, and ridicules the idea of therapy in nearly the same breath—"I ought to send you to the psychologist"—as she works to correct Silvia's trajectory.

The conversation continued with a discussion of formalization. Silvia then expressed her desire to move the store to the highland village of Caylloma, where she had family, further confirming Fabiola's sense of her indecision. Fabiola worked to dissuade her from this.

> But Silvita, first organize this nicely with your promotions. . . . You have problems with organizing and the problem with marketing. You haven't developed business cards. You are missing all that. So first finish all of that well, and then you can go to Caylloma. One day at a time, as they say. Right?

In this interaction, Silvia's concerns about standard recipes, her location, and having to stay in one place were individualized, rendered unacceptable manifestations of indecision. An alternative possibility, which would be consistent with other testimonies I recorded, was that Silvia was not an indecisive, timid young person but rather someone who was uncomfortable being immobilized in the provincial capital and who felt the need to diversify her engagements and be closer to kin who lived throughout the region.

As Fabiola recorded Silvia's "commitments" on the clipboard, Silvia asked, with a tone of concern, "What are you writing down, Señorita?" Fabiola responded, "What we have done [today]. . . . I'll let you know when you are going to see our next visit. How much do I owe you for the cakes?"

### Accountability: Ludgardo

Ludgardo Suni, Liliana's younger brother, was one of the thirty participants who won advising but not seed capital. I accompanied Fabiola on a one-on-one visit with Ludgardo in November 2013, while he was still in the early stages of putting his carpentry business together. We met in the village of Achoma, where Ludgardo studied carpentry at the Escuela Taller (trade school), an initiative of the Spanish Agency for International Development Cooperation. Fabiola quizzed Ludgardo on where he would locate demand for his products and services. Together, they came up with a plan. He would search out three to five clients in need of furniture construction or repair. Then, Fabiola asked, "Will you need credit to get this business off the ground?" He answered, apparently not having thought of it, that credit sounded like a good idea, "to complement what I can afford."

As Fabiola saw it, credit was the default tool for making the initial investments necessary for starting a business. It also occasioned a pedagogy of business planning. Fabiola told him that to take out credit, he had to make "a series of commitments" and set concrete, achievable goals for the next three months. The goals he set were to have a fully operational workshop and five customers by the end of January, which is when he would receive his first credit. As a device to commit Ludgardo to these goals, Fabiola had him write them down and sign his name beneath them in his notebook. She then took a picture of his signature with her digital camera.

This was a gesture that enacted Ludgardo's growth trajectory while, at the same time, submitting his responsible dreaming to NGO surveillance. The rural Andes is a region where the written word and, especially, the signature, are imbued with significant authority.[52] Fabiola's disciplinary practice of taking a picture of Ludgardo's commitments rendered his enterprise's growth attainable if he followed specific steps, projecting those steps as inevitably leading to entrepreneurial expansion. It also rendered him a personal failure if he did not follow those steps. Success was something Ludgardo *owed*; not accumulating clients was recast as an unmet professional commitment to an NGO staff member.

### Assets: Pati

Liliana and I visited Patricia Cusi Cusi's restaurant in the high-elevation village of Tuti to conduct an audit of her incomes and expenditures registry. This was another rainy afternoon in March 2014. Her restaurant is located in Tuti's plaza. With the help of her mother, Narcisa, who at the time was a participant in the Sierra Sur project, Pati opened a restaurant in her mother's home called Cusicoyllor Snack Ecológico (Cusicoyllor Ecological Snack). Cusicoyllor, the name of the Inca ruler Pachacútec's daughter and a play on Pati's surname, was devoted to organic, natural, and local foods. Pati's specialty was quinoa cakes. Quinoa is one of Tuti's flagship products; Tuti is the rare community in Caylloma whose quinoa has been certified as organic.

She aspired to attract tourists curious about Tuti's quinoa-centric Collagua cuisine, but the venue was mainly frequented by teachers, construction workers, and other professionals who worked in Tuti. With her seed capital, Pati bought an oven, tables, and earthenware dishes. Her mother owned the space. Like many other participants, Pati did not need to pay rent.

Upon arriving, Liliana and I found Pati in the restaurant with her 3-year-old son. She was seven months pregnant at the time. She swiftly asked her child to leave and then hurried to the kitchen to boil water for our tea. Our visit was clearly disruptive to Pati's afternoon. The first step in the meeting was a discussion of the incomes and expenditures notebook. After Liliana found it only minimally filled out, as was the case on every other visit I joined, Liliana gently reminded Pati of the importance of tracking her budget, because the Fondoempleo supervisor would likely ask to see her notebook. Pati then orally reported that customers only came rarely. Her statement contradicted Tuti resident Reynaldo Churro's confident appraisal of Tuti's prospects for entrepreneurship (see Chapter 3).

However, Liliana expressed concern only that Pati had not filled out the notebook, appearing more interested in the pedagogical model than in what the notebook might have said. Then, Liliana closed the nearly empty notebook. "Now tell me. How are you *really* doing?" Liliana's register switch from project audit to care for a young woman's well-being was how she managed the personal development that she saw as the more fundamental target of her intervention. Pati demurred. Liliana asked how Pati was physically during the pregnancy. "Fine," she shyly replied, her one-word answers marking the catechism with a quiet staccato.

After a pause, Liliana asked, "Does your husband ever help you with business tasks?"

"Sometimes," Pati responded, reluctant to detail their household routines.

Intervening directly in the intimate space of the family unit, and offering advice as an older mother to a younger one, Liliana urged Pati not to be too critical of her husband in the rare moments when he offered his help. After, she continued to probe Pati's family dynamic, seeking to ensure that the family functioned as an entrepreneurial team.[53] The team included Pati's toddler, whose role in the enterprise could be as simple as cleaning up his toys. But, Liliana stressed, he too had to learn responsibility. And, she implied, he too was part of the inspection.

As Liliana veered from the audit of the books into care for Pati as a whole "entrepreneurial self,"[54] she engaged the family unit as a substrate of growth. Pati's daily life, home, and child were resources. In this specific growth-making encounter, Liliana pressed Pati to speak about intimate dimensions of her life in a fashion that was at once empathetic and evaluative, reflecting the simultaneous tenderness and violence of extractive care. Turning to the personal, Liliana connected to participants by subtly tacking between disciplinary pedagogy and care at an intimate level that still factored into Desco's evaluations. My presence likely contributed to Pati's reticence. But the meeting also made clear that this audit was designed to be a scene of salutary humiliation before an NGO staff member whose gestures of gentle care were part of an affective extraction.

### Extractive Care

Desco's *visitas* are moments of unsettlement that can be generative, even if they are also quietly violent and humiliating, as I read the audits with Silvia, Ludgardo, and Pati to be. Inspections tied attitude to economic growth with pedagogy that was simultaneously a judgment of character. Staff surveillance of the registry and other homework could be poor fits with villagers' daily rhythms. The audit phase affords an interval when initial entrepreneurial results must become a performance that felicitously demonstrates that the original investment had been a good idea. During this period, signs of an Indigenous entrepreneurial self must begin revealing themselves.

Tania Murray Li has critiqued "the will to improve" in development interventions that render structural concerns as problems that can be solved through technical means.[55] Recent research into feminized microfinance development suggests that such a will to improve endures through efforts to enfold subaltern women into financial flows.[56] My fieldwork made clear that technified improvement could also apply to the psyche. Some participants, Liliana told me, were survivors of sexual abuse from family members. Others faced mental health difficulties. Liliana took the NGO's job to mean helping young people overcome *internal* barriers to their simultaneously economic and psychological flourishing. Consistent with the purposefully underfunded, austere approach to care visible in post-welfare spaces, which Barbara Cruikshank calls "Liberation Therapy," Liliana's mission was to build self-esteem and interiority into multiculturalist development work, which she sought to constitute as a strong relationship of "self-to-self."[57]

This interiority was key to building attitudes that would be compatible with and help to expand a booming national economy.

## Debt

The Desco project ended in May 2014. This month of closure was when participants worked to settle up, completing their financial and affective obligations to Desco and Fondesurco.

### Paradigm: Rogelio

Rogelio performed Desco's vision of what Fabiola called the entrepreneurial paradigm by framing his progress as a narrative arc of maturity achieved by overcoming internal obstacles to become a local business leader. Through repeated cycles of taking out and repaying credit, Rogelio demonstrated his growing skill as a young Indigenous entrepreneur far beyond the program's end. As late as 2018 Rogelio was deploying Facebook to expand his clientele (Figure 4.5). He posted a photograph to advertise his business, showing a section of his massive pen. "Good, Delicious, and Succulent Guinea Pigs," he writes, followed by an additional description: "Asprocel:[58] productive organization from the District of Lari that promotes care for ecological guinea pigs, realizes the sale of guinea pigs individually and in bulk. Well-skinned guinea pig carcasses and guinea pigs to raise." These are followed by two mobile phone numbers, smiley face emojis, and the English word "Delivery."

Rogelio expertly demonstrated Desco's theory of neoliberal citizenship. With credit capacity and an empowered interiority, young people could create new markets, extending the field of capitalist practice in ways that established sellers tended to miss. Rogelio was enacting the utopian future that Desco crafted through its emphasis on localized, heritage-validating enterprise, promoted through a creative recombination of resources at his disposal. He used the tools of globalized social media and microcredit to profit off of a gastronomic symbol of Indigenous Andean abundance that would also enable him to thrive in his village.

Compared with the other project participants, Rogelio came from a peasant family that had more land than many in Lari. As Fabiola later put it bluntly, "Rogelio has money!" He was, at the same time, highly motivated to become a competitive entrepreneur and a person of influence in his community, in no small part because of his recent membership in the Evangelical church. He told me that before his libertine days, he was a top student and elected mayor of his high school. This project was thus a kind of redemption.

Rogelio Taco

April 23 · 🐵                                                                    •••

BUENOS, DELICIOSOS Y SUCULENTOS CUYES.
Asprocel: organizacion productiva del distrito de Lari que promueve la
crianza de cuyes ecologicos, realiza la venta de cuyes al menor y por
mayor.
Cuyes carcaza bien peladitos y cuyes para recria. Contactenos,
990105774 —
993255676. 😊 S. Delivery:)

FIGURE 4.5 Rogelio Taco takes his guinea pig business to Facebook.

### Excess: Pedro, Felix, and Marcos

I did not often hear direct participant critiques of the project. But as
it closed, several participants implemented Desco's values in ways that
subverted the NGO's mission. Pedro and Felix, two of Desco's Lari participants, were twin brothers who went outside the program's mandate

to find their entrepreneurial success. They largely neglected "Los Peters" Dairy Products, the business for which Felix won seed capital to supply milk to the dairy conglomerate Gloria and special Lari-made yogurt products to vendors in Chivay. Instead, they opportunistically cornered an unexpected market: operating an internet café and electronics business in a prime location on Lari's plaza, for which demand from local children and teenagers was astronomical. Although the new business exemplified the opportunistic entrepreneurial sensibility that Desco staff members were training participants to cultivate, in practice the venture worried the Desco staff because of how much it diverged from the project they had agreed to fund. Fondoempleo's rigid, de-diversifying prescriptions for empowered development ignored the opportunism that was part of entrepreneurship as Pedro and Felix practiced it. In this case, going beyond the document represented the wrong attitude.

In a second case, Marcos drew inspiration from Desco's project to become an entrepreneur in informal moneylending, whose illicit status would also represent the wrong attitude. The enterprise for which he won seed capital was an appliance resale business in Chivay, not far from Silvia's cake shop. I first encountered him as I made the rounds with Fabiola, where he recounted at length his performance of a *pago a la tierra* in the store as a way of asking for its blessing. Friends were with him at the shop; one explained that "you have to do it with a lot of faith." He later told me how he strayed from his Desco-authorized business plan, noting the obstacles to reselling dishwashers, vacuums, and sound systems.

> I realized that when you buy used items, there is always a small risk that the things won't work like they're supposed to. I can't turn it on, so, so, I realized that we could lend. There is not too, too, too much to lose. Maximum loan is up to 500 soles [$170] and the minimum might be 50, 20, 10 soles [$17, about $7, a little more than $3, respectively].

Informal microlending presented lower financial risk to Marcos than his original Desco-approved plan. It was not likely to be authorized by SUNAT[59] and ran the risk of being shut down by state auditors, but Marcos was certainly expanding the scope and inclusiveness of capitalism with an energetic attitude. This is how he pitched the advantage of his services over a microcredit bank like Fondesurco: "Here, it's much quicker, because there, you have to complete paperwork to get credit, some 3, 4 days of paperwork, and only then do you get credit, and there are people that need cash right away." Marcos proposed to overcome the frictions of formal finance.

These divergences from Desco's program elucidate its competing aims, where an attitude of entrepreneurial expansiveness, the imperative to formalize, and staff concerns about youth indecision came into tension.

### Bankruptcy: Vanessa

With its emergency fund, Desco protected participants from the devastating realities of failing to settle up. But what did debt look like beyond Desco? Failure to repay is extremely rare, Fondesurco's Plinio Trelles told me. In that event the bank forces a client to liquidate their assets and can seize their home if they own one. It also puts a client's name onto a list of insolvent debtors kept by Infocorp (a firm owned by the U.S.-based Equifax), what Fabiola called *la lista negra* (the blacklist). Plinio described this as the doors of credit closing on a person because of their own failure to plan for the future. Although bankruptcies were rare, villagers certainly gossiped about people who engaged in aspirational credit-based spending that would keep their families in long-term debt.

Vanessa, an artisan friend of Anacé's, experienced that closure after failing to repay a loan in Arequipa. She rented a store along the main pedestrian mall in Chivay, where she sold Collagua- and Cabana-themed artisanry, jewelry, and other items aimed at tourist customers. She declared bankruptcy and was, at the time we spoke, blacklisted on Infocorp. Still, she firmly attached her hopes to the credit economy.

> I'm in bankruptcy four years now, and just now I'm pulling myself out of it, as here [in Chivay] the rent costs less [than it does in Arequipa], and, like, there are also tourists, not many but there are always some; so there is a path to opening up, once you believe that there is work to be done, maybe, I have—I'm going to grow more, more capital, then I can return to Arequipa. . . . Right now, I can't take out loans, because when I declared bankruptcy four years ago, I had credit from the banks, but when I was in bankruptcy, I couldn't pay the bank and right now [*ahorita*] no institution can lend to me. And it's because of this that I'm delayed in growing, because the bank is a great support. With a bank I would have been able to lift myself up in a year, in a year. Right now I would have had a house. Right now I would have been really good. But now I'm renting in a little room.

> I pay 50 soles [or $17 per month]. . . . I also don't have a husband, I'm a single mother.

Vanessa elided economic and personal growth with the phrase "I'm delayed in growing," demonstrating how brutally her lack of options has injured her self-worth. Later in our conversation, she proudly identified herself as an ideal independent entrepreneur in terms of the prevailing ethics of neoliberal growth: "I have never received any support from any government, from anywhere, never. I went alone. I sold in the street, in the street, and there I go gathering a little merchandise, another little bit of income, for my children, another little bit so we can eat. Yeah, you keep searching." She elaborated on what a new loan would do for her: "The bank loan is super great because that's a support. You invest capital and it leaves you profit and it gets paid. This is really good. But because I can't do any of these things, nothing stays with me."

Vanessa's testimony demonstrates the stakes of Antonio's no-alternatives logic. She was completely reliant on Peru's credit infrastructure to continue her livelihood, which was a toxic promise that left her hardly able to stay afloat.[60] Invoking the euphemistic *ahorita*, which diminishes the Spanish word for "now" (*ahora*) to indicate that this was merely a temporary situation, Vanessa registered her growth as a salvation only possible within the temporality of credit and debt. Credit was the only way out of a problem that credit caused. Her testimony reminded me of Liliana's argument that development is simultaneously economic and psychological; this is as much the case when development succeeds as when it fails. Vanessa was beholden to that no-alternatives logic. With credit, Vanessa was certain that her business would take off instantly. Without it, she had difficulty imagining an economic future.

## Conclusion: The Invisible Labor of Inevitable Development

Desco staff members enacted growth as the result of intimate and invasive behavioralist extractivism. Despite ideologies that framed a generation of individuals as easily able to extract from the worlds around them, I found that growth accomplished by the cultivation of financially adept Indigenous entrepreneurs requires, in practice, the laborious interactional work of extractive care. The project used face-to-face encounters to compose Peruvian economic growth in a place it recognizes as a margin of capitalism by training villagers in capitalist behavior and packaging that behavior as an inevitable manifestation of maturity. In these scenes, making growth feel real was the product of feminized labor by NGO staff and plenty of other unseen labor from participants. Invisibilized affective labor was vital to Desco's neoliberal project of pairing minimal spending with maximal demands on project participants. Highlighting this labor reveals some of the uneven hidden costs that enacting capitalism requires.

After the project closed, Fabiola was responsible for analyzing its results in a document called the *Sistematización* (assessment). This internal audit document, which was distinct from the audits that occupied much of the Desco staff's work, was geared toward generating helpful insights for future NGO initiatives. The evaluation had to balance critique with the imperative ultimately to legitimate the project. The document's "Findings" section highlights positive outcomes. It indicates that most participants did ultimately formalize their business and take out credit, despite a widespread "fear of formalization." It also positively assesses the capacity building sessions:

> *Impact of the capacity building in its surrounding context:* Not only did it improve the youths' management of their enterprises, but it also "contaminated" their previous family businesses. And in the enterprises themselves, the other members of the family who were involved also use the tools conferred in the capacity-building sessions.[61]

This was one of Desco's main growth missions. "Contaminate" was a word that Fabiola frequently used; Liliana would speak of "infecting." Both of these organic metaphors of positive contagion framed an inevitable extension of practices that would foster psychological development in young people while creating local jobs and stemming migration to Arequipa. As for employment, 70% of participants generated at least one new job but "with spouses and family members being the direct beneficiaries of these newly created positions." This means that the project ultimately entrenched many participants' roles within their kinship groups and communities. Entrepreneurs strengthened the bonds of kinship while relying on kin as invisible infrastructure for enterprise, but they did not become structural engines of a democratized prosperity.

Fabiola's report then turned to a section called "Lessons Learned," where she was invited to critique the project. Here is what she wrote: "The capacity-building program turned out to be 'rigid.' The initial model—designed with its reference urban youth who had more formal educational experience—should have been shaped according to local conditions. Having to adapt this model wore on the team."[62] This last point suggests that the project's emphasis on independence came into tension with its modular approach to youth as a universal category. Fondoempleo erroneously imagined a generic young person in Peru. Fabiola also implicitly indicts the project's fundamental ideology that growth will always occur so long as certain psychological conditions are met.

Desco's staff worked to enact a growth beyond mining that mining companies supported and that took a similar extractive shape to mining. They strove to enfold young people into Peruvian prosperity through the mechanisms of formal finance. But financialized development occludes certain problems and burdens: its modular standards, practices, and visions of youth and the future; the affective extraction, from villagers and staff alike, inherent to its functioning; and the irreversible damage that credit-based entrepreneurship can cause when it is posited as the only option for young people to thrive. In its wake, the Desco project left a constrained market space in which entrepreneurship was, to many of the people who had adopted its entrepreneurial imperative, the single option, without alternatives, for an empowerment that helps a participant flourish materially and mentally. But on its own terms, the project was successful. The staff did not mean to offer a structural intervention or establish a new situation of equality. For them, growth was about ambient paradigms, shared attitudes, and seeding the continued promise of a coming region-wide prosperity that resulted from restrained but well-targeted investments in just a few exemplary individuals.

# 5

## Extractive Care

### Cattle, Contamination, and Climate Change at the Tintaya Mine

FREDDY'S LEFT ARM WAS UP to his elbow inside the cow's rectum. The cow groaned in protest and squirmed in discomfort as Freddy, a veterinary technician, felt through the rectal wall for the long metal rod of the insemination gun, which he had inserted and was bracing with his external right hand. Each touch was slow and gentle. Yet this was undoubtedly a scene of violence, a violation.[1] The cow's legs were tied before the procedure; Freddy's two technical assistants had been holding her body in place since Freddy started the insemination by scooping out her feces. I watched as he slowly traced his gloved fingers up the muscular wall, following the outline of the rod until he could grasp the cervix through the rectal tissue to guide the rod through it. Freddy then shot a column of chilled sperm imported from a Brown Swiss bull named Bruno through the insemination gun. After that, maintaining his grip through the rectal wall, he gently pulled the gun out with his right hand and removed his left arm. Finally, his assistants untied the unwilling Andean cow, putting an end to the violence. She swiftly ran away from the veterinary team as Bruno's "enhanced" European sperm entered her uterus.

Over just a few minutes, several intimate touches between a veterinarian and a cow constituted an act that extended growth into rural Peru's capitalist margins. Here, in the highlands outside the town of Espinar, cattle inseminations meant face-to-face interactions between a veterinary team and a peasant family (Figure 5.1). They formed part of a broad package of veterinary care meant to open Indigenous livelihoods to new growth in livestock and dairy markets. Inseminations feature in a variety of agricultural

FIGURE 5.1 Freddy Panuera preparing to inseminate a cow.

development projects around the world.[2] In the southern Andes the genetic "improvements" they promise are a popular means of augmenting household productivity. They build income-generating potential through higher milk production, larger animals, and increased adaptability to climate change.

Unlike the livestock enhancement programs that once dominated agricultural development in the Andes, however, this 2017 insemination was the conspicuous work of a mine. The nearby Tintaya Mine, owned by the Swiss company Glencore, deployed inseminations and veterinary assistance to demonstrate care for the people who surrounded it. This work by a copper mine to make a nation's growth feel real by nurturing adjacent human and animal lives exemplifies the project of extractive care I explore throughout this book. At once tender and violent, extractive care attends to those domains of well-being that foster dominance over exploitable resource abundance. It encompasses acts of care that expand the scope of resource extraction.

So far, I have analyzed small-scale development projects to actualize Indigenous entrepreneurs and producers as nodal points in Peru's new rural growth. The investments I addressed in Chapters 3 and 4 worked to inculcate a self-plundering wealth extraction as a learned entrepreneurial skill. In this chapter I show that private mining companies also engaged the work of extractive care to make growth palpable, but in distinct ways. I base this chapter on my fieldwork with corporate agents and anti-mining Indigenous rights activists, mostly in 2017 and 2019. Focusing on the mining sector, where Peru's silver, copper, gold, and zinc deposits were at the heart of the country's massive aggregate growth between the 1995 privatization of mining and the 2020 COVID-19 outbreak, I build on recent research in feminist science studies that shows how "the exercise of power operates through care."[3]

In Peru, mining expansion is both entangled with and partly diverges from entrepreneurial empowerment discourses. As I have suggested throughout this book, I see extractive care as an approach to growth in a mineral-rich region that takes all aspects of daily life as potentially exploitable resources. Here, I show extractive care at work as a set of practices vital to the representation of growth in the *immediate vicinity* of a mine. This is a context that draws another dimension of extractive care into focus: It also indicates care for extracted minerals themselves, which requires instrumentally providing for the objects and lives around them to ensure their profitability. In this iteration of extractive care, medicalized violence committed against a cow with tender touches that give way to extreme violation is packaged as salutary for its owner household. Extractive care facilitates a macrolevel structural and ecological violence that becomes clear once one appreciates the scope, timescale, and impacts of mining-based growth. Extractive care also works to mitigate against a resistant politics of indigeneity flourishing in certain villages near the mine by actively associating Indigenous livelihood with improvements that are the conspicuous results of a mine's presence.

We were at a peasant family's home outside the town of Espinar (also known as Yauri), the provincial capital and urban center of Espinar Province. This was one of many artificial inseminations that Freddy Panuera conducted as part of his daily work as a veterinarian for the Tintaya Foundation, the Tintaya Mine's corporate social responsibility (CSR) outfit. Freddy and his team offered comprehensive medical care to the province's cattle, with inseminations as their signature contribution. By seeding Espinar's cattle with Brown Swiss genes, Glencore branded a conspicuous Swiss influence both above and below the ground as the medium for an inclusive growth. The Swiss brand would, in turn, be a useful partner in the work of building the Peruvian brand—Marca Perú—as "The Richest Country in the World."

The everyday, intimate, face-to-face work of creating what Freddy called an "improved" breed of hybrid Euro-Andean cattle enacts the Tintaya Mine "as an agent of sustainable development."[4] This veterinary work allows the corporation to stage growth as evidence of its own *responsibility*. Like *celebration* and *maturity* in the previous chapters, responsibility is not an objective condition but an aspirational claim.[5] It is far from inevitable that a mine should enlist productive cattle in its CSR regime. But concrete technical interventions such as inseminations remind villagers of a time of greater provision of material goods by development institutions and the state. They were popular, especially compared with entrepreneurial training. This promised improvement was a means of offsetting the mine's pollution. Cattle were the synecdoche of the mine's claim to an ethos of responsibility for rural market lives.

In this chapter mines enact economic growth through face-to-face encounters characterized by an extractive care for bovine and, by extension, human life. This enactment centers improved cattle as a figuration: a "performative image" that gives material and semiotic form to an object of desire.[6] Here, the figure of healthy cattle stands in for the vision of a thriving rural community near a mine that was able to feel the full benefits of growth in the form of bustling businesses and warm, hygienic homes free from want. Drawing feminist science studies into conversation with affect theory, I argue that for Peru's private mines, making growth feel real meant cultivating a "cruel optimism" in the mine's surround. Lauren Berlant describes a relation of cruel optimism as a relentless attachment to an object that either does one harm or is so unattainable that the attachment itself is toxic.[7] Here, the mine worked to toxically attach highland peasants to a sense of health, progress, and abundance that depended on its own profitability. Mining company staff members such as Freddy performed a future world in which a mine's growth meant well-being for villagers, even though that growth was, in the present, a source of heavy metal leakage, land grabs, and other harms. Mining companies such as Tintaya worked to affectively actualize a future of harmonious coexistence in abundance.

I proceed in this chapter by contextualizing the role that mines and their accompanying development schemes have recently played in building Peru's booming economy. Then I turn to three face-to-face encounters where growth was actualized and contested alongside mine expansions in Espinar and Caylloma. As with the previous two chapters, growth was enacted through interpersonal interactions. The first of these encounters, a veterinary visit, took place as the Tintaya Mine in Espinar made its daily case for the benefits of its presence to villagers living in its surround by routinely working to shape a sense that potential wealth existed both below and above the ground. In Freddy and his team's veterinary rounds, the prime nonhuman figure of resource abundance was thriving hybrid cattle, a synecdoche for growth through vibrant animal life in what was historically a highland economy centered on herding and livestock. The second encounter was a participatory feedback session in Espinar, where a government agency presented its analysis of an Environmental Impact Assessment (EIA) for an expansion of the Tintaya Mine. Protestors disrupted the session by centering a distinct figuration: a mangled sheep carcass they mobilized as embodied evidence of heavy metal contamination, arguing that it was this same water-stressed highland pastoral economy on which the mine had put intensified pressure. Tintaya's public, focused on the figure of resilient cattle, and its counterpublic, focused on the figure of dead sheep,[8] demonstrate how the mine's promises of growth through expanded extraction, climate adaptation, and transparency were contested. A final section draws us back over the provincial border into Caylloma. There, a third site of encounter was a temporary public exhibition in Chivay showcasing the benefits of mining. The exhibition staged Caylloma's Colca Valley region as an active frontier of extraction, representing mining as inevitable and mining communities as sites of ambient growth. Villages closer to Colca's potential mining projects, meanwhile, contested these promises of growth.

But first, we turn to a long-standing obsession.

### Interest in Cattle: Expertise and Technical Improvement in the Andes

Opening his famous chapter on the importance of cattle for the Nuer, E. E. Evans-Pritchard writes, "Most of their social activities concern cattle and *cherchez la vache* is the best advice that can be given to those who desire to understand Nuer behavior." He later adds, "Their social idiom is a bovine idiom."[9] Evans-Pritchard offers the advice to seek out cattle as though he were telling colonial anthropologists to "follow the money" in a place they assumed to be "premodern." Today, that advice is helpful for understanding the similar obsession of development projects with cattle in much of the rural world.[10]

Bovines were introduced into the Andes in the late 1500s alongside the region's many other European invaders.[11] In recent decades bovines have become an obsession in technocratic development projects. They are a kind of blank canvas for modernist development's resource logics of household productivity, efficiency, and market orientation, which means transforming *cows* and *bulls* into *cattle* and *livestock.* This discursive move characterized the Green Revolution, a global rural development paradigm starting in the 1950s that prioritized incremental improvements to agricultural production driven by Western breeding, planting, and agronomy science and implemented by technical experts throughout the global South.[12] More recently, cattle care, insemination, and other Green Revolution–style improvements have tended to be welcome in rural Espinar where, as in Caylloma, the state often felt absent. They were also significantly more satisfying to villagers than the behavioralist training of entrepreneurial empowerment described in the previous two chapters, which pushed subjects to invest, risk, and de-diversify their livelihoods but did not distribute immediately tangible benefits. Cattle were a recognizable source of rural livelihood. Cattle have also long served as a rural insurance policy around the world. By the end of the 2010s in the Andes, climate change and severely diminished cash-crop markets were driving peasants from agriculture to livestock. Tintaya's effort to care for cattle was well received but also uneven in the region.

Cattle came to Espinar with the mine. In Freddy's telling, the mine helped peasants raise and house cattle soon after its 1985 launch in Espinar. Espinar is about 4,000 meters above sea level, higher in elevation than both Yanque and Chivay. This elevation places ecological limits on agriculture. Before the mining company entered, residents were largely devoted to alpaca and sheep herding, wool trading, and subsistence livestock care, similar to other residents of the region's high slopes and plains. Since the mine's arrival, as the mining town of Espinar expanded rapidly, villagers in the rural highland environments surrounding the Tintaya complex have tended to be small livestock farmers. Although some live there year-round, others commute to seasonal labor obligations in Espinar, the mine, or elsewhere in the Cuzco or adjacent Arequipa region.

Writing in 2004, Chris Shepherd suggested that in rural Peru, "many community projects still bear the insignia of the GR [Green Revolution] style with an emphasis on greater productivity through high-yielding seed and hybrid animals, chemical inputs and irrigation technology."[13] However, the emphasis on entrepreneurship I observed in Peru in the 2010s appeared to be moving away from the technology transfer, service provision, and other forms of redistributing state resources that characterized Green Revolution interventions. In its deployment by a mine, that older model became useful for the effort to mobilize an ambient feeling of growth to neutralize agents of resistance. By "enhancing" bovine livestock, the mine distributes a benefit that is at once tangible and symbolic in a zone it figures as a space of lack, pushing small farmers out of subsistence and into the space of the market. Shepherd finds that development in Peru is fundamentally the work of shaping desires. Noting similarities to development everywhere, he observes that development work in Peru engages the structural power of urban-based expertise to construct subject identities as inferior, defective, and lacking in technical knowledge.

This face of growth, the private mining corporation, deploys inseminations as privatized technical assistance that meets desires for market productivity that the mine itself has shaped. Such a reduction of structural complexities to solvable problems is an example of what Tania Murray Li calls "rendering technical."[14] Inseminations constitute one small act in the ongoing work of making growth feel real and extending the reach of extractive capitalism, which, as Hannah Appel memorably writes, "is not a context; it is a project."[15] Inseminations help to build this representation of growth in a national atmosphere in which massive private mines are encouraged to thrive and given the freedom to expand. In contrast to the donor-constrained Sierra Sur and Desco investments, a corporate investment like Tintaya's was freer to be generous with material goods and services as part of its effort to cultivate attachments to the mine.

The Brown Swiss cattle breed is known for its productivity, its ability to withstand weather extremes, and its longevity. It is one of the oldest and most popular breeds in the world. According to the Brown Swiss Association, these cattle "yield large volumes of milk"; they offer "an ideal fat to protein ratio for cheese-making," and "Brown Swiss producers often receive more money per 100 pounds of milk than owners of other breeds."[16] Brown Swiss breeds are also important because of how they help Andean villagers face what mining companies have begun to point out as the Andes' true environmental threat, in which all are implicated: climate change.[17] In a recent study of livestock and climate change, Melissa Rojas-Downing and her co-authors acknowledge that climate change is likely to have an immense impact on livestock: "Changes in breeding strategies can help animals increase their tolerance to heat stress and diseases and improve their reproduction and growth development."[18] Hybridizing Andean cattle with Brown Swiss genes figures the resilient bovine as an animal project perfectible through European science.[19] These are climate-ready cattle.

James Ferguson describes development, from the perspective of the institutions he analyzed in Lesotho, as "largely a matter of changing values and attitudes, of winning over individual Sotho hearts and minds."[20] Development functions as a project to win hearts and minds in Tintaya's surrounding communities by working to affectively offset industrial toxicity. It was Tintaya's move to offer technical interventions that would conspicuously actualize a new sense of abundance in an era of climate change. By salvaging bovine genetics into its expansion project, the mine recruited villagers to align with its existence.

## Corporate Social Responsibility and the Mineral Frontier in Peru

Our presence brings lasting benefits for the regions in which we operate.
—Glencore, current corporate owner of the Tintaya Copper Mine

For my friends, everything. For my enemies, the law.
—Attributed to Oscar Benavides, president of Peru (1914–1915, 1933–1939)

Peruvian national law requires substantial royalty contributions to each local and regional government in which mineral exploitation takes place.[21] This *canon minero*, or mining royalty system, has become the mechanism by which the state redistributes funds from mining profits. In the abstract this redistribution is a recognition of the fact that mining enterprises make substantial profits by unearthing minerals on a specific community's land, both taking away most of that potential value and altering the surrounding environment. Mining royalties come from 50% of the taxes that "title holders of mining activity pay for the use of mineral, metallic, and non-metallic resources" in the prior fiscal year.[22]

The Cuzco region, where Espinar Province is located, collected 81 million soles ($25 million in 2018 dollars) in mining royalties in 2017.[23] Espinar receives the highest portion of any Cuzco province.[24] The Arequipa region, which has more extraction zones, receives significantly more in total royalties: 259 million soles ($79 million) in 2017. Mining companies have long met their *canon* requirements in Peru by offering project backing to NGOs such as Desco and local development initiatives. In 2017 mining royalties increased for regional and local governments across Peru by 24.4% from the previous year, to nearly 2 billion soles ($569 million), indicating an upswing in mineral production and profit.[25] In 2019, Pablo de la Flor, head of Peru's national mining lobby, predicted an increase to 3.2 billion soles ($900 million).[26]

However, my fieldwork revealed that many communities near mines do not tend to see much of that revenue up close. Testimonies indicate that royalties subsidize the region as a whole more than the specific province, municipality, or individuals directly exposed to potential contamination. Village-wide improvements promised by Andean mines tend to manifest themselves as several community members coming into money after their valuable land is bought out and as a trickle of visible local projects in a few lucky districts in the affected zone. Royalties are routed to regional and municipal governments, where leaders often invest the money in projects, a way that contemporary conventions of development suggest it will go farthest. These projects work to create a sense that mines are agents of growth and that, thanks to the mine, growth is visible and possible. But they do not call for substantial compensation or redress. In Espinar I encountered significant skepticism that royalties came back as sufficiently redistributive growth investments for directly affected communities. As one attendee at a July 2017 public presentation of an EIA put it to the audience, "Nobody's given *me* any compensation."

Mines work to produce an atmosphere of trust through two specific pathways: meeting legally mandated prior consultation requirements and engaging in voluntary CSR. Many scholars have written about prior consultation,[27] a human rights mandate to engage potentially affected Indigenous communities before extraction begins, enshrined in Convention 169 of the International Labor Organization (1989). The concept suggests that permission and social license to operate must come before mining can begin. In Peru, prior consultation was ratified in 2011 as Law 29785.[28] This law states in part that "it is the right of Indigenous or Originary groups to be previously consulted about the legislative or administrative measures that directly affect their collective rights, regarding their physical existence, cultural identity, quality of life, or development" (Article 2). Article 3 elaborates on the meaning of "consultation."

> The purpose of consulting is to reach an agreement or consent between the State and Indigenous or Originary groups with respect to the legislative or administrative measure that affects them directly, through an intercultural dialogue that guarantees their inclusion in the state's processes of decision making and the adoption of respective measures from their collective rights.

The related doctrine of Free, Prior, and Informed Consent for development on Indigenous land is also featured in the 2007 UN Declaration on the Rights of Indigenous Peoples, which Peru ratified. In practice, however, mandated consultation and dialogue can be circumvented by questioning a group's Indigenous or Originary status. This has been exploited in the Andes, where the indigeneity of Quechua-identifying groups would be cynically called into question, given decades of official institutionalization of Andean groups as peasant communities instead of native ones. Only in 2015 were the first Quechua groups recognized in court as formally Indigenous for the purposes of prior consultation. However, the Tintaya Mine began operations in 1985, decades before the UN declaration or Peru's prior consultation law. Ximena Málaga Sabogal and María Eugenia Ulfe show that as the Tintaya Mine expanded, Espinar residents faced cynical questions about their own apparent identity "invention" as they declared membership in the K'ana Indigenous community, which would entitle them to prior consultation rights.[29]

Mines must also follow a host of environmental regulations. Regulatory burdens range from verifying the absence of archeological remains to EIAs. The apparent cumbersomeness of these regulations is meant to be indexical of accountability and transparency to the state.[30] Within Glencore, the world's largest trader of commodities,[31] these regulations have spurred an expansive internal bureaucracy of professionals.

In contrast to prior consultation and environmental regulations, CSR programs entrench a climate of extractive industry investability and inevitability.[32] In their voluntary mission to create local stakeholders through CSR and dialogue-based forums, these programs are often highly selective in the communities and local representatives they work with.[33] CSR programs are engaged to prevent resistance and to serve as an investment in social stability. They can also serve as a public relations misdirection away from critiques of contamination. For example, many mines in Peru conspicuously highlight their work to address climate change. CSR projects can also backfire, especially when they are perceived as unethical. They can cause rather than prevent conflict and intensify local struggles rather than alleviate them.[34] Earning the social license to operate thus often means that a mine must cultivate relationships of dependence.

Peruvian *canon* regulations stress the obligation for mines to invest in sustainable development in the relevant zone.[35] "Sustainable" here is an open-ended concept that implies a type of development that, in contrast to mining, does not cause potentially irreversible devastation to the environment. In practice, it describes investments that economically and morally offset such devastation. CSR projects cannot result in profits, although publicizing an orientation to social responsibility is vital for any mining company's brand. For instance, Glencore's 2015 Sustainability Report frames its mines as vital to local economies and promises "lasting benefits to the regions in which we operate," including "local employment," "training and skills development," and "invest[ments] in local communities, health, education and infrastructure."[36]

CSR assembles distinct and sometimes conflicting discourses of development as it endeavors to "buy" stability in surrounding communities.[37] CSR scholars make clear that this work is meant to smooth a company's and an industry's expansion. But by training my own focus on specific interpersonal interactions near mine sites, my analysis engages the affective substance of how the mine's face-to-face development work creates the feeling of a region characterized by growth, which places Andean *campesinos* perpetually on the cusp of prosperity.

## The Tintaya Foundation

Operations began at the Tintaya Mine when it was established in 1985 as a state mining enterprise. Mines throughout Peru were privatized in the 1990s under President Fujimori. In that wave of mass privatization and foreign investment, BHP Billiton, an Australian-held enterprise, bought the Tintaya property in 1996. The Espinar community protested BHP for years because of its lack of interest in addressing their concerns. As a response, BHP, community representatives, and NGOs formed what they called the Dialogue Table in 2002, a permanent deliberative forum to negotiate corporate contributions and harm reduction. However, many residents of Espinar and the smaller surrounding villages continued to feel excluded. Meanwhile, mine expansion was outpacing consultation. Tensions came to a head after the 2002 construction of the Huinipampa tailings dam near fields where cattle and other animals grazed; Espinar residents claimed that they had not been properly consulted. A group of 1,000 protestors from the town of Espinar stormed the mine's gates in May 2003. As a result, BHP and local representatives forged the Tintaya Framework Agreement, in which the company agreed to contribute 3% or at least $1.5 million in pretax revenues annually to the province. BHP then went further by setting up the Tintaya Foundation in December 2004, a fund to support sustainable development in the region.[38]

Still, the sentiment that the Dialogue Table was simply for show persisted. After more tensions and a sit-in at the mine site in 2005 to protest BHP's unresponsiveness and uneven distribution of benefits, BHP committed to improving its environmental protections and engaging in land transfer or compensation. This struggle came to a halt in 2006 when BHP sold the Tintaya Mine to the British company Xstrata Copper, which in 2013, merged with the Swiss-based Glencore to become Glencore Xstrata PLC, since renamed Glencore PLC. Glencore owns the mine's operating firm, Compañia Minera Antapaccay.[39] Like BHP before it, Glencore is regulated by the "soft law" framework of "dialogue" meant to empower companies' voluntary self-regulation, indexing the neoliberal tendency to replace "government" with "governance."[40] Local residents suggest that Glencore has been significantly less receptive to dialogue.

The Tintaya Foundation survived the sale and merger. It is housed on a campus next to the mine complex, about a twenty-minute drive from the Espinar town center. Its purpose is to convey the mine as a receptive agent of responsibility. However, the foundation building is guarded by a high metal gate topped with barbed wire and surrounded by security cameras. Its projects are designed according to an institutional projection of what local actors are capable of doing to impede mining. By caring for Espinar's nonmineral assets, the foundation both makes the case for the mine's presence and masks the fact that most of its profits leave the region.

### Professional Investments: Freddy

Freddy Panuera Mejía is the husband of Liliana Suni Condori, who was employed as the clinical psychologist for Desco's youth entrepreneurship program (see Chapter 4). They live together in the Caylloma village of Yanque and share similar ideas about the merits of independent entrepreneurship for development. Both drew steady salaries from their employment but dreamed of being full-time owners of the Sumac Wayra Hotel (Beautiful Wind Hotel), which they had been building on their property. Since 2015, Freddy's work with the Tintaya Foundation has had him regularly commuting to the highlands of Espinar Province, a trip that involves catching two separate buses and that can take over six hours.

Freddy was born in Tacna to a Spanish-speaking family with rural Quechua forebears. The family lived in the highland city of Puno until Freddy turned 8, when they moved to Majes at the western end of Caylloma Province. Majes is a bustling commercial town where dairy cattle, livestock farming, and the commercial dairy industry, anchored by a Leche Gloria plant,[41] form the core of the local economy. Having come of age in this milieu, Freddy studied veterinary and zootechnical medicine at the private Catholic University of Santa María in Arequipa. With his professionalization and social mobility facilitated by an urban university education, he worked various jobs as a veterinarian, forming part of the Colca Valley's increasingly technified agronomy sector. Early in the 2010s, Freddy began working as a veterinarian for mining corporations, which was significantly more lucrative but came with an important cost.

> I'm getting used to it now. I wasn't used to leaving home before. The first time I left, it was for the Buenaventura Mine, where I stayed 20 days for 10 rest days. So there I felt it, because I was alone. I had little communication with my family, and I wasn't doing well. I'm really attached to my family. So this hurt a lot, so I had to quit that month. I was there one month. I quit, and I came here. I applied for the opportunity to work for the mine here, Tintaya, and now I'm doing better.

Freddy worked hard and, aside from the obligation to spend time away from his family, appeared to enjoy it. After watching him interact with animals, my sense was that Freddy was significantly more passionate about the intimate interspecies care work his job required than he was about serving as a technocratic intermediary between a mine and a community. His current position with Tintaya involves work that takes place in stretches of nine workdays, where he lives in a rented bedroom near the mine in Espinar's town center, followed by five days of rest in his Yanque home. Ultimately, he said, the intense work was an investment for the hotel. He described entrepreneurship as a family ethic: "We are an entrepreneurial family. Here with my wife. And my kids, right? They're still little." Freddy's sense of an entrepreneurial household is reflective of Liliana's work to push Desco participants to extend entrepreneurship to the conduct of family life. Freddy dreamed of quitting the mine to attend to the hotel full-time and work as a private livestock veterinarian in Yanque. When we talked in 2015 in his house, he speculated on when that might take place.

> I'll have to see. I will need to come and take the baton here [in the home and hotel]. This will begin to grow. Now maybe I'll buy a car for tourism, or, like, the ideas are still just dreams, but I think they'll

happen in their moment. . . . Now, because of debt, I'd maybe need
to work at least two more years there in the mine.

He noted that the family faced 250,000 soles ($85,000) in debts for the
construction of the hotel. When we spoke four years later in 2019, he said he
planned to work for another three to four years, his time horizon continuing
to recede. Freddy's veterinary work for the foundation was partly fulfilling
labor with animals and partly an investment in his own entrepreneurial
ideal. The substance of that work, however, frequently came into tension
with this ideal.

## Making a Daily Case: The Veterinary Visit

Freddy Panuera's job is to circulate the cold, windswept highlands surrounding Espinar in the Foundation's Toyota Hilux, traveling between farms and
fields to make sure that villagers' livestock do not become ill, to care for sick
cattle, and to inseminate cows with Brown Swiss sperm. This is Freddy's
small role in rendering the mine a conspicuous instrument of growth. He is
part of an army of professionals employed to maintain Tintaya's social license
to operate by making a daily case for the mine as a responsible enterprise
that brings growth to those who inhabit its surrounding environments.
Their technical assistance was an effort to shape desires[42] and, as such, was
a *messaging tool*. They conveyed the constant message that the land was barren and that its people were poor until the mine transformed it. "Before,"
Freddy told me, "when there was no mine, there was not much livestock.
There weren't many jobs. They didn't seed much barley, right, and you saw
that time you went [to Espinar]? The economy has grown more."

Freddy and his assistants made their rounds wearing baseball caps and
uniforms that prominently displayed the foundation logo, a large red T built
of bold square blocks reminiscent of K'anamarca, a site of pre-Inca ruins in
rural Espinar. Behind the T was a yellow circle that resembled a sun and a
halo, allowing it to double as an angel (see Figure 5.1).

Freddy invited me along for a day of veterinary rounds. On a cold
morning in July 2017, I joined some thirty veterinarians and technicians
who had gathered at 6:00 am for breakfast in the Espinar town center. This
was how Freddy's long workdays in the highlands began. He would awaken
in the room he rented in Espinar and walk to a nearby cafe for a bleary-
eyed breakfast with all the foundation's technical teams. The role of each

professional was to care for the animals and lands in what the corporation determined to be the area potentially affected by the mine.

Quiet conversations started as staff came to life with crumbly bread, butter, Nescafé, and tea. I spoke with one of Freddy's supervisors, learning that she, too, lived far away; most of these workers were, like Freddy, on a nine-five plan and lived elsewhere. She was about 40 years old and supervised all the foundation's veterinary teams. She indicated that her family lived in the city of Tacna, which meant a nine-hour commute on several buses. Staff spoke about the ups and downs of spending so much time so far away from home and family. The pay, they implied, was sufficiently lucrative to justify their homesickness.

That morning, a frost, biting even by the standards of the late Andean July, had hit Espinar's highland desert landscape. Five of us stuffed into the white Toyota Hilux. Freddy sat up front, beside his driver, Melitón Umasi. In the back seat were a veterinary assistant named Adolfo Cabrera, a U.S.-based anthropologist named Stefanie Graeter, who was also conducting fieldwork in the region, and me. Condensation covered the windows. The interior was initially as cold as the high-altitude town itself, whose inhabitants had begun their weekday bustle in the streets, stores, and markets nearby. The heat was on high in the truck. It was equipped with vaccines, antibiotics, medical equipment, and a refrigerated tank containing the Brown Swiss sperm that I had to hold upright between my knees.

Our oversized vehicle rumbled awkwardly through the narrow urban streets hastily built over the last two decades as the mining economy rapidly drew migrants to Espinar. The truck's high wheels positioned our bodies above many of the storefronts and cement walls we passed. Slowly, we pulled out of the town center, whose boundary was clearly marked by the transition from two-story cement buildings to a small ring of shanties and impermanent settlements and, then, by an open highway surrounded by rolling desert hills topped with highland shrubbery. As the truck pulled away from the town, Freddy and his staff began talking excitedly about the visits on the schedule, discussing which family's cows were sick and which might have cows in heat and wondering whether they might get any last-minute emergency calls.

At each of the ten households we visited that day, Freddy and the team touched, soothed, poked, and prodded cattle. Our first stop was a small peasant home where a middle-aged woman and her daughter were waiting for us. She reported a sick mother and baby cow to Freddy. They walked together to the animals under an icy blue sky. The woman removed the heavy alpaca blankets she used to keep the animals warm. Freddy gently felt along their bodies for swollen glands, checked their heartbeats with his stethoscope, and injected the mother with a dose of antibiotics.

Freddy's veterinary bedside manner consistently displayed an expert warmth and a human-animal connection that exemplified the microlevel tenderness of extractive care. In scenes like these, the team brought conspicuous signs of company care and veterinary technology to what they described as extremely remote rural households. The team was kind, cordial, and professional with people they dignified as "clients." They made their rounds between 6:45 am and 11:45 am, and then again between 3:00 pm and 7:00 pm, with a mid-afternoon staff meeting at foundation headquarters that I was not privy to.

At one stop, the team met another client, who identified himself as León. He was the male head of a sprawling rural household whose cattle the team gave a medical checkup and, for one of his cows, an insemination of Bruno's Brown Swiss sperm. León owned several pickup trucks and produced milk for Peru's large dairy conglomerates. His prosperous family qualifies for foundation aid because his home is near a creek downstream from the mine site, which puts his household in the zone of influence. When I asked him about the effects of the mine on his land, I expected to hear about contamination and other environmental damages. This was perhaps naïve, given that I was there with Tintaya Foundation staff. Instead, León told me that "before, there was never access to technology and resources like this in the *campo*, and unfortunately, most other *campesinos* do not know how to take advantage of them." Here, León registered the mine's presence as a palpably positive provider of growth and access to abundance and implied that neighboring villagers were depriving themselves of an opportunity when they opposed the mine. He said he was satisfied with the services that the foundation provided.

Freddy and his team knew the roads, the landscape, the climate, and the population well. Their superiors, meanwhile, knew every turn their Hilux made; supervisors used GPS tracking to monitor the truck's location and speed as it traced the dirt roads through the steep rocky hills. The foundation managed technician conduct to engineer every infinitesimal choice the team made to conspicuously indicate the company's posture of responsibility. Driving at an excessive speed would be a sign of the mine's ignorance of the fact that these roads are populated by herds of sheep, cattle, and alpacas and by small moto-taxis that transport people between homes and pastures. By managing their conduct through an economy of signs of sharing the terrain and collaborating in its overall prosperity, the team positioned its work as providing growth on a scale that would not be possible without the mine, as they had done effectively with León.

Freddy's driver, Melitón Umasi, lived on land bordering the mine. He showed us a video on his phone of explosions during a recent expansion that covered his home and fields in red dust. The others joked with him about the spectacular wealth he would come into as soon as he decided to sell his land to the mine. The jokes implied that such a decision was inevitable. He laughed with the group but remained silent about his plans. They were ultimately correct; he has since sold his land to the mine. His very job as a driver for the foundation was also part of its effort to appease the surrounding population with prosperous entanglements, transforming them into stakeholders and conspicuous beneficiaries of the mine's presence.[43] This was a relatively lucrative position for which the foundation gave priority to people who lived close to the mine.

The top-down imperative toward stability reinforced foundation staff discipline. Freddy told us that on rounds and visits to peasant homes, they were not allowed to use the word *contamination* or even hint at the possibility that Glencore had any responsibility for toxic environmental conditions. They were told that this could be used as evidence against the mine; it also risked riling up community members and creating a precarious situation for foundation workers. He was prohibited from working on days when conflict was percolating, because he risked damaging the truck, the equipment, and his person. One worker at breakfast told me that despite the foundation's work, they did not think Tintaya was a responsible mine.

Freddy labeled certain communities in Espinar, such as the Indigenous-identifying Originary Community of Alto Huancané, especially combative because of their proximity to the mine and the leverage it buys them. "The people who are close to the mine," Freddy explained, "have negotiating power, not just for terrains but also so that their children's enterprises can set up work with the mine. There are many ways to negotiate like that." Freddy claimed that Alto Huancané has many inhabitants who have benefited immensely from the mine, whereas others "are discontented because they simply want to bother the mine. . . . The people always want to take advantage, more advantage of the mine." If Alto Huancané's citizens can negotiate, so can the mine: Freddy indicated that negotiation is an ongoing process that usually leads to the mine expanding in the way that it wants to. As occurs with other Andean mines, negotiations would take place in small meetings in each peasant community, with strategic microlevel promises from the mine often made on a case-by-case basis to fracture anti-mining organizing. Although some residents close to the mine did receive priority for CSR projects,[44] residents of Alto Huancané and other well-mobilized activists did not receive routine attention because the foundation cynically labeled them threats to their safety.

Freddy's team visited other highland households as the morning's biting cold gave way to a scorching midday heat. Freddy had a list of families he planned to visit. Several others called the team and asked them to conduct a checkup on a sick bull or to inseminate a cow that was in heat, requests they obliged. Many homes had only women and children present; the men were often out with their animals, working somewhere far from home, or at work in the mine.

"I tend to the bovine livestock," Freddy opened in our 2015 interview, before I traveled into the field with him, in the register characteristic of the Andes' technocratic professional class. He might have said, more informally, "I look after cows and bulls." But register was essential to his effort to draw a distinction between his status as a technocrat and the villagers he was employed to aid. He continued, "All that is affected by the theme of environmental impacts, we attend to all of that around the mine, so for the *campesinos* that have their cattle up there, to mitigate these issues of impact." Note Freddy's use of the word *impact*. Where *contamination* is a negative word, *impacts* can be ambiguous. The term is often a euphemism for *contamination* in mining company parlance.[45]

Freddy's positionality as an agent of extractive care was one of intermediary between the mine and the community. His ambivalent role in Espinar's mining economy was echoed by an ambivalence about the clients to whom he brings his veterinary services. In a more recent interview, Freddy defined his clients as

the community members from the mine's surroundings, who we consider "affected by the mine." So [the company] gives them things. It gives them the service of education, health, this veterinary or agriculture and livestock service, as well as seeding, the hygiene aspect. This is the part that the mine works. To avoid social conflicts. And all of this is free.

Whereas written CSR materials from Glencore depict a magnanimous affective investment in the communities in which it works because of its devotion to responsibility, Freddy is blunter about the purpose of CSR: "to avoid social conflicts." He portrays Tintaya's social context as having gradually calmed from the heightened tensions between the mining venture and the community during the deadly protests of 2012. Acute tensions have since given way to more chronic ones between a corporation and what Freddy depicts as stereotypically wheedling Indigenous peasants who believe that they are entitled to more than they deserve.

Freddy's tender care for Espinar's cattle and his professionalism with his clients came in stark contrast to the exasperation he would later express to me behind the scenes at the way peasant households interacted with the foundation. He suggested that *campesinos* would cynically claim, at what seemed to be every possible opportunity, to be hurt by the mine's extractive activities. *Campesino* associations made claims to Freddy and other employees from a position of entitlement to their help because of the mine's presence. His description of the mine-society interface recalled a common critique of peasant *asistencialismo*, or welfarism, that runs across the investments I analyze in this book. *Asistencialismo* connotes a dependence on handouts, in which people do not have to put in any of their own effort to earn the benefits of development. Interestingly, this discourse never seemed to apply to mining corporations, which are existentially reliant on state land concessions, tax breaks, and other government benefits.

Freddy suggested that peasants made these claims regardless of the mine's fault for problems that any herder or cattle farmer might face in a region already vulnerable to the risks of an unpredictable and rapidly changing highland desert climate. Because the scale of interaction between institutional abstractions of state and corporation differs from that between technical assistant and peasant, it is significantly easier and more immediate for foundation employees like Freddy to accuse peasants, but not the corporation, of projecting an excessively entitled posture.

"*Exigen*," Freddy told me with exasperation. "They constantly demand." With any "social problem," he said, "people complain." Meetings would be called, Freddy explained,

to review all of the social problems. If an animal dies, for example,
the people complain. There it is not our problem, but all the same, we
have to communicate with community relations, so it is not our fault
as health experts, but the people blame us. That is where we get the
more intense problems, right? The people don't understand.

This statement evokes Freddy's own liminal position. As a foundation veterinarian at the far edges of the corporate hierarchy, he knows that *he* personally is not at fault for the externalized consequences of extractive industry.
But the blame he receives is rooted in public sentiment toward the mine,
directed at its ubiquitous foundation representatives instead of its absent
company leaders. Similar to how Sierra Sur staff embodied the state, Freddy
stands in as the metonym for the corporation, both when his work registers
positively as the conspicuous enactment of rural growth, as León read it,
and when other Espinar-area residents see Glencore as a contaminating
entity that unjustly extracts wealth from the region, as I discuss in the next
section. *Campesinos*, in Freddy's view, seemed to want everything without
earning it—food for their cattle, seeds, trucks, better attention from mining
personnel—and "they ask for scholarships for their children, demand other
things." He also suggested that local leaders take advantage of CSR benefits
at the expense of their own constituents.

Freddy continued, protesting the demands that peasants put on him:
"You can't give money just like that [*así no más*]. You have to have social
projects. And the people don't want it that way. They would say, better to
give and that's it. They don't understand anything." Freddy bristled at this
interest in cultivating relationships of mutual obligation with the corporation, an effort that resembled how Caylloma villagers approached Sierra
Sur. But despite his own personal investments in neoliberal self-sufficiency,
Freddy is part of a professional structure that encourages Green Revolution–style technical assistance, which means, in his view, inculcating dependence on the mine. Repeating his refrain that villagers "don't understand,"
Freddy reproduces a colonial hierarchy between the givers and receivers of
development, its "knowers and not-knowers."[46] The investments Freddy
makes ultimately deploy technical support as a means of entanglement. The
mining corporation's presence provides a development that the corporation
understands as sustainable not only in its ostensible care for climate change
impacts but also by equipping villagers with enduring tools for growing on
their own alongside the mine.

CSR, Freddy concluded, "works really well to avoid social conflicts. But people sometimes take advantage of the work, right? They take advantage. Sometimes they call for no reason, right? 'My cow is sick,' they say, and their cow is fine. It's mostly to bother the mine." Freddy's frustration with the population surrounding the mine exemplifies deeper tensions between the idealization of entrepreneurship as a reigning framework for rural growth and the messy practicalities of perpetuating a mining boom. But his exasperation behind the scenes was nowhere to be found in the field. There, he exhibited a caring affect, characterized by an upstanding professional treatment of his clients and tender interactions with their cattle. He demonstrated that face-to-face conversations and hand-to-cowhide intimacy were crucial affective instruments for enacting a sense of growth by rendering the benefits of a mine conspicuous. In this way, extractive care generates Peruvian capitalism.

## Espinar's Sacrificial Lamb: Contesting Growth at a Participatory EIA Session

This capitalism was far from frictionless. Framed as the easy exposure and capture of new capital, representations of nonmineral growth near the Tintaya Mine were contested compositions on the ground. The Tintaya Foundation strategically deployed the promise of genetically enhanced cattle as its conspicuous figuration of progress. During several days of protest in 2017, anti-mining activists in Espinar mobilized a deformed baby sheep carcass as their own counterpublic figure of contamination. The small corpse was skinny and limp. It had no eyes. It appeared to have a gaping hole where its mouth should have been. Activists claimed that the sheep was born with genetic mutations and lived a short and miserable life as a result of heavy metal contamination. They had mobilized other similarly deformed dead sheep in prior anti-mining protests in the 2010s. They argued that they did not see corpses like these before the mine's presence and that their ability to repeatedly use this provocative symbol was evidence of a trend of continued contamination.

In this section I follow the sheep carcass through acts of protest and refusal in the Espinar town center. The dead body oriented a mobilization against the corporation that came in three distinct public activities, none of which involved any direct interaction with Glencore executives: filing a claim at the corporation's social claims office; marching in a street protest; and participating in an EIA dialogue session with a state supervisory agency, an encounter vital to Glencore's expansion in the region. Demonstrating how growth is contested, messy, and riddled with friction, I end this section with a dramatic showdown at the EIA session.

### Filing a Claim

In July 2017 I met several leaders of the Originary Community of Alto Huancané (Pueblo Originario de Alto Huancané), members of the K'ana Nation, in the Tintaya Mine's Oficina de Gerencia Social (Office of Social Management) in downtown Espinar. This office was a distinct public face of the corporation. Here, community members could approach low-level company representatives face to face and file direct complaints or make claims for assistance. The office was separated from the street by a glass wall and door, symbols of transparency that revealed only a small waiting room. Opposite the glass wall was a reception area. Deeper in was another office and a conference room. By one of the couches where people waited to address a company representative, I found a series of pamphlets available in a small wooden box nailed to the wall, each of whose titles marketed the mine's ethical pillars: *Responsibility*, *Simplicity*, *Transparency*, and *Entrepreneurial Spirit*. These branding devices projected the mine as an elegant, frictionless release of capital. They were, perhaps ironically, meant to be perused while enduring the long waits required to speak to a representative.

Stefanie, who was also visiting Espinar, and I entered the waiting room on a Monday morning. I had initially planned to ask a representative about how they interacted with the community. There in the waiting room were the Alto Huancané leaders. While the community president, Flavio Huanqqe, spoke with the receptionist, we began a conversation with David, Mario, and Melchor,[47] activists who said that their community had been trying for years to seek relief from the mine's contamination. This was their latest attempt to "dialogue" with the company about accessing job opportunities, CSR projects, and environmental remediation. As we sat in the waiting room, David said:

> The biggest issue for us is poverty, right? How everyone lives, with all of the mining around us. Neither they nor their children have the opportunity to work in the mining center. And with the contamination, their animals have died. Or to put it another way, they [the mine] have taken everything, right? They promised us opportunities, and so it seemed like it would be nice [*bonito*] living next to the mine. But

it's not like that. Instead, what the people there say, is that they live more impoverished.

As David indicates, the mine cultivates cruel optimism, a "cluster of promises" that organize the expectation that life will improve.[48] Another Alto Huancané activist, a woman named Edith Díaz, later corroborated David's story, indicating that her fellow villagers are

> scared to talk of contamination. When we say, "There's contamination," [company representatives] fire right back, "What contamination? There's nothing. Be happy. There's nothing." But how are we going to be happy in this sad life? There's no water, the sheep die . . . so what should be making us happy?

The activists described a dynamic where neither the company nor the state appeared to follow through on their promises of transparency, responsibility, and economic development that were supposed to result from the mine's presence near their homes and fields. "The company leaves us divided," David said, indicating that the Office of Social Management legitimates only a select number of claims from villagers throughout Espinar and directs the benefits of CSR, such as Freddy's veterinary team, to only a disappointing few villagers who need it. Alto Huancané directly borders the mine site. Given that Freddy had claimed that such communities hold significant leverage over the mine, I was curious to see how strategically advantaged they felt. They said that their village has faced years of dispossession, pollution, and health crises as a result of the mine's presence. This was the opposite of leverage.

In contrast to Glencore, Tintaya Mine's previous owner, BHP Billiton, had been open to dialogue, even though it too was frequently in tension with the surrounding community. Indeed, what seemed to be an eminently dysfunctional relationship during the BHP ownership period was almost an object of nostalgia: BHP would listen and at least minimally engage locals, especially after representatives from rural villages in the province stormed the mine's heavily guarded gates in what they tactically described as an effort at "dialogue."[49] In contrast, Glencore did not even pretend to be interested, according to the Alto Huancané activists.[50] David had never seen any social project carried out by the company in his community. That day, the group was working, in vain, to force the company to make good on its promise of *tierra por tierra* (land for land), an exchange of plots for equally good land elsewhere. Such a program had been promised by BHP and conformed to World Bank voluntary safeguards, which advise that forced resettlement because of a mining project should not make residents worse off when it comes to income and production systems.[51]

In a study of the factors that tend to motivate resistance to mining, Condé and Le Billon tracked mine-community interactions around the world.[52] Among the factors they found to correlate with conflict were highly visible ecosystem damage, low outreach by the mine to people in its vicinity, and a distribution of royalties, profits, or projects through channels judged to be corrupt. The Alto Huancané representatives expressed frustration along all these lines as they waited to be heard. After a long delay, Flavio was called to file his latest appeal for a meeting with the corporation, an act that amounted to no more than leaving a letter with the officer who dutifully registered its receipt. Then we left the office and walked down the street to continue our conversation over a lunch of alpaca soup. As we spooned at the warm, grain-rich soup, the activists described the intersecting economic and environmental problems that the Originary Community of Alto Huancané faced as the mine sought to expand. Mario, another member of the group, elaborated on the community's struggles.

> The Originary Community of Alto Huancané doesn't have potable water, right? And that's in terms of human consumption. It also doesn't have water that's treated in some way for animal consumption. For example, we have cattle, sheep, and camelids there. So all of the live-stock that's there, animals, in Pacpacco and Inomayo sectors, all of Alto Huancané, just drink from the tailings pond, which obviously has, could have, right, an impact. Of course we don't know what per-centage of heavy metals or other things could be in that water. This is what we're facing in terms of our water resources.

Espinar residents have long reported similar and as yet unaddressed con-cerns about increased concentrations of heavy metals in the soil and water. Their concerns manifested in various protests over the years, including deadly protests in 2012. One protestor in 2012, Alberto Huallpa, claimed that "contamination caused by the mine" was making its way "into water courses and streams."[53] In subsequent years, studies were published with evi-dence confirming those claims of unmitigated heavy metal contamination, specifically with lead, cadmium, mercury, and arsenic.[54] This contamination ultimately resulted in only a small fine for the firm.[55]

BHP Billiton had obtained Alto Huancané land for its expansion in the early 2000s through what David called "illegal purchase." In David's telling, BHP failed to obtain sufficient signatures, so they deceived people into signing the petition twice. Later, more land grabs in Alto Huancané were facilitated by a second deceit: the false promise of a land-for-land deal. The land they received was even higher in the mountains and inadequate for farming and herding. As they described it, in the early 2000s some people in the community "fell for the trap for reasons of work, economy," said Mario. The fact that part of the community did approve of the mine allowed BHP to frame a narrative of community dialogue. The company's ubiquitous language about dialogue and responsibility, according to these men, amounted to no more than nice words that divided and conquered. "They do not want to dialogue," David said. "They just send their representatives" to interact on a bilateral, ad hoc basis with the few villagers willing to be bought. Flavio put it more bluntly: "Here, they have forgotten us."

In this space, forgetting and remembering run together. David said that the company keeps a blacklist with the names of protestors banned from future employment with or other direct benefits from Glencore. David and Mario indicated that they saw neither job prospects nor CSR projects in Alto Huancané. They exemplified the gaps in the uneven neoliberal logic of competition and paradigm creation. Unlike Sierra Sur's public investment competitions, conducted partly in the name of state transparency, here, winning CSR investment projects was, in practice, corrupt and opaque, according to these activists. David and Mario described the effort to secure projects as "a dark game" (*un juego oscuro*), an interpretation consistent with local critiques of the BHP Dialogue Table a decade earlier.[56] As Mario elaborated:

> The *canon minero* goes to the departmental or regional level, right, which is the Region of Cuzco, which the Originary Community of Alto Huancané belongs to. From there it comes to the provincial governments, to the province of Espinar, and then it passes to the districts, and only after that does it come to the communities in what's now only a minimal percentage. Sometimes we don't see anything. This is what we're dealing with in terms of the *canon minero*.

Funds are allocated this way as a product of Peru's neoliberal decentralization, a project ongoing since the early 2000s.[57] Importantly, Alto Huancané
does not receive a greater share of the *canon* than other municipalities in the
province. This failure on the part of local governments to justly distribute
CSR and state-imposed mining royalty funds is one of the crucial factors
for the unrest that Condé and Le Billon point out.[58] Nor is the mine a
visible source of employment. Mario, an industrial technician, had work
experience with the Peruvian construction giant Graña y Montero. He told
me that 20% of the village had university or technical training. However,
the mine treated community members as though they had no education or
qualifications to work there.

The fourth person in the group was an elderly man named Melchor.
His main concern was his wife, who had cancer and could no longer walk.
He expressed how difficult it was to find treatment for her. The hospital in
Espinar did not have specialists, and the mine was no help. The men referred
to their lack of access to essential medicines as a "tremendous abuse" by the
mine. They believed that many in their community had died as a result of
their inability to access cancer care, which the group linked to the mine.
Belying the mine's messaging about responsibility, the province, said Mario,
is in "a crisis of health and education."

Edith Díaz' testimony accentuated this sense of crisis, offering a framing
that opposed Freddy's representation of a landscape that was barren until
the mine brought prosperity. We met later that evening in the single-room
apartment she rented in Espinar. She described how her son was arrested
at a protest and elaborated on her personal experience of contamination.

> "What solution is the mine going to give us?" This is what my son
> asked them. So, we have deformed sheep, [the face] a ball without
> eyes, with a sheep's body. It happens like that every now and then: A
> cow or sheep is born, exactly the same, without feet; another is born
> with its hands intertwined, its hind legs don't lift; they're dragging
> like snakes. Animals like this are born. Then, there are times that for
> no reason, cats die, yelling, "meow, meow," they say. Puppies too.
> Well, before, it wasn't like this. Everything was good, fine, nothing.
> Sometimes before they also died, but not like now always. Because
> I live here by the [mine's industrial] mill, there's no more life now.
> Totally, grass doesn't grow, wheat doesn't grow, potatoes don't grow,
> sheep, nothing. Unfortunately, I find myself sad. Look, given all this,

I don't even have a hat and am all old now. We no longer have what it takes to live. . . . What do I have to sustain myself now? . . . I don't know how to read, but I live by my animals. But now I don't have my animals, given all the contamination.

Edith expressed a trauma rooted in a mine whose expansion meant dismissing her and her child as disposable. She and her son failed to perform as palatable subjects to extractive capital. Her feeling of toxic exposure was widely shared, as a gathering of activists demonstrated.

### Marching

Later on the day that we met in the office, the leaders of the Originary Community of Alto Huancané reconvened in Espinar's central market. Some fifty people gathered to await the verdict of a criminal trial against three Espinar anti-mining movement leaders. Oscar Mollohuanca, ex-mayor of Espinar Province, Herber Huamán, president of the Espinar Defense Front, and Sergio Huamani, the vice president, were all charged with violating civil order in the 2012 protests. Upon learning of their exoneration, the accused and their supporters celebrated with raucous cheers inside the market. Then, they moved outside to the adjacent plaza, giving triumphant speeches before a jubilant impromptu march through downtown. A municipal worker happened to be spray painting a bus stop shelter nearby, which showered a green cloud of intoxicating dust on the gathering. Their speeches concerned Glencore's lack of interest in "dialogue," a term these activists appropriated from the mine. Herber told the assembled that "these are *our* mineral resources, natural resources. They say that *we* should suggest solutions. But *they* should offer the solution. Because we are not the ones promoting contamination."[59]

Activists distinguished between mining in general and the specific acts of Glencore. Many suggested that they were simply asking the company to take responsibility for environmental harm and conveying that they deserved a real share in the benefits the company reaped from their land. Sergio Huamani argued that "we are not rejecting mining. We accept that mining will continue, but not like this with its contamination." This distinction indicates the profound power that mining enterprises have to set the terms of debate about growth, rendering it outlandish to suggest that no foreign company should mine land in one's community. In this way, the corporation builds the discursive infrastructure for its own accumulation.

According to the activists, mining in general was not the problem. It was violence, pollution, and the company's deceptive stinginess about the opportunities it promised. Huamani told me shortly after his speech that Glencore was different from a normal mine: "Unfortunately, I think the mining enterprise needs to go away. It has become a murderer, a criminal, in the ways it acts." Other speakers mentioned the insecurity that people in the mine's vicinity felt: a double threat of contamination and police violence that met their attempts at what they saw as dialogue. Since the activist deaths in 2012, a climate of fear pervaded the region. As Díaz told me, "We go to the police and mention the mine. There's no justice. Where, where should we go to complain?"

Oscar Mollohuanca took the microphone to argue that the young people of Espinar should be able to enjoy the possibilities of mining-enabled progress, as mining executives had: "Just as those who take away our natural resources get to progress, all of us have the right to progress, without contamination, without transgression, without criminalization, here in the Province of Espinar, better, with liberty, with justice." Each activist spoke into the microphone as a partner would hold up the sheep carcass. They pitched its concave face upward so that it could be visible as evidence of the mine's harm. Speakers made sure that protestors, armed with phones and social media, and the press, with cameras and zoom lenses, could see the limp figure.

### Participation: Growth as "Listening"

The sheep carcass reappeared as a symbol of protest the following day. The Originary Community of Alto Huancané's contestation reached its climax at a feedback session hosted by agents of the National Service for Environmental Certification for Sustainable Investments (SENACE), the state organization that authorizes EIAs. Villagers from throughout the province gathered in Espinar's municipal auditorium to hear from these regulatory technocrats, who had flown in from Lima. They convened to a backdrop of chants from the *plaza de armas*, sounds of the teachers' union protests that were happening throughout Peru at the same time in 2017.

One woman and three men, all middle-aged, made up the SENACE panel. They sat wearing beige vests that marked their agency affiliation over crisp button-down shirts. The audience maintained a respectful silence as the panelists began their PowerPoint presentation. The slides featured walls of text. They first painstakingly laid out their specific place in the national bureaucracy, careful to distinguish their office in the Ministry of the Environment from other parts of the state and from any pro-business orientation. They told the audience that the Ministry of the Interior is in charge of prior consultation. SENACE, by contrast, deals exclusively with the EIA process by evaluating only specific studies for approval. Their narrow ambit of intervention and their claims to scientific objectivity were constant themes to which they returned to deflect criticism.

The main feature of their presentation was a discussion of the EIA for the Coroccohuayco extension, which would be a new offshoot of the Tintaya Mine. To authorize the extension, SENACE needed to find a grade of "Insignificant Impact," which means an adequately low level of contamination in bodies of water, population centers, and archeological remains. The EIA was a key document demonstrating that the expanding mine took responsibility to minimize harming its surroundings. SENACE announced their finding that Glencore had so far failed to reach an acceptably low level of projected impact. This was ostensibly good news. SENACE's slides were extremely technical and seemed as though they would be difficult to interpret for most audience members untrained in environmental science or anybody unfamiliar with the complex requirements of an EIA. SENACE demonstrated the importance of *form* and *process* in the display of environmental accountability.[60] This was their priority; it took precedence over clearly communicating the *content* of their findings and the *significance* of their decision not to authorize the extension yet.

This projection of official compliance was an essential dimension of the violence of extractive care. Fabiana Li has suggested that in sites of conflicted mining expansion, state-sanctioned transparency can both reveal and conceal.[61] Li and others have analyzed transparency as more an articulation of a particular political project than the apolitical, disinterested information sharing it purports to be.[62] Here, conspicuous gestures of transparency were essential to a mineral growth project, routed through the state, that removes decision making power from Espinar residents in the guise of extending information to them. The SENACE participatory feedback session was one example of how, as Li writes, "the state's regulatory structures facilitate resource extraction in the context of neoliberal governance."[63] Although the SENACE agents conveyed comprehensive information about the agency's mandate and the study findings, their presentation failed to speak directly to the community's urgent concerns about human and animal health. Instead, in the name of a transparency that, in practice, obscured a clear understanding of how the expansion project would tangibly affect their lives, representatives directed attendees to the web. There, they could download the full, several-hundred-page EIA report as a PDF. Far from every participant had their own computer or internet access. But for those who did, this apparent transparency would have led them to a dead link. I failed to find any PDF when I tried to replicate the search. This new reliance on digital information supposedly in the name of transparency is a further misdirection, as documents are, at best, overwhelmingly long, intricate, and technical and, at worst, absent, buried, or inaccessible because of limited digital access or literacy. Audience members expressed frustration at their inability to access this supposed transparency. One attendee said, "You are all mentioning these previous studies about heavy metals in our bodies, but we don't have access and haven't seen these studies."

After the presentation, the audience was invited to participate. Attendees expressed their discontent with the state's stewardship of the mine, corroborating findings elsewhere in Peru that there was "great distrust in state supervisory authorities."[64] One asked how SENACE had even been able to conduct its preliminary impact studies without prior consultation. The answer to this was that "direct impact" of the expansion project was not deemed to affect any state-authorized Indigenous community—even though, as I described in the Introduction, the state effort to build a national database was incomplete and ongoing. Alto Huancané leaders' declaration of their own Originary K'ana status meant that the district should have at least been considered for its legal claim to prior consultation as Glencore sought to expand its operations.

Tension rose when Flavio, the community president, stood up to intervene. With a canvas bag in his hand, Flavio turned his back on the agents and faced the audience. He said the following in Quechua, his voice increasing in volume:

> We tried to speak with them. To dialogue. They didn't want any of it. Now, we say to them, we say to SENACE, you need to know this. You need to remember this. The harms of the company have come to our land. To the Indigenous [he used the Spanish *indígena*] nation of Alto Huancané . . . to our sector.

Explicitly identifying his community's indigeneity, Flavio's confrontation reached its height as he produced the sheep carcass from the bag and held

**FIGURE 5.2** Flavio Huanqqe holds the sheep carcass during his speech at the SENACE session.

it high so that the whole room could see it (Figure 5.2). A murmur of shock reverberated through the meeting room. He continued:

> Look at this dead sheep. Look at its deformed body. Seeing this, how could you not say that this is because of the contaminated water? . . . You decide not to help us, for nothing. Don't tell us you are safeguarding the environment looking, looking with your eyes at what you see here.

At this, the audience laughed and cheered approvingly. The four SENACE presenters' faces went blank. They appeared not to understand the Quechua. Flavio ended—still in Quechua—by inviting the SENACE representatives to witness firsthand how the mine has impacted his community. "Come tomorrow to Alto Huancané," he concluded, so that he and his fellow community members could show them the mine's damage up close. This invitation was also met with loud applause.

Flavio was clearly aware that the Lima-based experts did not speak Quechua. He deployed the language as a defiant enactment of his community's indigeneity that only one of his two audiences in the room was meant to understand. Laura Graham has noted how bilingual Indigenous actors weigh strategic choices between referential and indexical content in advocacy speech.[65] Describing an anti-mining protest in Cuzco's central plaza, Guillermo Salas Carreño reads the use of Quechua public speech alongside Spanish as a tactical indicator of implicit indigeneity. Quechua allows speakers to place their political concerns on an equal footing with those of urban-based power holders while avoiding the disparagement that explicit identification might risk.[66] But here, Flavio embraced and politicized his indigeneity explicitly. Speaking *only* in Quechua, he turned his back on the SENACE presenters to address his audience. He also mobilized a feature of Quechua grammar that requires claims to come with evidential markers (in this case, evidence is in a shared sight: "*looking, looking* with your *eyes* at what you *see* here"), repeatedly emphasizing sight to argue that the sheep makes contamination clear to the eye.[67] In doing this, Flavio was *refusing* a state-brokered mining expansion as Audra Simpson has used the term: an embodied denial of colonial regulatory frameworks of recognition, biopolitical care, and resource distribution.[68] Dialogues had been afoot since the early 2000s, to no avail. Flavio's use of Quechua meant refusing dialogue while remaining in the room.

It also undercut the Lima-centric, Spanish-based idioms of technical legitimation rooting a normative epistemological framework that those assembled did not need to accept, for its methods never seemed to serve them. Mobilizing the same sheep carcass that had been used in the prior day's protests meant putting forth a community figuration of damage that offered tangible scientific evidence of contamination (Figure 5.3), enabling Alto Huancané residents to question regulator expertise with their own longitudinal observations, their own science.[69]

The presenters' initial response was silence. They simply called on other speakers, whose interventions supported Flavio's speech. One questioner expressed anger that SENACE workers were well-paid employees who came from Lima every two years to do essentially nothing for them. "Okay, enough already with the abuse from these companies," said another. In response, presenters returned to the theme of SENACE's narrow mandate. They made clear that they were not the people responsible for determining whether the currently operational and long-since greenlit Glencore holdings were causing genetic mutations in animals and cancer in humans. From their perspective, the panelists were simply examining the corporation's compliance with Peruvian environmental law. This was their version of extractive

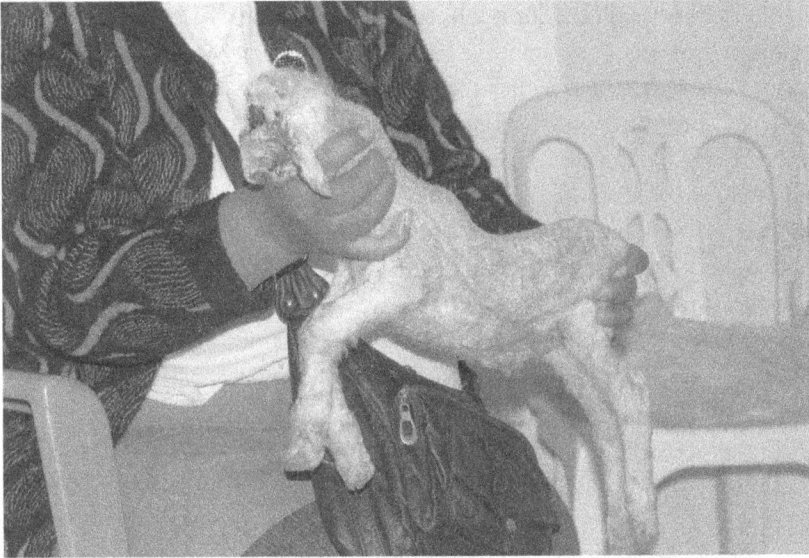

FIGURE 5.3 Activists from Alto Huancané passed the sheep carcass around to one another during the SENACE presentation. Holding the body evoked a mix of horror and morbid curiosity.

care: projecting a sense of minimized harm according to protocols rooted in an ostensibly national democratic process, in which mining corporations held significantly more clout than the residents of Alto Huancané.

"We have listened. My job is to listen," said one representative, in a vain effort to calm the crowd.[70] She said that they made visits to surrounding communities to collect residents' concerns. There was no discussion of what they did with this collected data. Yet underneath SENACE's evasions was the fact that they consistently failed to make attendees feel heard or to legitimate their anxieties. To many in the audience, SENACE demonstrated no specific evidence of having carried out any meaningful regulation. The state affects of confident technocratic authority I described in Chapter 3 reappeared here and failed to evoke public feelings of trust and security.

This was an encounter meant to enact growth in the rural Andes. Growth, here, took the form of a discrete expansion project on a mining company property accomplished with accountability. It was temporarily stalled, which meant that Tintaya staff would need to make changes to meet the state's environmental standards for mining. Halting the process was ultimately not inimical to the project, which has since resumed. Rather, it demonstrated that the Coroccohuayco expansion would proceed in a way that was conspicuously *responsible* as a result of transparent regulation and expert authorization. In the face of this effort to render growth real, the activists offered their own tangible evidence for the argument that the mine was responsible for taking away a nonextractive agrarian abundance. Such abundance could in theory exist alongside a mine. For them, an abundant landscape was one not of booming wealth and colonial resource logics but an abundance of ways to be self-sufficient and forge relations with other beings, in which mining might be just one part of a diverse, thriving economy. They conveyed that mining should not be so dominant that its contamination would pose an existential threat to the lives in its vicinity.

## An Advancing Mineral Frontier: The Public Exhibition

The Alto Huancané community's protests were on my mind two years later. It was 2019, and I was back in Chivay, on the other side of the Cuzco-Arequipa border. My U.S.-based student research assistants and I had just walked into a freshly built two-story building, called Misti Wasi (Quechua for Misti House), at the end of the market street.[71] Inside was a massive exhibition hall. Its white tile floor and elegant marble walls resembled an aesthetic that I would expect in Lima's upscale districts or the several five-star resorts tucked into the hillsides between Colca Valley villages. The exhibition was an effort to introduce communities to the benefits of mining, a new public face of mining's "economy of appearances" in Peru.[72] Although mines have long occupied the Colca Valley's edges, I had never seen anything like this in the provincial capital.

Signs throughout the valley announced the nine-day event, held from July 2 to July 11, called Casa Abierta (Open House). This title was a nod to a transparency distinct from SENACE's technocratic information sharing. Here, the democratic ideal of transparency framed a glossy public relations campaign that advertised an exciting new future for the region's growth. The event was put on by the National Society of Mining, Oil, and Energy (SNMPE), Peru's extractives lobbying organization, with the idea that mining is easily disparaged before people know all the facts. Its displays were presented under the guise of "merely" offering Caylloma citizens the full range of information about mining.[73] The Casa Abierta came to Chivay as part of a nationwide campaign called Mining for All, whose tagline was, "If we listen to each other, we can come together: United we build a better Peru."[74] This phrase echoes the emphasis on dialogue and listening that pervades asymmetric mine-community encounters; its implication is that unity only means approving of new mining projects. In the invitation that SNMPE representatives sent to institutions throughout the province, they describe their intention to

> generate a dialogue with the population regarding formal mining in the country. . . . This museum-style event seeks to share extensive information on diverse aspects of mining activity, in addition to understanding the perspective of citizens. It is directed to the general public and is free to enter.[75]

Mining certainly had had its place in Caylloma before this. The right bank of the Colca River has been home to a number of mining projects. An active mine exists in the highland district also named Caylloma, owned by the Canadian concern Fortuna Silver Mines Inc. The downriver district of Madrigal is home to an inactive mine. But this Chivay exhibit represented something new as a discursive form. It announced that mining was no longer relegated to the Colca Valley's distant edges. Mining was now in the provincial capital, making its presence known as the expanding frontier of an industry ready to fill the vacuum of a climate-stressed agricultural market. Indeed, according to the exhibit, the Peruvian company Buenaventura "successfully produced its first bar of gold in December 2016" in the new Tambomayo mine in the small agrarian village of Tapay, which thanks to that mine was connected by road to the rest of the province only in the last ten years.

We entered the exhibition on a chilly Chivay afternoon. A woman named Carla dressed in a down jacket bearing the SNMPE logo warmly greeted us and invited us on the standard forty-minute exhibition tour. As she began her remarks, an older woman dressed not in the SNMPE uniform but in a Cabana sombrero and a colorfully embroidered vest handed us cookies and Styrofoam cups of instant coffee. She appeared to embody the employment opportunities that mining companies could bring. Cradling the hot cup in my hands provided welcome relief from the stone building's frigid indoor temperature.

Carla walked us through the exhibit, giving us a guided lecture on each display. Her explanations were interspersed with short videos on flat-screen televisions. A number of the informational videos were in cartoon form; the bright colors would be especially appealing to children or people

of low literacy. As we toured, we saw school groups listening intently to
other guides. The displays and Carla's lecture emphasized that this was
what *formal* mining looked like in Peru. "Formal" means mining that is
approved by the state, undergoes an EIA, and follows all environmental and
economic regulations; in practice, the term usually connotes the work of a
large corporate entity. In contrast, Carla presented "informal" or artisanal
mining as ad hoc, small scale, opportunistic, not state authorized, and
unsafe. Formality put extractive growth in the comfortable apolitical light
of regulation, accountability, and transparency. Contrasted with images of
informal mining as a sketchy criminal enterprise, state-permitted mining
was a means of dispelling potential unease among exhibition attendees.
Exhibition displays implied that any negative news the public had heard
about mining was relevant only to informal mining.

The opening information panels emphasized formal mines' commitment to human rights (Figure 5.4). "Right from the beginning," one of
my students observed in their fieldnotes, "we could tell this was going to
be a biased exhibit." The exhibition purported to inform viewers of the
entire mining process, illustrating the stages of an extractive venture from

FIGURE 5.4 A video of a rural dialogue session on display at the exhibition, beside
an information display indicating that formal mining "RESPECTS Human Rights,"
"PAYS Taxes and Royalties," and "RESPECTS the Environment."

exploration to closure, depicting the many precautions a formal mine must take and emphasizing how seriously Peru's mines take dialogue and CSR. Displays appealed to young eyes with bright colors, clear depictions of order, cleanliness, green landscapes, and images of immaculate hulking machinery.

Signs depicted the ubiquity of mined materials that accompany "us" throughout each day. Mined commodities were as close at hand as "our" smartphones and laptops, technologies that far from every Caylloma resident owned. Minerals were also vital for medications, musical instruments, and environmental technologies, such as solar panels. The viewer was invited to weigh the profound economic importance of mining against the fact that, as the campaign's online interface put it, "all human activities have the potential to generate environmental impacts."

A timeline spanning several meters on the wall revealed that Peru always had some mining, back to at least 700 BCE. One item on the timeline highlighted the metal jewelry adorning the well-preserved Inca-era mummy Juanita, discovered on the nearby Mount Ampato in 1995. The young girl's elaborate metal adornments, signs that she was likely an Inca sacrifice, were reframed for this publicity campaign as evidence that mining had been occurring in the region since before Spanish colonization. Other placards marked the 1990s as the dawn of modern mining, in which regulations, technological sophistication, and human rights were being prioritized. This was, of course, the same historical moment that the current boom began with the massive privatization of Peru's mines under President Fujimori.

At one stop we were shown an animated video that walked viewers through the EIA process. The EIA, we were told, was rooted in "participatory workshops" that were always initiated by the mine. These workshops were meant to record all comments and address "doubts from the population." There was no reference to the possibility that a mine might opt not to proceed with its exploration in light of these "doubts" or that a village could definitively refuse a mine in or near its territory. EIA approval was, the video implied, inevitable if a company judged the project to be profitable. Most of the three-minute video was set against the cartoon backdrop of a bright green landscape pleasantly populated with trees, houses, and dutifully concerned citizens. Carla then played us the Quechua version of the video, showing off the campaign's ability to cater to all potential "stakeholders" in Colca Valley mining.

The exhibition portrayed the seemingly endless economic advantages of mining, arguing that mining expansion could entail a multidimensional investment in indigeneity. One placard revealed that six indirect local jobs were created for every single formal mining job in Peru. Taxes, royalties, and fees were routed back to the communities to improve schools, hospitals, and other public institutions. Many displays described contemporary formal mines' implementation of environmentally protective practices, such as reforestation and desalination. These conspicuously environmentalist measures staged what Gökçe Günel calls a "status quo utopia," a vision of a prosperous, apparently sustainable society that does not alter any of the fundamental structural problems that come with mining, such as uneven development, persistent inequality, and the slow violence of contamination.[76]

Closely following this, another section of the exhibit continued building the local investment theme. It was titled "We Bet on Sustainable Development" (*Apostamos por el Desarrollo Sostenible*), featuring the investor language of speculative attachment identical to that of Sierra Sur, Desco, and Fondesurco. The section displayed several implicitly Indigenous Andean products, such as alpaca textiles, weavings, cheeses, and chocolate developed for sale by CSR projects in Cuzco and Cajamarca. It promised similar investments for Colca if mining were to expand there.

After the tour, visitors were invited to "Express yourself" with markers on a large piece of paper pinned to a wall. The comments I saw were largely positive. I imagined that local students on school trips were encouraged by their teachers to write messages. One comment read, "I am very happy to learn about formal mining and that it does not contaminate, that's prohibited." Another: "Mining is an important source [of income] for our country." This praise stood in contrast to the anti-mining sentiment percolating at the same time in the region.

Visitors were then invited to write their questions on one side of a postcard. On the other side, they were to fill in their name and email address, with the promise that the SNMPE would respond within a month. There was no limit to how many questions visitors could ask. The campaign website has posted over 300 questions from the public,[77] with extensive, multiparagraph answers. This gesture of transparency was followed by the gift of a tote bag displaying the campaign's logo, along with a coffee mug, pen, and pad of paper, all with the same logo.

I decided to participate in the question-writing exercise. This was my first question: "What negative climate change impacts does mining have, and how does a Peruvian mining enterprise remedy these impacts?" Two months later, I received the following answer by email:

The increase in accumulation of greenhouse gases (GHGs) in the atmosphere, a consequence of natural and human processes, is causing increases in temperature and, as a result, changes in the climate. Now, Peru emits 0.4% of global emissions, and the industrial sector (in which we find mining) for its part emits 4% GHGs; given that industrial emissions are less than 0.01% of global emissions, Peru and mining in Peru are micro-sources of GHGs. Facing that, the Peruvian mining and energy sector has spent years adapting diverse methods of mitigation that have contributed to reducing emissions. These actions include the recycling of waste, technological changes in primary productive processes, management for achieving energy efficiency and the development of a clean electric grid, among others. We also work in methods of adaptation like the efficient use of water, the construction of reservoirs, afforestation and reforestation programs, construction of water treatment plants, conservation of forests and wetlands, among others. These efforts demonstrating the commitment of mining and energy enterprises to reducing GHG emissions and adapting to climate change have been compiled by the [SNMPE] in a bulletin on 'The mining-energy sector and climate change,' which can be downloaded at the following link: [dead link].

This answer exemplifies the practice of extractive care. It makes clear that the public co-production of environmental and economic responsibility with prosperity are essential in the effort to stage a sense of mineral-driven growth. It also identifies real environmental problems while minimizing the mining company's responsibility, emphasizing acts of mitigation and adaptation and gesturing toward transparency that, as in the Espinar EIA session, leads to a dead link.

My other question asked whether companies used the database of Indigenous communities compiled by the Ministry of Culture (see Introduction). The staff member collecting questions read it and shook her head at my apparent naïveté. She told me that the database was woefully incomplete. A mining company representative had to *see* a community directly to verify whether it merited consideration as an Indigenous group. Indigeneity was apparently something the corporation could recognize on an ad hoc basis and without oversight. Questioning the database's validity was consistent with the work that mining corporations undertake to downplay "inventions" of indigeneity and to prevent distinctly situated communities from building shared identity connections. If previous chapters showed that indigeneity was praised for the growth it promised rural entrepreneurs, here, indigeneity was disavowed when it posed a threat to potential growth.

Before I left, I asked a representative why the exhibition was happening now. She candidly told me that we were standing on mineral-rich land and that people should have the right kind of information at the ready if mining companies came to them attempting to expand. Yet nowhere in the exhibit was the procedure of seeking permission to mine detailed, which the representative indicated was a "negotiation" that was distinct in every possible site of exploration. She strikingly compared mine-community negotiations to how a parent might persuade a child to eat their vegetables. This paternalistic framing reflects the behaviorist idea from previous chapters that sacrifice is necessary to enjoy the benefits of growth, represented, once again, in the idiom of a life-course intervention. Just as a child grows by eating vegetables, this logic goes, villagers who live amid mineral abundance must responsibly endure a mine's temporarily unappealing presence to enjoy their own healthy economic growth.

The exhibition was a costly and solicitous public relations campaign to recruit hearts and minds to the expansion of Peru's mining economy into the Colca Valley proper. At the scale of face-to-face encounters, it worked to extend the cruelly optimistic feeling that widespread growth was coming. It pitched mining as an unexpectedly gentle industry. The exhibition showed corporate care for surrounding communities and environments, manifested in generous investments in implicitly Indigenous development that aggressively avoided explicitly identifying Indigenous land. This demonstrates the cynical opposite of Guillermo Salas Carreño's distinction between explicit and implicit indigeneity as a subaltern tactical decision.[78] Supporting the SNMPE's figuration of mining as a source of universal promise were subtler paired figurations that curated a sense of mining as an inevitability: naïve questioner and expert answerer, formal and informal mining, and the condescending figuration of mine and community as a parent-child relationship.

## Agro Sí, Mina No

A distinct face of mineral-driven growth appeared at the high-elevation edges of the district of Lari, where Buenaventura is seeking to begin operations on a new mine. When my research assistants and I visited Lari, we encountered another sight I had not previously seen in Colca: a row of flags lining Lari's main avenue bearing the messages *Agro sí, mina no* (agriculture yes, mining no) and *Agua sí, mina no* (water yes, mining no). These flags populated anti-mining protests throughout the Arequipa and Cuzco regions. They marked the Colca Valley as a new site of tension.

A group interview with Lari's *regidores* (council members) revealed that the community was allied against the encroaching corporation. Despite their role as district authorities, they expressed pessimism that they would have the power to prevent Buenaventura's entry. The prospective mine site was located in Lari's high-elevation northern edge, alarmingly close to the mountain origin of its irrigation water (and close to the site Lari claims as the source of the Amazon River). An expanding extractive economy into the central Colca Valley is also an awkward development, given its UNESCO designation as a Global Geopark (see Map). That status—hard-won by tourism entrepreneurs big and small in the region—marks the valley as a space of "international geological significance" that must be "managed with a holistic concept of protection, education and sustainable development."[79]

*Regidora* Julia Quispe Panta told me that "it's a problem, right, for our district, because in the end the mine is going to contaminate us. And apart from that, our eyes of water [springs] will dry out" as a result of the mine's presence. "We don't want the mine in our district. The whole population is against the mine." Quispe's fellow *regidores* Eusebia Chavez and Isidro Chipa Pilares echoed her position. Chavez elaborated:

> We are not going to say, "You know what, it's fine, I will eat gold."
> I'm not going to say, "I will eat gold." I think that, right, to live, we're
> not going to think only about the immediate. We have to think from
> here to the years to come.

Buenaventura began its new exploration in 2017 and had been attempting to expand since then. "Like always," Chipa said, "the mine has this strategy of dividing us, the population." Referring to Lari's isolated high-elevation sector, Chipa indicated that "they have worked two, three people up there. They did a participatory information workshop, and afterward, they called it dialogue." This was consistent with the practices of division that the Alto Huancané representatives described. Buenaventura appeared to be exploiting the autonomies visible in many Andean villages divided by moiety between higher-elevation and lower sectors. The mine proved persuasive to several residents in Lari's high sector. But the *regidores* noted that most of their constituents were against the mine. Chavez continued:

What's better? Water will always give life. Meanwhile, does a mineral give life? It could improve momentarily, maybe, situations, okay,
improve conditions, but even in this . . . they have not known, um,
how to compensate for those resources that they take. They don't
compensate the population.

Here, Chavez opposes mining to life and then identifies her perspective as
part of Lari's long-standing Collagua heritage. Her evidence for the false
promise of mining was the neighboring village of Madrigal, which once
boasted a "beautiful surrounding environment" that a now-defunct mine
"ruined with tailings. They ruined everything." Chavez described the place
as completely abandoned: "There is no development in Madrigal District."
Her testimony reflected a similar sense from Espinar's activists that compensation and development were empty promises. She finished by tracing
her own timeline of mining in the Andes back to the colonial project.

The Spaniards plundered what is today called Peru. They took gold,
silver, everything that they could. They looted. And we continue almost
the same situation of the corporate giants, which is their exploitation. And it's sad. . . . We prefer, ourselves, for them not to touch our
natural resources.

### Conclusion: Contesting Extractive Care

In this chapter I have built an ethnography of growth out of the mining
corporation, the type of institution that is most directly responsible for Peru's
economic boom. Marina Welker describes the corporation as a distributed
network of people, discourses, and institutions that is constantly enacted.[80]
Following multiple points of tension and curation in one such corporate
network, I have sought to theorize economic growth as it takes a specific
corporate form and corporate feel within the broader field of Andean capitalist expansion. Mining corporations build their own growth through a
performance of responsibility by conspicuously nurturing a sense of ambient
possibility for villagers in their surround. The Tintaya Foundation did this
with investments in resilient cattle, extending the reach of global capital
through violently intimate acts of extractive care. In CSR projects such
as these, as Michelle Murphy writes, "accumulation and dispossession are
knitted together through affect."[81]

Cattle and sheep frame the terms of a broader debate in the region about what it means to be wealthy at the immediate margins of a mining boom. Caring for cattle was, to the Alto Huancané protestors, a front for the mine's violence. Their acts of protest suggested that their bodies and the animal bodies they live and work with have become part of the mining complex. As Stefanie Graeter—with whom I traveled in Espinar in 2017—writes in her study of the port city of Callao, people who live among lead dust, toxic runoff, and the other leakages resulting from Peru's mining economy are "human infrastructures of extractive capitalism."[82] If mines promise care for rural well-being to extract minerals from the rural Andes, villagers, against their will, are forced to care for mineral-driven growth with their injured bodies. This is the ultimate end point of extractive care for those whom its uneven benefits fail to reach. Edith Díaz demonstrates the stakes of this cruel arrangement, where mining penetrates the skin: "My whole body hurts. I'm not in good health. . . . My body must be full of minerals."

At stake in the contestation between these two animal figures— "improved" cattle and "degenerate" sheep—is how promises of growth mediate feelings of abundance in a mineral-rich space. Mines actively cultivated certain kinds of implicitly Indigenous livelihoods to benefit from growth, rendering them palatable to capital and compatible with the promises of Marca Perú. These were less overt but still forceful in Freddy's veterinary visits and clearer in the glossy Chivay exhibition. This palatable indigeneity was consistent with the celebrated regional Collagua and Cabana heritage on display in the business pitch competitions convened by Sierra Sur and in Desco's financial success stories, such as Rogelio Taco's guinea pig farm.

On the other hand, a second indigeneity took shape in capital's way that follows a counterhegemonic thread woven throughout this book. This version defied the status quo utopias and cruel optimisms of mining-induced growth. If the subtler resistors worked to make Freddy and his colleagues' days difficult, more activist practitioners refused to act within the fields of practice and representation that capital organized for them. K'ana and Collagua counterpublics mobilized rootedness in their terrains in the hope of viscerally destabilizing the mining industry's promises of abundance. Their refusal to feel growth as a result of resource extraction may not lead to the end of mining in Espinar and Caylloma, but it highlights that growth is an argument and not a fait accompli.

# Conclusion

## Returns

### Wealth

The Marca Perú brand launched in 2011 with a viral video in which a busload of the nation's most famous celebrity chefs, actors, musicians, and athletes travel to a Nebraska town also called Peru. These cultural ambassadors humorously awaken a depressed community in the backwoods of the country with the world's highest GDP to the lively economy and culture that is "Peru." As though the Midwestern United States were a region of the global South in need of market penetration, the ambassadors task themselves with "making sure that Peru, Nebraska, is not forgotten or left behind." By now, scholars have widely documented the humor, brand diplomacy, and ecstatic commodification of this fascinating mediated encounter.[1] But to me, a specific detail stands out. A brief scene, during a montage, shows a resident reaching into the *Omaha World-Herald* newspaper rack to find, instead of the *Herald*, a Spanish-language paper with this headline: "Economy at Full Throttle: Grows 10% and Salaries Rise 4%." In the next shot, a display of fireworks—an assemblage of spinning sparklers in the Rube Goldberg–like *castillo* (castle) that accompanies fiestas in Peru—spells out "10%," illuminating the night outside the humble Bank of Peru.

The message here is that "Peru" should be associated with growth. Colorful clothing, vibrant music and dances, and delicious food stand in relief as signs of growth against the backdrop of a depressed U.S. Midwest. If growth is a project rooted in representation, this scene represents growth as both a number and a feeling that emanates from Peru and Peruvians. In the years since the brand's launch, Peru's association with growth has appeared in advertisements for more corporate audiences. Identifying Peru as "one of the best countries to do business in," for example, the PromPerú website describes "export sectors (raw materials, manufacturing, and agribusiness)" as reliable sources of the country's stable growth next to a picture of the sleek glass Westin Hotel in Lima, one of the country's tallest buildings.[2]

In 2017 a new version of the campaign for the narrower tourist audience was launched in London at the World Travel Market. Coming at a time when GDP growth had slowed, the updated campaign offered a distinct take on Peru's wealth. The brand suggested that prosperity meant much more than GDP, even though Peru's GDP was still rising. A narrator redefines wealth for the potential tourist as images of Peru flash across the screen.

> They say that nowadays, being rich is not about having lots of things. It's about enjoying timeless moments. Moments that can only be experienced in one country: Peru. A country blessed with the most precious riches of all. Riches measured in terms of harmony with nature. Riches experienced when savoring food that also feeds the soul. Or when the sun sinks below the horizon, but its glow lingers on in your heart. Today Peru invites you to experience true riches. The kind you treasure on the inside. Welcome to Peru, the Richest Country in the World.[3]

These distinct iterations of Peru, in 2011 and 2017, as a place of wealth, bookended much of my fieldwork there. Both destabilize expectations. Both also evoke feelings. The 2011 advertisement pokes fun at geopolitical power imbalances, positing a spectacularly growing Peru as an ironic inspiration for how the global North might achieve its own development. Addressing Peruvians, its final message is that "we are all" brand ambassadors. If the viral video represented Peru as a desirable "commodity image" to be consumed,[4] it was also a recruitment tool for Peruvians to join the brand's affective project. The 2017 advertisement asks the consumer to rethink what it means to be and to feel rich. It highlights an "experience economy" appeal,[5] but more fundamentally, it reflects the message that Peru's wealth is so ubiquitous that you can feel it "in your heart." That feeling is only possible, as I have argued in this book, because of the specific affective labor and representational work of disciplining Andean people, practices, gastronomy, geology, histories, and environments into riches available for market consumption.

The peculiar forms by which material wealth comes to be promised, generated, found, distributed—or, crucially, *not* distributed—and messily debated have preoccupied this book. As an ethnography of economic growth, my core preoccupation has been to ask what it means to transform Peru's glossy national self-identification as a rich country into a daily life oriented by the potential to extract new wealth at that country's margins. I found that potential wealth started with a certain kind of self—the imagined Indigenous entrepreneur—and moved outward as an encompassing logic of appropriation that could extend Peru's emerging mining frontier. I followed the affective labor required to figure Andean communities as sites of extractable wealth where growth was not just an expanding statistical aggregate but a feeling, an atmospheric charge that could be enacted in face-to-face encounters.

The development agents who worked to extend growth mobilized affect as the connective tissue that intertwined extraction and production. This work took the form of resource-oriented development interventions in which rural residents were sold spectacular promises of generating entrepreneurial production out of an expanded extractive gaze.[6] Growth and its associated institutions of financialized development, entrepreneurial pedagogy, and corporate social responsibility manifest beyond the neat bar graph and the urban boardroom as a fact of rural daily life. Tracking the representations that growth engaged reveals the immense affective labor that it takes to make growth feel real, and it offers a glimpse into the real-life slippages of a theoretical growth orthodoxy as it is put to work in the world.

The ironic coexistence of mining that violently extracts from the land and small-scale Indigenous entrepreneurship that is meant to commodify harmony with nature as two complementary forms of wealth frames tensions around Peru's brand in Caylloma and Espinar Provinces. Mining and Indigenous entrepreneurship position the southern Andes as a frontier of growth by way of a proposition that unites the principles of neoliberal multiculturalism and extractive capitalism. The proposition is this: The southern Andes is a region whose cultures, traditions, and geologies are abundant. These "assets" simply need to be brought to life. If that argument holds, it follows that failing to benefit from Andean abundance is a personal failure and not a structural one.

Starting from wealth, then, ultimately opens four overarching contributions to our understanding of what it means and how it feels to grow in a site of uneven development. First, taking wealth seriously as an assumed economic fact reveals the frameworks that development creates to represent its own success. In my ethnography I found that the opportunistic neoliberal premise that wealth is present but latent is more of an aspirational claim than an empirically accurate description of daily life. This does not mean that rural Peru is objectively or uniformly poor, only that extractable wealth was not a widely shared local framework for engaging terrain, connecting with kin, or making a life. However, it was exactly as an aspiration that this neoliberal premise did important affective work. Often underwritten by mining investments, this idea activated a resource-centric optimism that moved some people to labor, as individuals, toward new kinds of accumulation without addressing the structural obstacles of uneven development. Neoliberal entities deny the uneven macropolitics of growth through micropolitical encounters where they project its achievement as irrelevant to the marginalizations of capitalism.

Second, beginning from the problematic of wealth reveals a specific mode of belonging in a nation that self-identifies as rich. In efforts to inculcate the investor-investee relation that neoliberal nation making prioritizes as a mode of citizenship, rural villagers were tasked with behaving like entrepreneurs in order for the state, NGOs, and corporations to appreciate them as full citizens. Belonging to a nation experiencing an aggregate economic boom was not a matter of access to benefits, protections, or fairly redistributed wealth but of market agency, of one's capacity to become an individual entrepreneur—the neoliberal unit of growth.[7] Following how villagers subverted this idealized investor-investee relation even as they took up aspirations for getting ahead reveals each of these institutions as contested sites of care and affect.

Third, resource logic becomes influential in marginalized spaces when there is an ongoing, purposeful, labor-intensive effort to inculcate it. Over the course of my fieldwork, I realized that the NGOs, the state, and the mine had all been selling a fundamentally decontextualized vision of Indigenous entrepreneurship as a generic search for generic treasure. Despite decades of critiques of development interventions generated in far-off donor offices and NGO conference rooms, these projects of "do it yourself development"[8] recapitulated a *modular* orientation to economic growth.[9] For these projects all entrepreneurship looked the same, economic actors were ironically generic in their Indigenous uniqueness, and local context was simple raw material to extract, rebrand, or "salvage," to invoke Anna Tsing's term.[10] Far from a seamless release of capital, this decontextualized extractivist ideology was difficult to implement and extend in practice, opening frictions and tensions that villagers could play to their advantage.

Fourth, resource logic is a capitalist ontology that sees itself as mutually exclusive of other ways of being in its efforts to expand. However, like colonial invaders,[11] the corporation,[12] and the state,[13] resource logics are not all-powerful or perfectly dominant. Andean relational logics can also be incorporative and voracious.[14] Such logics are not just the purview of formal ritual practitioners outside the realm of capitalist development. In this book I have detailed scenes where markets, cash-cropping, mining, and engaging with urban institutions also become important sites for building relations, forging obligations, and imagining Andean lives and futures that intersect with capitalist trajectories but are not overdetermined by them.

Riches are representations. Marca Perú cultivates a cluster of promises that do not, alone, alter conditions of uneven development and relative poverty on the ground. The microlevel interactions that the national brand framed during the 2010s condenses a "neoliberal structure of feeling" rooted in an aspirational sense of ubiquitous wealth.[15] We can understand this structure of feeling in its full ethnographic complexity by reading growth not as a happy natural by-product of market exchange or an ambient economic context but as a deliberate project.[16]

## Growth on Hold

Projects, unlike contexts, can be put on hold. On March 16, 2020, the Peruvian growth project suddenly stopped. Then-president Martín Vizcarra implemented one of the world's earliest and strictest lockdown orders as a response to the COVID-19 pandemic. Public health experts around the world declared Peru a paragon of infection control. For a brief moment, I watched with envy from a rudderless United States as Peru's national quarantine went into effect. So-called nonessential businesses—restaurants, tourist sites, mines—were locked down. Travel was restricted. Infection rates were, at first, low. A pandemic aid package that amounted to just over $100 per family was programmed to pay some 9 million "vulnerable" Peruvian citizens not to engage in their usual day labor.[17]

This moment of promise was brief. It was not long before Peru's exemplary response gave way to a rapid rise in infections, overflowing intensive care units, and deaths.[18] The Peruvian experience of the pandemic has been one of the world's most tragic, although that is a devastatingly crowded category. It also became clear that a long-term quarantine was incompatible with the face-to-face work that most Peruvians engage in to make a living. To many of the most precarious workers in the informal sector and to many rural families, pandemic aid, delivered to bank accounts, was inaccessible. Thousands of urban residents migrated to rural regions where relatives lived, some engaging in agricultural labor for the first time in their lives.[19] Peru's GDP dropped by 30%, one of the steepest declines in the world.[20]

What happens to a place when growth stops and there is no alternative? "The pandemic has lain bare the fragility of existing economic systems," write Giorgos Kallis and his colleagues in the degrowth movement.[21] More specifically, as Peru's ex-minister of health Víctor Zamora has suggested in a criticism of his own government, "The pandemic is an expression in capital letters of the failure of the neoliberal model . . . of our fixation on three indicators: growth, inflation, and fiscal deficit."[22] Despite decades of astronomical aggregate economic growth, Peru's pandemic has revealed what years of neoliberal privatization and extractive care have obscured: that a long-term disinvestment in public goods, political disunity and distrust, racist anti-rural disparagement, and underfunded medical infrastructure made unreliable foundations for fundamental well-being.[23] This became starkly clear to me in an April 2021 Facebook Messenger conversation with Fabiola Dapino, who seven years earlier was convinced that poverty did not exist in the Colca Valley. Fabiola has become a good friend since my fieldwork with Desco. I asked about her health, her family, and whether she would soon have the chance to receive a COVID vaccine. She acknowledged that she likely faced a long wait and added, "I swear that now I finally understand that we're a poor third-world country."

Given the precarities it has exposed, the COVID-19 pandemic suggests that it is urgent to rethink our existing growth orthodoxies. I have made clear throughout this book that people employed by and beholden to neoliberal institutions in Peru tend to see no alternative to an individualistic capitalist growth. Yet in Peru and around the world the pandemic has rendered that no-alternatives logic untenable for most of the people who have suffered through it. Scholars associated with degrowth and environmental justice conversations incisively critique the disingenuous neoliberal thesis that there is no alternative.[24] They argue against the globalized premise that economic growth must be pursued at all costs. There is a tendency among some of these scholars, however, to see capitalism's boosters as unequivocally powerful, overlooking the fact that this ideology of growth has always been unstable. It needs to be taught and evangelized. It encounters frictions. I have sustained the argument that growth is an interactional, face-to-face project, both in the way it is presented as a priority and in the way it is enacted. It is extended through acts of *investment*, a mode of alignment that blends the economic, the financial, the extractive, and the affective. While invest*ors* tended to hold hierarchical power, in practice I found that invest*ees* opened room for renegotiating the terms of that power. Growth relies on—and *is*—an obscured, shifting infrastructure of in-person care work and meaning making.

As I write these words in the late summer of 2021, however, face-to-face encounters also remain the single most dangerous means of virus transmission for most of the world. Growth projects have long been sites of potential violence and danger, reverberating with the legacies of colonial plunder. In their new link to the threat of contagion, the essential affective building blocks and interdependencies fundamental to market life and capitalist growth have been drawn violently into relief. Any recovery that centers genuine well-being must attend to these newly visible interdependencies.

In a recent conversation, Yeny Huánaco Huerta, the owner of a Yanque restaurant called Willariy and one of my closest friends in the village, told me not to worry about her or the community, despite Caylloma Province's dramatically underfunded health care infrastructure. Yanque *campesinos*, she said with wry laughter, "have always been socially distancing." Viral infection was much worse in Peru's cities, she told me. But of course I worry, even as Yanque residents begin to receive their vaccines. I also wonder about the days ahead. Months of a national quarantine that proved difficult to enforce, distrust of a scandal-ridden national public health infrastructure, and the agonizingly slow struggle to vaccinate the country may invite a shift in local priorities away from resource logics. Or it may mean the consolidation of those logics. This remains to be seen. The pandemic is likely to shape economic life for years to come in Peru and around the world. If the pandemic, the quarantine, and the uneven impacts of both challenge existing growth orthodoxies, then, as I have argued in this book, the pandemic is far from the only such challenge. Indeed, everywhere I witnessed growth being made, I saw contestations, messy overlaps, and entanglements between ideologies of independence and interdependence, empowerment and patronage, and resources and relations.

### Returns

The evangelizers of capitalist growth may have worked hard to represent resource-extractive entrepreneurial individualism as the sole pathway to prosperity, without any possible alternative. But I have sustained throughout

this book that capitalism is not a complete project and that alternatives proliferate through daily life at the margins of a booming capitalist economy.
Our last scene returns us to the fields of Yanque, where agriculturalists
composed a mixed tableau of relational and resource logics. It was another
cold July, this time in 2019. It was my last visit to Peru. Several days later, I
would return to the United States to prepare for the coming academic year.
Just a few months after that, the pandemic would begin to radically reorder
global priorities, suspending my plans to return.

Night was falling. I stood on a terraced terrain called Collota. We were
near Gerardo's *chakra* Ch'ela. On one of the terraced walls behind us, I
could see painted white letters spelling out "Desco" on stones that the
vegetation had mostly overtaken, a relic of the NGO's effort to revive the
valley's terraced agriculture about fifteen years earlier. My weeks of interviews
and conversations in Yanque in 2019 about plummeting crop prices and
intensifying climate change led me to believe that agriculture was a waning
practice here. I was surprised, then, to find myself among a large group of
agricultural workers. We had just finished a day of seeding fava beans and
quinoa in the *chakra*. This was the *michka*, a brief session of seeding that
some families engage in before the main sowing season in mid-August. The
large group gathered, after the day's labor drew to a close, to sing to the land.

Mario Checca was leading the Hialeo chant. He was about 35 years old
and was one of the sons of Gerardo Huaracha's close friend Máximo. Mario
is related to the many other Checcas that populate Yanque. His words to
the twenty people in the work party marked the conclusion of a day of
work and chicha drinking.

> With the Lord's blessing, we are planting here in the hearth, the Pa-
> chamama, holy land, Collota-mama. . . . So as they say, we are going
> to call forth the energy [*ánimo*] of the *chakra*, and its care, so that it
> gives us a good harvest, so that it gives us a good product too. Good
> production and also her blessing. Yes?

The others, slack with fatigue but in the mood to celebrate, cheered their
assent. Then, Mario shouted his calls of praise, to the crowd's increasingly
raucous responses of "Hai le!" This was a group of young and old people
from Yanque. Most of them had other jobs in tourism, construction, mining, or urban day labor; agriculture was not a regular means of income for
any of them. Yet like the thousands of city dwellers who would soon board

buses for one-way trips to the rural Andes after the pandemic lockdown, this group of kin, partners, and friends was able to return to Yanque for a day of convivial labor. Collota belonged to the Checca family and was worked and supplied with the offerings that would enable its crops to thrive. It formed part of the heterogeneous economic assemblages that each person present organized for themselves, "adapting and recombining" lives rooted in Yanque in different ways.[25] The Hialeo chant was not the extracted confession of an interior conversion to Indigenous entrepreneurship. Nor was it the cry of protest against mining that is increasing throughout the Arequipa and Cuzco regions.

The song was part of a different kind of relationship, which also had constantly to be composed and maintained: that between humans and terrain, through which abundance is temporarily sustained by fragile cycles. This relationship's future may be in doubt, given declining crop prices and increasingly extreme weather changes. Its future may also be tested, given that Collota sits on the Colca River's mineral-rich right bank, where mining companies are expanding their mission to "build a better Peru."[26] Its future may also see renewed commitment if the pandemic forces a new generation of Yanque villagers to pursue agricultural labor. But that day in July 2019 land and workers helped one another thrive in a world beset by the uncertainties of lingering coloniality and late capitalism.

This is therefore not a romanticized happy ending. Neoliberal capitalism comes with significant structural violence and neglect, felt sharply at its margins. Resource logics can violently interrupt relational logics. But this final song draws capitalism into perspective, demonstrating that multiple logics can be engaged within the same economic lives. Capitalism is not the only structure of feeling generated in a system we might generalize as capitalist. Nor is it necessarily dominant, even for people who engage with its markets. Andean relational logics and sensibilities are also able to incorporate diverse frameworks and still thrive. The joy of this Hialeo song tells us that resource logics and extractive care are far from the only roads to a sense of abundance. To fully understand how these resource logics work as actually existing social forms, we must be careful not to ascribe too much power to them or loosen them from their own ethnographic contexts. This is why, in the end, I have focused on the labor of enacting growth as a discourse, a material arrangement, a feeling. I have hoped to put growth in its place.

# Notes

## Introduction: The Richest Country in the World

1. Unless otherwise indicated, I use real names throughout this book, as my interlocutors usually asked to be on record. I indicate where I use a pseudonym.

2. Benavides (1983).

3. "Bench of gold" is a phrase from Peruvian Italian explorer Antonio Raimondi (1824–1890) that circulated widely in urban Peruvian public life. According to Fabiana Li (2015), the idea "placed the blame on Peruvians who seemed unwilling or unable to make effective use of the country's bountiful resources" (13). A related notion is ex-president Alan García's famously indignant descriptions of anti-extraction environmentalists and villagers as "the dog in the manger, who prays: 'If I don't do it, let nobody do it'" (García Pérez 2007).

4. According to the Ministry of Economy and Finance poverty mapping initiative, the 2018 monetary poverty rate for Caylloma Province was between 14.4% and 20% (INEI 2020), and its extreme monetary poverty was 6.1% (CEPLAN 2017). Monetary poverty in Espinar Province ranged between 23.9% and 38% (INEI 2020), with an extreme monetary poverty rate of 5.2% (CEPLAN 2017).

5. De Soto (2000), 4, 6.

6. Lossio Chávez (2018).

7. Beck (2017); Bornstein (2005); Ferguson (1990); Mosse (2005); Radcliffe (2015).

8. Nixon (2011).

9. See Ross (2001) for a paradigmatic example of the resource curse framework. Appel (2019) critiques this literature, as does a robust tradition of scholarship in political ecology. See, in particular, Tubb (2020), Watts (2004), and Watts and Peluso (2014).

10. I use *village* as a translation of the Spanish *villa* or *pueblo*, used in the region to designate a settlement that has a name, whether that means a municipal district (such as Yanque) or an autonomous annex to a district (such as Taya).

11. García (2021).

12. Puig de la Bellacasa (2017).

13. Murphy (2015), 719.

14. Murphy (2015), 721.

15. Hochschild (1983), 7.

16. Salazar Parreñas (2018), 6.

17. Cookson (2018).

18. Wenzel (2020), 148. See also Escobar (1999) and N. Smith (2010). Jason Moore (2016) scales this framework up to capitalism as a whole, which he reads as a means of organizing nature.

19. Galeano (1973).

20. Tsing (2015b).

21. Marx (1990), 727.

22. Bunker (1985), 20.

23. Himley (2012).

24. Freeman (2014, 57) mobilizes this concept, based on Raymond Williams's "structures of feeling" (1977, 132), to track how the categories, desires, and marginalizations of neoliberal capitalism press into the intimate texture of everyday life in Barbados.

25. Ethnographic quotations in this book were originally uttered in Spanish unless noted otherwise.

26. Distrito.pe (2020).

27. Callon (1998).

28. Appel (2019); Ho (2009).

29. Appel (2019), 212.

30. Mirowski (1989).

31. Hodgson (2005).

32. Marx (1990); Paulson (2017), 428.

33. Chertkovskaya and Paulsson (2016) identify three dimensions of contemporary growth: increasing biophysical throughput, capital accumulation, and the imperative for national economies to expand.

34. This resonates with Claudia Castañeda's (2002) analysis of the figure of the child. See next section.

35. Silverstein (1998).

36. Murphy (2017), 117.

37. Mezzadra and Neilson (2015), 7.

38. Tsing (2000).

39. Gómez-Barris (2017), xvii. See also Simpson (2014) and TallBear (2019).

40. Bear et al. (2015). For examples of research into the continual and often unseen labor of generating capitalism, see also Bear (2015), Rofel and Yanagisako (2019), Schuster (2015), Tsing (2015a), and Yanagisako (2002). Gibson-Graham (2006) was influential in these inquiries, offering a framework for economic diversity that actively resists "capitalocentric" economic discourse.

41. Ahmed (2004), 119.

42. W. Brown (2015); Morton (2015).

43. Ferguson (2015).

44. *Primitive accumulation* is a term Karl Marx (1990, 873–76) mobilized to describe the first possessive enclosure of nature as something that can be owned, which, he argued, transformed people who worked the land into an impoverished proletariat. This interpretation offered a critical update from Adam Smith's simplistic thesis that the basic act of accumulating useful things from nature must come before the higher-order establishment of capitalist economic principles. Scholars have debated and updated Marx's use of this concept. Throughout this book, my analysis continually returns to Anna Tsing's update— *salvage accumulation*—which moves away from the problematic historical implications of the "primitive" and instead places specific emphasis on the ongoing present-day transformations from noncapitalist relations into capitalist ones that contemporary globalization demands (Tsing 2015a). Salvage and extraction are similar actions and can overlap (Han 2019). Here, I read *salvage* as an act that can be considered extractive as soon as the object or concept to be salvaged (or found, recovered, or rescued) is viewed as raw material for capitalist activities. One of Merriam-Webster's definitions of *salvage* is "something extracted (as from rubbish) as valuable or useful" (Merriam-Webster 2021). The sense of extracting a found object to perform capitalist work is the definition I mobilize for *salvage* in this book.

45. Gómez-Barris (2017), xvi. See also Farthing and Fabricant (2018).

46. Kimmerer (2015), 111.

47. M. Smith (2017).

48. Sahlins (2017).

49. Bataille (1991).

50. Haraway (2018), 11. See also Castañeda (2002).

51. Vich (2007), 1.

52. Lossio Chávez (2018), 63.

53. Lossio Chávez (2018), 60.

54. Cánepa (2014). I thank Fabiana Li for pointing me to this arena of public debate.

55. Cuevas Calderón (2015).

56. See Ramos (1994, 160) for a discussion of "model Indians" in Brazilian environmental advocacy.

57. De la Cadena (2000); Mendoza (1999).

58. D'Argenio (2013), 29.

59. D'Argenio (2013), 28.

60. Aronczyk (2018), xi.

61. Flores Galindo (2010); Galeano (1973).

62. T. M. Li (2014); Tubb (2020).

63. Escobar (1995). See also Beck (2017), Bornstein (2005), Ferguson (1990), Mosse (2005), and Radcliffe (2015).

64. Andolina et al. (2009); Colloredo-Mansfeld (1999); DeHart (2010).

65. Harvey (2005).

66. This was not the case with all of Peru, however, where only 56.6% of homes had potable water as of the 2014 census (Cookson 2018, 16).

67. Bury (2005).

68. Morton (2015), 1291.

69. Roy (2010). See also Cooper (2020).

70. In 2013 the upper-middle-income threshold was a gross national income (GNI) per capita of $4,086.

71. Cookson (2018).

72. UNESCO (2015).

73. UNESCO (2017).

74. This idea extends the insights of other recent scholars on indigeneity in Peru who parse various encounters where indigeneity comes to matter in the Andes. See Cánepa (2018), Greene (2009), and Mendoza (1999).

75. Larson (2014); Yashar (2005).

76. García (2005), 176.

77. Mayer (2009).

78. García (2005).

79. For the official declaration founding the Indigenous Community of the District of Yanque, see Comunidad de Indígenas de Yanque (1961); and for the official state recognition, see Ministerio de Trabajo y Asuntos Indígenas (1965). Both documents can be found in the Gerardo Huaracha Archive, which is my name for the collection of documents, records, artifacts, and relics collected by Gerardo Huaracha in his Yanque home.

80. Sánchez Dávila (2019).

81. Ministerio de Cultura (2020).

82. Rojas-Perez (2017).

83. Postero (2007).

84. Martinez Novo (2014).

85. Jackson (2019).

86. Starn (1999).

87. Hale (2004).

88. Comisión de la Verdad y Reconciliación (2003).

89. Callirgos (2018).

90. Noriega (2020).

91. Taj (2015).

92. Cervantes (2019).

93. See Pajuelo Teves (2019).

94. Eve Kosofsky Sedgwick (1990) reads the act of coming out of the closet as queer to be a fraught gesture that is fundamentally revealing of deep public anxieties around sexuality. I thank Jay Sosa for this connection, as Richard Chase Smith's notion of an Indigenous "coming out" similarly frames a moment of revelation, destabilization, and anxiety in Peru.

95. Alejandro Diez Hurtado, personal communication, 2017. See also de la Cadena (2000). Jackson (2019) describes a similar phenomenon in Colombia.

96. Drinot (2011); Portocarrero (2007).

97. Graham and Penny (2014).

98. Ministerio de Cultura, "Los pueblos indígenas del Perú," PowerPoint presentation, 2013. This presentation was shared with me during an interview with Leonor Cisneros in the ministry. The slides were used in various meetings the ministry held.

99. The title of Florence Babb's article documenting this phenomenon, "The Real Indigenous Are Higher Up" (2020), reflects Leonor Cisneros's quote almost verbatim.

100. Salas Carreño (2020), 9. Salas Carreño emphasizes that "implicit indigeneity" is his own analytic term, not a concept claimed by the Andean communities he works with.

101. Whyte (2016).

102. "The Quechua" is an umbrella category that designates diverse groups that were under Inca rule at the time of the Spanish invasion of the Andes. It includes the Collaguas and Cabanas in the Caylloma area and the K'anas in the Espinar area.

103. Greene (2009), 17.

104. L. T. Smith (2012); S. Wilson (2008).

105. Hoover (2017).

106. Orlove (2002).

107. Scholarly and archival sources I worked with from his collection have the designation "Gerardo Huaracha Archive" in my bibliography.

108. See Clifford (2013).

109. Million (2009), 61.

## Chapter 1: The Coloniality of the Resource

This chapter is a modified version of a previously published article titled "Mediating Indigeneity: Public Space and the Making of Political Identity in Andean Peru," in PoLAR: Political and Legal Anthropology, 39(1): 95–109. © 2016 by the American Anthropological Association.

1. Cook (2007).

2. Wernke (2013), 91.

3. The folios documenting the two colonial *visitas* to Yanque are catalogued in the Parochial Archive of Yanque as "#191. Visita a Yanquecollaguas Hanansaya. 1591. Fragment, 29 folios without number" and "#195. Visita a Yanquecollaguas Urinsaya. 1604. Incomplete, 361 folios. Transcript, unpublished." D. J. Robinson (2006) offers an extensive four-volume history of the Collaguas.

4. Femenías (2005).

5. Benavides (1989).

6. Alberto Flores Galindo (2010) details this search as a long-standing historical motif.

7. Among the many scholars who root capitalism in colonial institutions, I am thinking in particular of the work of Deborah Thomas (2019), Timothy Mitchell (2009), and Macarena Gómez-Barris (2017).

8. Gómez-Barris (2017), 2.

9. For understandings of foreign aid in Peru, see S. Brown (2019) and Chávez and Coe (2007). For histories of the Colca Valley, see Cook (2007), Wernke (2013), and Benavides (1983, 1994). Thomas Love (2017) presents a detailed history of Arequipa regionalism.

10. Navaro-Yashin (2012), 10, 17.

11. Benavides (1983).

12. See Morris (2013) for a discussion of Inca urbanism. Wernke (2007, 2013) notes that the Incas are insufficiently analyzed as colonists in their own right. His work traces a single trajectory of spatial and material manipulations spanning both Inca and Spanish colonialism.

13. VanValkenburgh (2017).

14. Galeano (1973).

15. Lowe (2015), 6.

16. Quijano (2000).

17. Maldonado-Torres (2007).

18. A robust conversation about the connections between resource extraction and ongoing colonial conditions is especially active among Indigenous scholars of North America. See, for example, Byrd (2011) and Estes and Dhillon (2019).

19. Thomas (2019).

20. Benavides (1989).

21. Shepherd (2004), 249.

22. Quijano (2000), 542 (my emphasis).

23. Gelles (2000), 29.

24. Flores Galindo (2010), 132.

25. Manrique (1985).

26. Wernke (2007), 131.

27. Wernke (2013), 57.

28. Benavides (1989). See Murra (1972) on the vertical archipelago concept.

29. Blenda Femenías (1991) details the relationship between clothing style and historical ethnicity in the Colca Valley. She suggests that today each village has certain unique stylistic motifs but, aside from sombreros, clothing is largely not a present-day means of distinguishing between Collagua and Cabana heritage.

30. Málaga Sabogal and Ulfe (2017).

31. Derechos Sin Fronteras (2017).

32. Allen (2002), 108.

33. De la Cadena (2010), 354.

34. Benavides (1994, 42n9) notes that *ayllu* organization faded in the late colonial era during the eighteenth century, which potentially corroborates Ulloa's 1586 speculation that the *ayllu* may have been an Inca imposition.

35. Cook (2007), 155.

36. Wernke (2013), 218.

37. Benavides (1989), 250.

38. Toledo (1986), 33.

39. Mumford (2012), 2.

40. Gose (2008), 122–23.

41. Abercrombie (1998).

42. "Caylloma Development Project," unpublished report, 1968, Archive of the Universidad Católica de Santa María-Museo de Yanque.

43. Cook (2007), 82–83.

44. The phrase Cook draws on comes from Flores Galindo (2010).

45. Scott (1998).

46. Cook (2007), 84.

47. Wernke (2010), 52.

48. Cummins (2002), 203 (my emphasis).

49. Wernke (2013), 161.

50. Benavides (1989), 258.

51. Llosa and Benavides (1994), 116.

52. Lefebvre (1991), 99.

53. Rafael (1988), 89.

54. Hagan (1979), 1.

55. Warner (2005), 122.

56. Rafael (1988), 87.

57. Benavides (1994).

58. Toledo (1986), 3435.

59. Jacobs (1961), 56.

60. Foucault (1995).

61. Benavides (1989), 244.

62. Cook (2007).

63. Benavides (1989), 244

64. VanValkenburgh (2017), 127.

65. Valderrama Fernandez and Escalante Gutierrez (1987).

66. Benavides (1998). Chapter 2 features Gerardo's firsthand narrative of the 1971 "Battle of Chachayllo," a recent eruption of those historical tensions.

67. See C. J. Robinson (1983) and García (2021).

68. Quijano (2000).

69. Mayer (2009).

70. Mayer (2009), 24.

71. Mayer (2009), 3.

72. Cf. Albó (1991).

73. Babb (2011), 5.

74. Urry (1990).

75. Colloredo-Mansfeld (1999) describes the stakes of uneven affluence from tourist markets.

76. Weiss (2018), 32, citing E. P. Thompson.

77. De la Serna Torroba et al. (2016), 320. This page details one participating household from Yanque, but the same household categories apply throughout the P>D report.

78. *Chakra* is Quechua for "terrain" or, if translated more broadly, "space of care."

79. Foucault (1991).

80. Hobsbawm and Ranger (1983).

## Chapter 2: Contesting the Resource

1. See Chakrabarty (2000).

2. De la Cadena (2015); Todd (2018).

3. Gose (2018), 501.

4. Starn (1991), 64.

5. The term *earth-being* conveys the notion of a sentient nonhuman being, such as a mountain or river, that forms a part of the local community and politics. Marisol de la Cadena (2015) has popularized this term in recent scholarly discussions.

6. Million (2009). See also Berlant (2011) on capitalism's cruel promises.

7. Comunidad de Indígenas de Yanque (1961).

8. Ministerio de Trabajo y Asuntos Indígenas (1965).

9. Yashar (2005).

10. Stensrud (2016).

11. Ocsa (2013).

12. Guillet (1994).

13. Guillet (1994), 182. See also Gelles (2000), Trawick (2001), and Valderrama Fernandez and Escalante Gutierrez (1988).

14. Seemann (2016).

15. Thorough treatments of specific Colca Valley villages' irrigation distribution systems and ritual practices as of the late 1980s can be found in Valderrama Fernandez and Escalante Gutierrez (1988) and in the edited volume *Irrigation at High Altitudes* (W. P. Mitchell and Guillet 1993), specifically, the chapters by John Treacy, Paul Gelles, David Guillet, and Karsten Paerregaard.

16. See Gelles (1994).

17. Stensrud (2018).

18. McDonell (2018).

19. Gelles (1994), 257; Paerregaard (1994), 195.

20. De la Cadena (2015).

21. Gose (2018), 493; Sax (2018), 109.

22. Bolin (1998).

23. Salas Carreño (2014), S202.

24. Treacy (1994), 109.

25. The *kuraka*, a local lord or *ayllu* leader, is a position dating back to the Inca era that endured into the twentieth century.

26. This section (and much of this chapter) draws on a series of nearly annual life history interviews that I conducted at least once per visit between 2008 and 2019.

27. As mentioned earlier, *chakra* is Quechua for "terrain," "field," or, more broadly, "space of care."

28. Benavides (1998) offers a full history of this conflict.

29. This echoes Gelles's (2000) reflection that the "earth's personality varies from one place to another" (82).

30. This idiom of attachment resonates with ethnographic observations of human-land relations elsewhere in the Peruvian Andes (Caine 2021; Salas Carreño 2020; de la Cadena 2015).

31. Brewing and serving chicha was a gendered act where women usually had control.

32. Alan Huaracha, Gerardo's youngest son, recently told me that chicha consumption was the reason that, in relation to urban Peru, comparatively few Yanque residents have contracted COVID-19.

33. Election day, for example, was officially a national dry holiday. However, in Yanque the dry law does not preclude chicha consumption, which makes election day a public celebration where competing local candidates drink together in a display of civility.

34. Mayer (1974).

35. Deere (1982).

36. Bolin (1994); Paerregaard (2017).

37. See Gershon (2019).

38. Laura Bear's (2015) study of austerity highlights a similar subsidizing along the Hooghly River.

39. Treacy (1994).

40. In his study of Huaynacotas in neighboring Cotahuasi Province, Trawick (2001) notes that using replacement laborers for communal water work "would be considered behavior befitting a valley landlord" and would violate the ceremony's egalitarian spirit (367).

41. A *topo* is about 3,500 square meters (Guillet 1994) or, as Gerardo described to me, the amount of land that two yoked bulls can plow in a day.

42. Sánchez Dávila (2019), 227.

43. Salas Carreño (2014), S198.

44. Allen (2016).

45. Stensrud (2016).

46. Amazonianists have focused extensively on concepts of consubstantiality. See Vilaça (2010) and Oakdale (2008). In the Andean context, Paulson (2006, 652) describes consubstantiation in a Bolivian ritual feast.

47. Allen (2016).

48. Sánchez Dávila (2019), 232.

49. Million (2009).

50. Babb (2018); Seligmann (2004); Weismantel (2001).

51. Babb (1996), 28.

52. The cantuta (*Cantua buxifolia*), a flower with long petals shaped like a trumpet, is Peru's national flower and is associated with Inca-era mythology.

53. This follows the common Andean practice of moving children from their parents' home to that of a better-off relative or godparent as a means of mitigating economic stress (Leinaweaver 2008). For discussions of multisited dwelling, see also Hirsch (2018), Paerregaard (2017), and Peluso (2015).

54. Beer is also a sign of contemporary regional integration: Yanqueños almost exclusively drink the beer branded "Cerveza Arequipeña."

55. Treacy (1994), 104.

56. Hirsch (2018); Paerregaard (2017).

57. Choy (2010), 28.

58. Tsing (2000), 143.

59. Cf. Tsing (2009).

60. Grillo Fernandez (1998), 133–34.

61. Salas Carreño (2014), S211.

62. Todd (2018), 61.

## Chapter 3: Staging Growth

1. But see Tsing (2000), who addresses performative spectacle as a constitutive aspect of globalized finance capital. In this chapter I follow spectacles of growth as they are scaled down and track the specific work it takes to render them meaningful in the everyday encounters that constitute a Peruvian development investment.

2. García (2021). See also Povinelli (2002).

3. Rasmussen (2016), 351.

4. Navaro-Yashin (2002), 4 (citing Aretxaga 2000).

5. Berlant (2011).

6. This phrase, *indio permitido* in Spanish, comes from the work of Silvia Rivera Cusicanqui (2008). See also Hale (2004).

7. Povinelli (2002).

8. T. Mitchell (1991), 94. See also Das and Poole (2004).

9. Rasmussen (2016). See also Tanaka (2002).

10. Many scholars have extensively debated what the state is and does and how it feels. That debate is beyond the scope of this book. Here, I emphasize "state affects" (as opposed to Ann Stoler's [2004] "affective states" or other recent formulations) to train ethnographic attention on specific public feelings evoked by and surrounding the state. In other words, this discussion is less about the state itself than about how a specific genre of affects come to be part of disputes about resource wealth and power relations.

11. Benavides (1983); Love (2017).

12. Tsing (2015b). See Introduction.

13. Bear et al. (2015).

14. Staging is an idea that also draws on Tsing's (2000) work on "economies of appearance" and the performative nature of financial spectacle.

15. Rasmussen (2016), 343.

16. The theme of reciprocity has received much attention in the anthropological and historical scholarship of the Andes. Exemplary works in this conversation include Allen (2002), Isbell (1985), Mayer (2001), Walsh-Dilley (2017), and Gose (1994).

17. For a classic ethnography of Andean patronage in contexts of peasant struggle, see Nash (1993). More recently, ethnographers have explored patronage in contexts of Andean development work (Cameron 2009; Harvey 2010).

18. Benavides (1983), 5. *Misti* is a racialized, "whitened" category of upper-class urban-based or mestizo people.

19. Condori Mamani and Quispe Huamán (1996); Gelles (2000); Leinaweaver (2008).

20. Rasmussen (2016).

21. https://www.ifad.org/en/web/operations/project/id/1100001240.

22. IFAD (2018).

23. Sierra Sur (2011); emphasis added.

24. Sierra Sur (2014a).

25. Framing these two categories of diversity together is also suggestive of the racist animalizing language long used to describe rural Andeans, as García (2021) elaborates.

26. See García (2005) for an analysis of contestations over Quechua-language instruction in Peru's Intercultural Bilingual Education program.

27. De la Cadena (2000).

28. Jackson (2019).

29. Sierra Sur's largest investment was in Cabanaconde. For six associations and a team of 200, it contributed 100,564 soles ($31,608.97, or $158.04 per person) to the associations' 20,086 soles ($6,313.37)—that is, 83.35% of the total budget of 120,650 soles ($37,925.97).

30. Abers (2000).

31. Susan Paulson (2015) highlights the often overlooked gendered labor expectations faced by working-class Latin American men.

32. In my back-to-back interviews in Arequipa headquarters with Sierra Sur's director and with former Desco regional director Oscar Toro, each disparaged the other organization as *asistencialista*.

33. Schwittay (2015), 6.

34. The exchange rate I use for late 2014 is 34 U.S. cents to the sol, based on historical exchange rates from Pound Sterling Live (https://www.poundsterlinglive.com/best-exchange-rates/us-dollar-to-peruvian-nuevo-sol-exchange-rate-on-2014-11-14).

35. Mosse (2005), 181.

36. Rasmussen (2016).

37. Gil Ramón (2020), 145.

38. Farbotko (2010), 50.

39. The discipline of anthropology's colonial origins and the ways it reproduces ongoing coloniality have been subject to substantial scholarly critique in recent decades (Asad 1995). In Lilia's case, perpetuating this binaristic modern-nonmodern hierarchy also entrenches Peru's strong urban-rural class and racial divides (Quijano 2000).

40. Orlove (2002) theorizes the violence of forgetting in the Andes.

41. See Hirsch (2018).

42. Scott (1990), 4.

43. Sierra Sur (2014a), 23. The hierarchical learning that oriented these competitions is clearly distinct from the co-labored teaching I discussed in Chapter 2.

44. Scott (1998). See also F. Li (2009) and Riles (2006).

45. Bourdieu (1984), 110.

46. See DeHart (2010).

47. Neyra (2017).

48. F. Li (2009).

49. Graham (2005), 625.

50. INEI (2014).

51. Bidwell (2020) details Tuti producers' engagements with regional and global food-based development initiatives.

52. See García (2021, 93–119) for a critical analysis of race, class, and difference in the Mistura festival.

53. Diario El Pueblo (2017).

54. Femenías (2005), 294. Several scholars have analyzed Barbie dolls as a site for shaping gender politics and cultural commodification (e.g., Babb 2018). I elaborate on Mercedes' Barbie doll in Hirsch (2020b).

55. Sierra Sur (2014a).

## Chapter 4: Economies of Empowerment

1. García (2021).

2. Roy (2010).

3. Freeman (2000), 3. See also Schuster (2015).

4. Radcliffe (2015); Sharma (2008).

5. Murphy (2017), 9.

6. Roy (2010), 6.

7. Searle (2016), 58.

8. MacKenzie (2008).

9. Zaloom (2006).

10. Chong (2018).

11. Appel (2019); Huang (2020); Kar (2018).

12. Stout (2016).

13. Wendy Brown (2015) characterizes neoliberalism as "the replacement of citizenship defined as concern with the public good by citizenship reduced to the citizen as *homo oeconomicus*" (39).

14. Elizabeth Povinelli reads the paired moves of abandonment and highly selective inclusion of the otherwise as a core working of late liberal power in her book *Economies of Abandonment* (2011), from which I draw this chapter's title. In a related formulation, Lisa Lowe (2015) theorizes the postcolonial liberal project as resting on an "economy of affirmation and forgetting" (3).

15. Lashaw et al. (2017).

16. Schuller (2012), 177.

17. Schuller (2009).

18. Ahmed (2010), 35.

19. Banner (2020).

20. Mauss (1990).

21. Krippner (2011).

22. Krippner (2011), 4.

23. Guyer (2007), 411.

24. Peebles (2010); Schwittay (2011).

25. Among these was Xstrata Tintaya, at that time the owner of the mine I discuss in Chapter 5.

26. ExxonMobil was one of Fondoempleo's largest donors later in the decade.

27. Desco (2012).

28. Desco (2012), 20.

29. Desco (2012), 17.

30. Desco (2012), 3.

31. For example, Babb (2011).

32. I use a pseudonym for this participant for reasons that become clear at the end of the chapter.

33. De Soto (2000); Elyachar (2012).

34. Huang (2020), 5.

35. T. M. Li (2007).

36. Cruikshank (1999), 88.

37. Cf. Mauss (1990), who reads the gift as a "total social fact," or a social form that intersects with every existing institution in a particular community.

38. See Salas Carreño's (2020) "explicit" and "implicit" indigeneity distinction.

39. Desco (2012), 11.

40. Fondesurco (2014).

41. Real Academia Española (2019).

42. West (2016), 72.

43. Tsing (2015b).

44. I elaborate on Anacé's and Rogelio's entrepreneurial experiences in Hirsch (2020a).

45. See Chapter 2.

46. Quijano (2000). See Chapter 1.

47. Kwon (2015).

48. See Alberti and Mayer (1974), Babb (2020), Deere (1982), and Mayer (2001).

49. Elyachar (2012), 496.

50. Huff (2014).

51. Desco (2014).

52. Salomon and Niño-Murcia (2011).

53. See W. Brown (2015) on the neoliberal ideology of framing a group of workers as a team.

54. Freeman (2014).

55. T. M. Li (2007), 1.

56. Kar (2018).

57. Cruikshank (1999), 89.

58. An entrepreneurial association that Rogelio formed after Desco's project ended.

59. SUNAT is the National Superintendence of Customs and Tributary Administration, Peru's taxation agency.

60. Berlant (2011).

61. Desco (n.d.), 43.

62. Desco (n.d.), 43.

## Chapter 5: Extractive Care

1. María Elena García (2021) highlights rape and sexual violence against animals as a routine aspect of modernist industrial animal agriculture in her discussion of Peruvian guinea pig production. See also Gillespie (2013).

2. Rojas-Downing et al. (2017).

3. Murphy (2015), 719.

4. Welker (2014), 97.

5. Fabiana Li (2015) distinguishes between vague claims of responsibility that mining corporations make and the more specific notion of accountability, which "refers to a corporation's obligation to answer to citizens and the state and provide evidence to show that certain outcomes have been achieved" (186).

6. Haraway (2018), 11.

7. Berlant (2011).

8. See Warner (2005).

9. Evans-Pritchard (1969), 16, 19.

10. Ferguson (1990).

11. Perez (1992).

12. Shepherd (2004); T. M. Li (2007); Welker (2012). Green Revolution–style assistance emphasizes the top-down imposition of genetic modification, high-yield varieties of seeds and grains, expert-driven farm optimization, and other modernization-focused technologies to augment agricultural production.

13. Shepherd (2004), 242–43.

14. T. M. Li (2007), 123.

15. Appel (2019), 2.

16. Brown Swiss Association (2018).

17. This was the opportunistic consensus among extractive industry representatives in a panel discussion about corporate social responsibility that I witnessed during the 2014 UN Conference of the Parties in Lima.

18. Rojas-Downing et al. (2017), 156.

19. Govindrajan (2018).

20. Ferguson (1990), 58.

21. Laws 27506, 28077, and 28322 set the specific rules for mining, hydropower, gas, fishing, logging, and petroleum royalties.

22. MEF (2015).

23. This figure is based on a report by the Department of Parliamentary Investigation and Documentation, an official transparency outlet of the Peruvian Congress. The report also—transparently—takes its figures from the national pro-mining lobbying organization (SNMPE 2018).

24. Dollar amounts come from xe.com, accessed July 31, 2018.

25. Gestión (2017).

26. Gestión (2019).

27. For discussions of prior consultation and the shifting interpretations of the UN-authorized concept of "free, prior, and informed consent," see Arellano-Yanguas (2011), Condé and Le Billon (2017), F. Li (2009), and Perreault (2015).

28. Congreso de la República (2011).

29. Málaga Sabogal and Ulfe (2017). Povinelli (2002) notes a similar mobilization of suspicion against Aboriginal communities in Australian land claims.

30. F. Li (2009, 2015).

31. T. Wilson (2017).

32. Goldstein and Yates (2017).

33. Newell (2005).

34. Condé and Le Billon (2017).

35. MEF (2015).

36. Glencore (2016), 8. In the same display depicting the company's commitment to "operating responsibly," one bullet point reads: "We identify, understand, and mitigate our environmental risks." This inadvertently gives away the game of corporate transparency, as mining companies tend to identify only those risks that they are able to address. See F. Li (2015). I discuss the concept of transparency in greater detail later in this chapter.

37. Amengual (2018).

38. Anguelovski (2011); de Echave et al. (2009).

39. Glencore stands for Global Energy Commodity Resources. During the research for this book, the ownership of the Tintaya mining complex changed and was reconfigured multiple times. The difficulty of tracking Tintaya's owners is but one small example of the growth of financialized rentierist complexity and its dispersal of accountability in late capitalism (Sassen 2014).

40. Welker (2014), 14–15.

41. Leche Gloria S.A. is Peru's largest dairy conglomerate.

42. Shepherd (2004).

43. See Gil Ramón (2020) and Salas Carreño and Diez Hurtado (2018) on similar examples of this effort in other Andean mining regions.

44. Gamu and Dauvergne (2018).

45. F. Li (2009), 223.

46. Shepherd (2004), 242.

47. Given the tense situation in Espinar, I use pseudonyms for any activist who was not a public figure.

48. Berlant (2011), 23.

49. Anguelovski (2011), 391.

50. This finding was consistent with other testimonies (Gamu and Dauvergne 2018).

51. World Bank (2013).

52. Condé and Le Billon (2017).

53. Bowcott (2017).

54. CooperAcción (2016).

55. Orellana Lopez and de Boissiére (2014).

56. Anguelovski (2011), 392.

57. See de Echave et al. (2009).

58. Condé and Le Billon (2017), 692.

59. De Echave et al. (2009) comprehensively detail the longer history of protest at the Tintaya Mine.

60. F. Li (2009).

61. F. Li (2015).

62. F. Li (2015). See also Hetherington (2011) and Ballestero (2012).

63. F. Li (2015), 186.

64. Gil Ramón (2020), 4.

65. Graham (2002).

66. Salas Carreño (2020).

67. Mannheim and van Vleet (1998).

68. Simpson (2014). Fabiana Li (2015) explores other sets of quandaries that surround strategies of refusal in the context of the Yanacocha mine expansion in Cajamarca.

69. F. Li (2015).

70. This is a common retort in EIA participatory meetings in Peru (F. Li 2009).

71. *Misti* is a volcano near the city of Arequipa. *Wasi* is Quechua for "house."

72. Tsing (2000).

73. This is an example of what Cori Hayden called "mere-ing" in a 2013 workshop at the University of Chicago.

74. See Minería de Todos (2019).

75. UGEL (2019).

76. Günel (2019), 13. See also Nixon (2011).

77. https://www.mineriadetodos.com.pe/.

78. Salas Carreño (2020).

79. UNESCO (2017).

80. Welker (2014).

81. Murphy (2015), 729.

82. Graeter (2020), 13.

## Conclusion: Returns

1. https://www.youtube.com/watch?v=RL9gsVy9gfU&t=18s. Babb (2018), Cánepa (2014), García (2021), Lossio Chávez (2018), and Silverman (2015), among others, have critiqued various aspects of the branding scheme.

2. PromPerú (2019).

3. PromPerú (2017).

4. Mazzarella (2003), 37.

5. Pine and Gilmore (2011).

6. Gómez-Barris (2017).

7. I owe this formulation to Caroline Schuster's (2015) notion of the social unit of debt.

8. Huang (2016), 1.

9. Escobar (1995) and Mosse (2005) classically sum up the critique of modularity in development projects.

10. Tsing (2009, 2015b).

11. Wernke (2007).

12. Welker (2014).

13. Rasmussen (2016).

14. Grillo Fernandez (1998).

15. Freeman (2014), 57.

16. This is a variation on Appel (2019), 2.

17. "Martín Vizcarra anuncia bono de 380 soles a familias que dependan de trabajos diarios," *La República*, March 16, 2020, https://larepublica.pe/economia/2020/03/16/martin-vizcarra-anuncia-bono-de-380-soles-a-personas-que-cumplan-trabajos-diarios. Aid was a one-time bonus of 380 soles ($106).

18. Kincaid (2020).

19. Chávez Yacila and Turkewitz (2020).

20. Kincaid (2020).

21. Kallis et al. (2020).

22. Noriega (2020).

23. Rondón (2020).

24. Paulson (2020).

25. Clifford (2013), 7.

26. Minería de Todos (2019).

# Bibliography

Abercrombie, Tom. 1998. *Pathways of Memory and Power: Ethnography and History Among an Andean People*. Madison: University of Wisconsin Press.

Abers, Rebecca. 2000. *Inventing Local Democracy: Grassroots Politics in Brazil*. Boulder, CO: Lynne Rienner.

Ahmed, Sara. 2004. "Affective Economies." *Social Text* 22 (2): 117–39.

———. 2010. "Happy Objects." In *The Affect Theory Reader*, ed. Melissa Gregg and Gregory Seigworth, 29–51. Durham, NC: Duke University Press.

Alberti, G., and E. Mayer. 1974. *Reciprocidad e intercambio en los Andes peruanos*. Lima: Instituto de Estudios Peruanos.

Albó, Xavier. 1991. "El retorno del indio." *Revista Andina* 9 (2): 299–345.

Allen, Catherine. 2002. *The Hold Life Has: Coca and Cultural Identity in an Andean Community*, 2nd ed. Washington, DC: Smithsonian Press.

———. 2016. "The Living Ones: Miniatures and Animation in the Andes." *Journal of Anthropological Research* 72 (4): 416–41.

Amengual, Matthew. 2018. "Buying Stability: The Distributive Outcomes of Private Politics in the Bolivian Mining Industry." *World Development* 104: 31–45.

Andolina, Robert, Nina Laurie, and Sarah Radcliffe. 2009. *Indigenous Development in the Andes: Culture, Power, and Transnationalism*. Durham, NC: Duke University Press.

Anguelovski, Isabelle. 2011. "Understanding the Dynamics of Community Engagement of Corporations in Communities: The Iterative Relationship Between Dialogue Processes and Local Protest at the Tintaya Copper Mine in Peru." *Society and Natural Resources* 24 (4): 384–99.

Appel, Hannah. 2019. *The Licit Life of Capitalism: U.S. Oil in Equatorial Guinea*. Durham, NC: Duke University Press.

Arellano-Yanguas, Javier. 2011. "Aggravating the Resource Curse: Decentralization, Mining, and Conflict in Peru." *Journal of Development Studies* 47 (4): 617–38.

Aretxaga, Begonia. 2000. "A Fictional Reality: Paramilitary Death Squads and the Construction of State Terror in Spain." In *Death Squad: The Anthropology of State Terror*, ed. Jeffrey A. Sluka, 46–69. Philadelphia, PA: University of Pennsylvania Press.

Aronczyk, Melissa. 2018. "Foreword." In *Branding Latin America: Strategies, Aims, Resistance*, ed. Dunja Fehimovic and Rebecca Ogden, ix–xiii. Lanham, MD: Lexington.

Asad, Talal. 1995. *Anthropology and the Colonial Encounter*. Washington, DC: Rowman & Littlefield.

Babb, Florence. 1996. "After the Revolution: Neoliberal Policy and Gender in Nicaragua." *Latin American Perspectives* 23 (1): 27–48.

———. 2011. *The Tourism Encounter: Fashioning Latin American Nations and Histories*. Stanford, CA: Stanford University Press.

———. 2018. *Women's Place in the Andes: Engaging Decolonial Feminist Anthropology*. Berkeley: University of California Press.

———. 2020. "'The Real Indigenous Are Higher Up': Locating Race and Gender in Andean Peru." *Latin American and Caribbean Ethnic Studies*, 1–22. doi:10.1080/17442222 .2020.1809080.

Ballestero, Andrea. 2012. "Transparency Short-Circuited: Laughter and Numbers in Costa Rican Water Politics." *PoLAR: Political and Legal Anthropology Review* 35 (2): 223–41.

Banner, Jessica. 2020. "Bodies of Colour as Bodies of Resistance: Affective Intermediaries and Gelatinous Collision in *The Woman of Colour*." *Journal of Literary and Cultural Studies* 1 (1): 13–20.

Bataille, Georges. 1991. *The Accursed Share: An Essay on General Economy*, Vol. 1, *Consumption*, trans. Robert Hurley. New York: Zone.

Bear, Laura. 2015. *Navigating Austerity: Currents of Debt Along a South Asian River*. Stanford, CA: Stanford University Press.

Bear, Laura, Karen Ho, Anna Lowenhaupt Tsing, and Sylvia Yanagisako. 2015. "Gens: A Feminist Manifesto for the Study of Capitalism." Blog post, *Theorizing the Contemporary, Fieldsights*, March 30. https://culanth.org/fieldsights/gens-a-feminist-manifesto -for-the-study-of-capitalism.

Beck, Erin. 2017. *How Development Projects Persist: Everyday Negotiations with Guatemalan NGOs*. Durham, NC: Duke University Press.

Benavides, María. 1983. "Two Traditional Andean Peasant Communities Under the Stress of Market Penetration: Yanque and Madrigal in the Colca Valley, Peru." Master's thesis, University of Texas, Austin. (Gerardo Huaracha Archive)

———. 1989. "Las visitas a yanque collaguas de los siglos XVI y XVII: Organización social y tenencia de tierras." *Bulletin Institute Frances et Andines* 18 (2): 241–67. (Gerardo Huaracha Archive)

———. 1994. "The Franciscan Church of Yanque (Arequipa) and Andean Culture." *The Americas* L3: 419–36. (Gerardo Huaracha Archive)

———. 1998. "Las batallas de Chachayllo: La lucha por el agua de riego en el Valle del Colca (Arequipa, Perú)." *Espacio y Desarrollo* 10: 78–93. (Gerardo Huaracha Archive)

Berlant, Lauren. 2011. *Cruel Optimism*. Durham, NC: Duke University Press.

Bidwell, Simon. 2020. "Cultivating What Is Ours: Local Agro-Food Heritage as a Development Strategy in the Peruvian Andes." PhD diss., Victoria University of Wellington, Wellington, New Zealand.

Bolin, Inge. 1994. "Levels of Autonomy in the Organization of Irrigation in the Highlands of Peru." In *Irrigation at High Altitudes: The Social Organization of Water Control Systems in the Andes*, ed. William P. Mitchell and David Guillet, 141–66. Washington, DC: Society for Latin American Anthropology and the American Anthropological Association.

Bolin, Inge. 1998. *Rituals of Respect: The Secret of Survival in the High Peruvian Andes*. Austin: University of Texas Press.

Bornstein, Erica. 2005. *The Spirit of Development: Protestant NGOs, Morality, and Economics in Zimbabwe*. Stanford, CA: Stanford University Press.

Bourdieu, Pierre. 1984. *Distinction*, trans. Richard Nice. Cambridge, MA: Harvard University Press.

Bowcott, Owen. 2017. "U.K. Mining Firm in Court over Claims It Mistreated Environmental Activists." *The Guardian*, October 31. https://www.theguardian.com/business/2017/oct/31/uk-mining-firm-in-court-over-claims-it-mistreated-environmental-activists.

Brown, Stephen. 2019. "Foreign Aid, the Mining Sector, and Democratic Ownership: The Case of Canadian Assistance to Peru." *Development Policy Review* 38 (S1): O13–O31.

Brown, Wendy. 2015. *Undoing the Demos: Neoliberalism's Stealth Revolution*. New York: Zone.

Brown Swiss Association. 2018. "Breed Attributes." https://www.brownswissusa.com/Breed/BrownSwissBreed/BreedAttributes/tabid/175/Default.aspx.

Bunker, Stephen G. 1985. *Underdeveloping the Amazon: Extraction, Unequal Exchange, and the Failure of the Modern State*. Chicago: University of Chicago Press.

Bury, Jeffrey. 2005. "Mining Mountains: Neoliberalism, Land Tenure, Livelihoods, and the New Peruvian Mining Industry in Cajamarca." *Environment and Planning A* 37: 221–39.

Byrd, Jodi A. 2011. *The Transit of Empire: Indigenous Critiques of Colonialism*. Minneapolis: University of Minnesota Press.

Caine, Allison. 2021. "'Who Would Watch the Animals?' Gendered Knowledge and Expert Performance Among Andean Pastoralists." *Culture, Agriculture, Food, and Environment*, 1–10. https://doi.org/10.1111/cuag.12261.

Callirgos, Juan Carlos. 2018. "Neoliberal Discourses and Ethnonormative Regime in Post-Recognition Peru: Redefining Hierarchies and Identities." *Cultural Studies* 32 (3): 477–96.

Callon, Michel. 1998. "Introduction: The Embeddedness of Economic Markets in Economics." *The Sociological Review* 46 (1, suppl): 1–57.

Cameron, John. 2009. "'Development Is a Bag of Cement': The Infrapolitics of Participatory Budgeting in the Andes." *Development in Practice* 19 (6): 692–701.

Cánepa, Gisela. 2014. "Peruanos en Nebraska: Una propuesta de lectura crítica del spot publicitario de Marca Perú." In *Sensibilidad de frontera: Comunicación y voces populares*, ed. Abelardo Sánchez León, 207–35. Lima: Fondo Editorial, PUCP.

————. 2018. "La paisana jacinta: Pensar la relación entre representación y discriminación racial." *Intercambio* 41. https://intercambio.pe/la-paisana-jacinta-pensar-la-relacion-representacion-discriminacion-racial/.

Castañeda, Claudia. 2002. *Figurations: Child, Bodies, Worlds*. Durham, NC: Duke University Press.

CEPLAN. 2017. *Información departamental, provincial y distrital de población que requiere atención adicional y devengado per cápita: Perú*. Lima: Centro Nacional de Planeamiento Estratégico. https://www2.congreso.gob.pe/sicr/cendocbib/con5_uibd.nsf/8CB9B-B79495ACE5F052582780056A821/$FILE/Informaci%C3%B3n-departamental-provincial-distrital-al-31-de-diciembre-VF.pdf.

Cervantes, María. 2019. "Indigenous Groups in Peru Are Suing Government over Oil, Mining Plans—and Winning." *Reuters*, June 27. https://www.reuters.com/article/us-peru-indigenous/indigenous-groups-in-peru-are-suing-government-over-oil-mining-plans-and-winning-idUSKCN1TS240.

Chakrabarty, Dipesh. 2000. *Provincializing Europe: Postcolonial Thought and Historical Difference*. Princeton, NJ: Princeton University Press.

Chávez, Susana, and Anna-Britt Coe. 2007. "Emergency Contraception in Peru: Shifting Government and Donor Policies and Influences." *Reproductive Health Matters* 15 (29): 139–48.

Chávez Yacila, Rosa, and Julie Turkewitz. 2020. "Highways of Peru Swell with Families Fleeing Virus." *New York Times*, April 30. https://www.nytimes.com/2020/04/30/world/americas/20virus-peru-migration.html.

Chertkovskaya, Ekaterina, and Alexander Paulsson. 2016. "The Growthocene: Thinking Through What Degrowth Is Criticising." Blog post, *Entitle Blog: A Collaborative Writing Project on Political Ecology*. https://entitleblogdotorg3.wordpress.com/2016/02/19/the-growthocene-thinking-through-what-degrowth-is-criticising/.

Chong, Kimberly. 2018. *Best Practice: Management Consulting and the Ethics of Financialization in China*. Durham, NC: Duke University Press.

Choy, Tim. 2010. *Ecologies of Comparison: An Ethnography of Endangerment in Hong Kong*. Durham, NC: Duke University Press.

Clifford, James. 2013. *Returns: Becoming Indigenous in the Twenty-First Century*. Cambridge, MA: Harvard University Press.

Colloredo-Mansfeld, Rudi. 1999. *The Native Leisure Class: Consumption and Cultural Creativity in the Andes*. Chicago: University of Chicago Press.

Comisión de la Verdad y Reconciliación. 2003. *Informe final de la Comisión de Verdad y Reconciliación*. Lima: CVR.

Comunidad de Indígenas de Yanque. 1961. "Libro de actas de la Comunidad de Indígenas de Yanque: Acta de fundación de la comunidad Indígena del distrito de Yanque." April 26, 1961. (Gerardo Huaracha Archive)

Condé, Marta, and Philippe Le Billon. 2017. "Why Do Some Communities Resist Mining Projects While Others Do Not?" *Extractive Industries and Society* 4 (3): 681–97.

Condori Mamani, Gregorio, and Asunta Quispe Huamán. 1996. *Andean Lives*, ed. Ricardo Valderrama Fernandez and Carmen Escalante Gutierrez; trans. Paul Gelles and Gabriela Martinez Escobar. Austin: University of Texas Press.

Congreso de la República. 2011. *Ley no. 29785: Ley del derecho a la consulta previa a los pueblos indígenas u originarios, reconocido en el convenio 169 de la Organización Internacional del Trabajo (OIT)*. https://sinia.minam.gob.pe/normas/ley-derecho-consulta-previa -pueblos-indigenas-originarios-reconocido.

Cook, Noble David. 2007. *The People of the Volcano: Andean Counterpoint in the Colca Valley of Peru*. Durham, NC: Duke University Press.

Cookson, Tara Patricia. 2018. *Unjust Conditions: Women's Work and the Hidden Cost of Cash Transfer Programs*. Berkeley: University of California Press.

Cooper, Melinda. 2020. "Anti-Austerity on the Far Right." In *Mutant Neoliberalism: Market Rule and Political Rupture*, ed. William Callison and Zachary Manfredi, 112–45. New York: Fordham University Press.

CooperAcción. 2016. "Espinar—Noviembre 2016." http://cooperaccion.org.pe/mapas/?region=espinar&reg=cusco&provincia=espinar.

Cruikshank, Barbara. 1999. *The Will to Empower: Democratic Citizens and Other Subjects*. Ithaca, NY: Cornell University Press.

Cuevas Calderon, Elder Alejandro. 2015. "Perú INC: La pugna por una nación a partir del Nation Branding." Master's thesis, Pontificia Universidad Católica del Perú, Lima.

Cummins, Tom. 2002. "Forms of Andean Colonial Towns, Free Will, and Marriage." In *The Archaeology of Colonialism*, ed. Claire Lyons and John Papadopoulos, 199–240. Los Angeles: Getty Research Institute.

D'Argenio, Maria Chiara. 2013. "A Contemporary Andean Type: The Representation of the Indigenous World in Claudia Llosa's Films." *Latin American and Caribbean Ethnic Studies* 8 (1): 20–42.

Das, Veena, and Deborah Poole, eds. 2004. *Anthropology in the Margins of the State*. Santa Fe: School of American Research Press.

De Echave, José, Alejandro Diez, Ludwig Huber, Bruno Revesz, Xavier Ricard Lanata, and Martín Tanaka. 2009. *Minería y conflicto social*. Lima: Instituto de Estudios Peruanos, Centro de Investigación y Promoción del Campesinado; Centro Bartolomé de Las Casas; and Consorcio de Investigación Económica y Social.

De la Cadena, Marisol. 2000. *Indigenous Mestizos: The Politics of Race and Culture in Cuzco, Peru, 1919–1991*. Durham, NC: Duke University Press.

———. 2010. "Indigenous Cosmopolitics in the Andes: Conceptual Reflections Beyond Politics." *Cultural Anthropology* 25 (2): 334–70.

———. 2015. *Earth Beings: Ecologies of Practice Across Andean Worlds*. Durham, NC: Duke University Press.

De la Serna Torroba, Juan, Jorge Luis Chávez Marroquín, and Jessica María Dulanto Martinez. 2016. *Programa de vivienda rural y desarrollo social en el Valle del Colca*. Lima: Programa de Cooperación Hispano Peruano.

De Soto, Hernando. 2000. *The Mystery of Capital: Why Capitalism Triumphs in the West and Fails Everywhere Else*. New York: Basic Books.

Deere, Carmen Diana. 1982. "The Division of Labor by Sex in Agriculture: A Peruvian Case Study." *Economic Development and Cultural Change* 30 (4): 795–811.

DeHart, Monica C. 2010. *Ethnic Entrepreneurs: Identity and Development Politics in Latin America*. Stanford, CA: Stanford University Press.

Derechos Sin Fronteras. 2017. "Espinar: 'Hatun K'ana tinkuy,' día internacional de los pueblos originarios." August 9. https://derechosinfronteras.pe/espinar-hatun-kana-tin-kuy-dia-internacional-de-los-pueblos-originarios/.

Desco (Center for Studies and Promotion of Development). 2012. "Development of Young Entrepreneurs and the Generation of Self-Employment in Caylloma Province, Arequipa." Institutional Project Proposal to Fondoempleo. Lima: Desco.

———. 2014. *Promoción de emprendimientos en Lari*. March 10. https://www.youtube.com/watch?v=hFU29WuJWag.

———. n.d. "Sistematización: Emprendimientos juveniles en el Valle del Colca—Arequipa. Linde, Mayo del 2014." Linde: Desco.

Diario El Pueblo. 2017. *Se redujo la pobreza a la mitad en el distrito de Tuti*. April 25. https://www.youtube.com/watch?v=7cQaM5obVAw.

Distrito.pe. 2020. "Ciudades y distritos del Perú." https://www.distrito.pe.

Drinot, Paulo. 2011. *The Allure of Labor: Workers, Race, and the Making of the Peruvian State*. Durham, NC: Duke University Press.

Elyachar, Julia. 2012. "Next Practices: Knowledge, Infrastructure, and Public Goods at the Bottom of the Pyramid." *Public Culture* 24 (1): 109–29.

Escobar, Arturo. 1995. *Encountering Development: The Making and Unmaking of the Third World*. Princeton, NJ: Princeton University Press.

———. 1999. "After Nature: Steps to an Antiessentialist Political Ecology." *Current Anthropology* 40 (1): 1–30.

Estes, Nick, and Jaskiran Dhillon, eds. 2019. *Standing with Standing Rock: Voices from the #NoDAPL Movement*. Minneapolis: University of Minnesota Press.

Evans-Pritchard, E. E. 1969. *The Nuer: A Description of the Modes of Livelihood and Political Institutions of a Nilotic People*. Oxford, UK: Clarendon Press.

Farbotko, Carol. 2010. "Wishful Sinking: Disappearing Islands, Climate Refugees, and Cosmopolitan Experimentation." *Asia Pacific Viewpoint* 51 (1): 47–60.

Farthing, Linda, and Nicole Fabricant. 2018. "Introduction: Open Veins Revisited—Charting the Social, Economic, and Political Contours of the New Extractivism in Latin America." *Latin American Perspectives* 45 (5): 4–17.

Femenías, Blenda. 1991. "Regional Dress of the Colca Valley, Peru: A Dynamic Tradition." In *Textile Traditions of Mesoamerica and the Andes: An Anthology*, ed. Margot Blum Schevill, Janet Catherine Berlo, and Edward B. Dwyer, 179–204. Austin: University of Texas Press.

———. 2005. *Gender and the Boundaries of Dress in Contemporary Peru*. Austin: University of Texas Press.

Ferguson, James. 1990. *The Anti-Politics Machine: "Development," Depoliticization, and Bureaucratic Power in Lesotho*. Minneapolis: University of Minnesota Press.

———. 2015. *Give a Man a Fish: Reflections on the New Politics of Distribution*. Durham, NC: Duke University Press.

Flores Galindo, Alberto. 2010. *In Search of an Inca: Identity and Utopia in the Andes*, trans. Carlos Aguierre, Charles Walker, and Willie Hiatt. Cambridge, UK: Cambridge University Press.

Fondesurco. 2014. "FONDESURCO: Primeros en inclusión financiera." http://www.fondesurco.org.pe/Noticias/PrimerosInclusionFinanciera/Inclusion.php.

Foucault, Michel. 1991. "Governmentality." In *The Foucault Effect: Studies in Governmentality*, ed. Graham Burchell, Colin Gordon, and Peter Miller, 87–104. Chicago: University of Chicago Press.

———. 1995. *Discipline and Punish: The Birth of the Prison*, trans. Alan Sheridan. New York: Vintage.

Freeman, Carla. 2000. *High Tech and High Heels in the Global Economy: Women, Work, and Pink-Collar Identities in the Caribbean*. Durham, NC: Duke University Press.

———. 2014. *Entrepreneurial Selves: Neoliberal Respectability and the Making of a Caribbean Middle Class*. Durham, NC: Duke University Press.

Galeano, Eduardo. 1973. *Open Veins of Latin America*, trans. Cedric Belfrage. New York: Monthly Review Press.

Gamu, Jonathan Kishen, and Peter Dauvergne. 2018. "The Slow Violence of Corporate Social Responsibility: The Case of Mining in Peru." *Third World Quarterly* 39 (5): 959–75.

García, Maria Elena. 2005. *Making Indigenous Citizens: Identities, Education, and Multicultural Development in Peru*. Stanford, CA: Stanford University Press.

———. 2021. *Gastropolitics and the Specter of Race: Stories of Capital, Culture, and Coloniality in Peru*. Berkeley: University of California Press.

García Pérez, Alan. 2007. "El síndrome del perro del hortelano." *El Comercio*, October 28, https://archivo.elcomercio.pe/edicionimpresa/Html/2007-10-28/el_sindrome_del_perro_del_hort.html.

Gelles, Paul. 1994. "Channels of Power, Fields of Contention: The Politics of Irrigation and Land Recovery in an Andean Peasant Community." In *Irrigation at High Altitudes: The Social Organization of Water Control Systems in the Andes*, ed. William P. Mitchell and David Guillet, 233–74. Washington, DC: Society for Latin American Anthropology and the American Anthropological Association.

———. 2000. *Water and Power in Highland Peru: The Cultural Politics of Irrigation*. New Brunswick, NJ: Rutgers University Press.

Gershon, Ilana. 2019. "Porous Social Orders." *American Ethnologist* 46 (4): 404–16.

Gestión. 2017. "Ingresos por canon minero en los gobiernos regionales y locales aumentaron 24.4% a Julio." *Gestión*, August 1. https://gestion.pe/economia/ingresos-canon-minero-gobiernos-regionales-locales-aumentaron-24-4-julio-140691-noticia/.

———. 2019. "Regiones y municipios recibirán adelanto de s/ 1,500 millones por canon minero." *Gestión*, February 6. https://gestion.pe/economia/regiones-municipios-recibiran-adelanto-s-1-500-millones-canon-minero-257954-noticia/.

Gibson-Graham, J. K. 2006. *The End of Capitalism (As We Knew It): A Feminist Critique of Political Economy*. Minneapolis: University of Minnesota Press.

Gil Ramón, Vladimir. 2020. *Fighting for Andean Resources: Extractive Industries, Cultural Politics, and Environmental Struggles in Peru*. Tucson: University of Arizona Press.

Gillespie, Kathryn. 2013. "Sexualized Violence and the Gendered Commodification of the Animal Body in Pacific Northwest U.S. Dairy Production." *Gender, Place, and Culture: A Journal of Feminist Geography* 21 (10): 1321–37.

Glencore. 2016. "Sustainability Report 2015." https://www.glencore.com/dam/jcr: 6fd34880–265c-4644-8208-220b29476a45/2015-Sustainability-report.pdf.

Goldstein, Jenny Elaine, and Julian Yates. 2017. "Introduction: Rendering Land Investable." *Geoforum* 82: 209–11.

Gómez-Barris, Macarena. 2017. *The Extractive Zone: Social Ecologies and Decolonial Perspectives*. Durham, NC: Duke University Press.

Gose, Peter. 1994. *Deathly Waters and Hungry Mountains: Agrarian Ritual and Class Formation in an Andean Town*. Toronto: University of Toronto Press.

———. 2008. *Invaders as Ancestors: On the Intercultural Making and Unmaking of Spanish Colonialism in the Andes*. Toronto: University of Toronto Press.

———. 2018. "The Semi-Social Mountain: Metapersonhood and Political Ontology in the Andes." *Hau: Journal of Ethnographic Theory* 8 (3): 488–505.

Govindrajan, Radhika. 2018. *Animal Intimacies: Interspecies Relatedness in India's Central Himalayas*. Chicago: University of Chicago Press.

Graeter, Stefanie. 2020. "Infrastructural Incorporations: Toxic Storage, Corporate Indemnity, and Ethical Deferral in Peru's Neoextractive Era." *American Anthropologist* 122(1): 21–36.

Graham, Laura. 2002. "How Should an Indian Speak? Amazonian Indians and the Symbolic Politics of Language in the Global Public Sphere." In *Indigenous Movements, Self Representation, and the State in Latin America*, ed. Kay B. Warren and Jean E. Jackson, 181–228. Austin: University of Texas Press.

———. 2005. "Image and Instrumentality in a Xavante Politics of Existential Recognition: The Public Outreach Work of Eténhiritipa Pimentel Barbosa." *American Anthropologist* 32 (4): 622–41.

Graham, Laura, and H. Glenn Penny. 2014. *Performing Indigeneity: Global Histories and Contemporary Experiences*. Lincoln: University of Nebraska Press.

Greene, Shane. 2009. *Customizing Indigeneity: Paths to a Visionary Politics in Peru*. Stanford, CA: Stanford University Press.

Grillo Fernandez, Eduardo. 1998. "Development or Cultural Affirmation in the Andes?" In *The Spirit of Regeneration: Andean Culture Confronting Western Notions of Development*, ed. Frédérique Apffel-Marglin and Proyecto Andino de Tecnologías Campesinas, 124–45. London: Zed Books.

Guillet, David. 1994. "Canal Irrigation and the State: The 1969 Water Law and Irrigation Systems of the Colca Valley of Southwestern Peru." In *Irrigation at High Altitudes: The Social Organization of Water Control Systems in the Andes*, ed. William P. Mitchell and David Guillet, 167–88. Washington, DC: Society for Latin American Anthropology and the American Anthropological Association.

Günel, Gökçe. 2019. *Spaceship in the Desert: Energy, Climate Change, and Urban Design in Abu Dhabi*. Durham, NC: Duke University Press.

Guyer, Jane I. 2007. "Prophecy and the Near Future: Thoughts on Macroeconomic, Evangelical, and Punctuated Time." *American Ethnologist* 34 (3): 409–21.

Hagan, Paul. 1979. "Qué espera el campesino cayllomino del sacerdote?" Paper presented at the 4th Congreso del Hombre y la Cultura Andina, Cusco. Document 050700025#35, Archive of the UCSM-Museo de Yanque.

Hale, Charles R. 2004. "Rethinking Indigenous Politics in the Era of the 'Indio Permitido.'" *NACLA Report on the Americas* 38 (2): 16–21.

Han, Lisa. 2019. "The Blue Frontier: Temporalities of Salvage and Extraction at the Seabed." *Configurations* 27 (4): 463–81.

Haraway, Donna. 2018. *Modest_Witness@Second_Millennium: FemaleMan©_Meets_Onco-MouseTM*, 2nd ed. London: Routledge.

Harvey, Penelope. 2005. "The Materiality of State-Effects: An Ethnography of a Road in the Peruvian Andes." In *State Formation: Anthropological Perspectives*, ed. Christian Krohn-Hansen and Knut G. Nustad, 123–41. London: Pluto Press.

———. 2010. "Cementing Relations: The Materiality of Roads and Public Spaces in Provincial Peru." *Social Analysis* 54 (2): 28–46.

Hetherington, Kregg. 2011. *Guerrilla Auditors: The Politics of Transparency in Neoliberal Paraguay*. Durham, NC: Duke University Press.

Himley, Matthew. 2012. "Regularizing Extraction in Andean Peru: Mining and Social Mobilization in an Age of Corporate Social Responsibility." *Antipode* 45 (2): 394–416.

Hirsch, Eric. 2018. "Remapping the Vertical Archipelago: Mobility, Migration, and the Everyday Labor of Andean Development." *Journal of Latin American and Caribbean Anthropology* 23 (1): 189–208.

———. 2020a. "Ethnicity as Potential: Abundance, Competition, and the Limits of Development in Andean Peru's Colca Valley." In *Ethnicity, Commodity, In/Corporation*, ed. George Paul Meiu, Jean Comaroff, and John L. Comaroff, 94–119. Bloomington: Indiana University Press.

———. 2020b. "Hidden Treasures: Marca Perú (Peru™) and the Recoding of Neoliberal Sustainability in the Peruvian Andes." *Latin American and Caribbean Ethnic Studies* 15 (3): 245–69.

Ho, Karen. 2009. *Liquidated: An Ethnography of Wall Street*. Durham, NC: Duke University Press.

Hobsbawm, Eric, and Terence Ranger, eds. 1983. *The Invention of Tradition*. Cambridge, UK: Cambridge University Press.

Hochschild, Arlie Russell. 1983. *The Managed Heart: Commercialization of Human Feeling*. Berkeley: University of California Press.

Hodgson, Geoffrey M. 2005. "Decomposition and Growth: Biological Metaphors in Economics from the 1880s to the 1980s." In *The Evolutionary Foundations of Economics*, ed. Kurt Dopfer, 105–48. Cambridge, UK: Cambridge University Press.

Hoover, Elizabeth. 2017. *The River Is in Us: Fighting Toxics in a Mohawk Community*. Minneapolis: University of Minnesota Press.

Huang, Julia Qermezi. 2016. "Do It Yourself Development: Ambiguity and Relational Work in a Bangladesh Social Enterprise." PhD diss., London School of Economics, London.

——. 2020. *To Be an Entrepreneur: Social Enterprise and Disruptive Development in Bangladesh*. Ithaca, NY: Cornell University Press.

Huff, James. 2014. "Pentecostalized Development and Novel Social Imaginaries in Rural El Salvador." *Journal of Latin American and Caribbean Anthropology* 19 (1): 22–40.

IFAD (International Fund for Agricultural Development). 2018. "Empowering People to Lead Their Own Development." https://www.ifad.org/en/approach.

INEI (Instituto Nacional de Estadística e Informática). 2014. *Estado de la población peruana 2014*. Lima: INEI.

——. 2020. *Mapa de pobreza monetaria provincial y distrital 2018*. Lima: INEI.

Isbell, Billie Jean. 1985. *To Defend Ourselves: Ecology and Ritual in an Andean Village*. Prospect Heights, IL: Waveland Press.

Jackson, Jean E. 2019. *Managing Multiculturalism: Indigeneity and the Struggle for Rights in Colombia*. Stanford, CA: Stanford University Press.

Jacobs, Jane. 1961. *The Death and Life of Great American Cities*. New York: Random House.

Kallis, Giorgos, Susan Paulson, Giacomo D'Alisa, and Federico Demaria. 2020. "The Case for Degrowth in a Time of Pandemic." Blog post, *Open Democracy*, May 14. https://www.opendemocracy.net/en/oureconomy/case-degrowth-time-pandemic/.

Kar, Sohini. 2018. *Financializing Poverty: Labor and Risk in Indian Microfinance*. Stanford, CA: Stanford University Press.

Kimmerer, Robin Wall. 2015. *Braiding Sweetgrass: Indigenous Wisdom, Scientific Knowledge, and the Teachings of Plants*. Minneapolis: Milkweed Editions.

Kincaid, Jake. 2020. "Despite Early, Strict Quarantine Measures, Peru Has Worst Covid-19 Death Rate In the World." *Miami Herald*, September 10, https://www.miamiherald.com/news/nation-world/world/americas/article245600805.html.

Krippner, Greta A. 2011. *Capitalizing on Crisis: The Political Origins of the Rise of Finance*. Cambridge, MA: Harvard University Press.

Kwon, June Hee. 2015. "The Work of Waiting: Love and Money in Korean Chinese Transnational Migration." *Cultural Anthropology* 30 (3): 477–500.

Larson, Brooke. 2014. "Indigeneity Unpacked: Politics, Civil Society, and Social Movements in the Andes." *Latin American Research Review* 49 (1): 223–41.

Lashaw, Amanda, Christien Vannier, and Steven Sampson. 2017. *Cultures of Doing Good: Anthropologists and NGOs*. Tuscaloosa: University of Alabama Press.

Lefebvre, Henri. 1991. *The Production of Space*, trans. Donald Nicholson-Smith. Malden, MA: Blackwell.

Leinaweaver, Jessica. 2008. "On Moving Children: The Social Implications of Andean Child Circulation." *American Ethnologist* 34 (1): 163–80.

Li, Fabiana. 2009. "Documenting Accountability: Environmental Impact Assessment in a Peruvian Mining Project." *PoLAR: Political and Legal Anthropology Review* 32 (2): 218–36.

———. 2015. *Unearthing Conflict: Corporate Mining, Activism, and Expertise in Peru*. Durham, NC: Duke University Press.

Li, Tania Murray. 2007. *The Will to Improve: Governmentality, Development, and the Practice of Politics*. Durham, NC: Duke University Press.

———. 2014. *Land's End: Capitalist Relations on an Indigenous Frontier*. Durham, NC: Duke University Press.

Llosa, Hector, and María A. Benavides. 1994. "Arquitectura y vivienda campesina en tres pueblos andinos: Yanque, Lari y Coporaque en el Valle del Río Colca, Arequipa." *Bulletin Institute Frances et Andines* 23 (1): 105–50. (Gerardo Huaracha Archive)

Lossio Chávez, Felix. 2018. "The Counter-Narratives of Nation Branding: The Case of Peru." In *Branding Latin America: Strategies, Aims, Resistance*, ed. Dunja Fehimovic and Rebecca Ogden, 59–78. Lanham, MD: Lexington.

Love, Thomas. 2017. *The Independent Republic of Arequipa: Making Regional Culture in the Andes*. Austin: University of Texas Press.

Lowe, Lisa. 2015. *The Intimacies of Four Continents*. Durham, NC: Duke University Press.

MacKenzie, Donald. 2008. *An Engine, Not a Camera: How Financial Models Shape Markets*. Cambridge, MA: MIT Press.

Málaga Sabogal, Ximena, and María Eugenia Ulfe. 2017. "Ethnicity Claims and Prior Consultation in the Peruvian Andes." In *Resource Booms and Institutional Pathways*, ed. E. Dargent, J. C. Orihuela, M. Paredes, and M. E. Ulfe, 153–73. London: Palgrave.

Maldonado-Torres, Nelson. 2007. "On the Coloniality of Being: Contributions to the Development of a Concept." *Cultural Studies* 21 (2–3): 240–70.

Mannheim, Bruce, and Krista van Vleet. 1998. "The Dialogics of Southern Quechua Narrative." *American Anthropologist* 100 (2): 326–46.

Manrique, Nelson. 1985. *Colonialismo y pobreza campesina: Caylloma y el Valle del Colca, siglos XVI–XX*. Lima: Desco.

Martinez Novo, Carmen. 2014. "Managing Diversity in Postneoliberal Ecuador." *Journal of Latin American and Caribbean Anthropology* 19 (1): 103–25.

Marx, Karl. 1990. *Capital: A Critique of Political Economy*, vol. 1, trans. Ben Fowkes. London: Penguin.

Mauss, Marcel. 1990 [1925]. *The Gift*, trans. W. D. Hall. New York: Norton.

Mayer, Enrique. 1974. "Las reglas del juego en la reciprocidad andina." In *Reciprocidad e intercambio en los andes peruanos*, ed. G. Alberti and E. Mayer, 37–65. Lima: Instituto de Estudios Peruanos.

———. 2001. *The Articulated Peasant: Household Economies in the Andes*. New York: Perseus.

———. 2009. *Ugly Stories of the Peruvian Agrarian Reform*. Durham, NC: Duke University Press.

Mazzarella, William. 2003. *Shoveling Smoke: Advertising and Globalization in Contemporary India*. Durham, NC: Duke University Press.

McDonell, Emma. 2018. "The Quinoa Boom Goes Bust in the Andes." *NACLA Report on the Americas*, March 12. https://nacla.org/news/2018/03/12/quinoa-boom-goes-bust-andes.

MEF (Ministerio de Economía y Finanzas). 2015. "Transferencias a gobierno nacional, regional y locales." http://www.mef.gob.pe/index.php?option=com_content&view=article&id=454&Itemid=100959.

Mendoza, Zoila S. 1999. "Genuine but Marginal: Exploring and Reworking Social Contradictions Through Ritual Dance Performance." *Journal of Latin American Anthropology* 3 (2): 86–117.

Merriam Webster. 2021. "Salvage." https://www.merriam-webster.com/dictionary/salvage.

Mezzadra, Sandro, and Brett Neilson. 2015. "Operations of Capital." *South Atlantic Quarterly* 114 (1): 1–9.

Million, Dian. 2009. "Felt Theory: An Indigenous Feminist Approach to Affect and History." *Wicazo Sa Review* 24 (2): 53–76.

Minería de Todos. 2019. "Quienes somos?" Minería de Todos and Sociedad Nacional de Minería Petroleo y Energía. https://www.mineriadetodos.com.pe/quienes-somos (accessed June 5, 2020).

Ministerio de Cultura. 2020. "Búsqueda de localidades de pueblos indígenas." Base de datos de pueblos indígenas u originarios. https://bdpi.cultura.gob.pe/busqueda-de-localidades-de-pueblos-indigenas.

Ministerio de Trabajo y Asuntos Indígenas. 1965. "Resolución Suprema No. 387." October 25. (Gerardo Huaracha Archive)

Mirowski, Philip. 1989. *More Light than Heat: Economics as Social Physics, Physics as Nature's Economics*. Cambridge, UK: Cambridge University Press.

Mitchell, Timothy. 1991. "The Limits of the State: Beyond Statist Approaches and Their Critics." *American Political Science Review* 85 (1): 77–96.

———. 2009. "Carbon Democracy." *Economy and Society* 38 (3): 399–432.

Mitchell, William P., and David Guillet, eds. 1993. *Irrigation at High Altitudes: The Social Organization of Water Control Systems in the Andes*. Washington, DC: Society for Latin American Anthropology and the American Anthropological Association.

Moore, Jason. 2016. *Capitalism in the Web of Life: Ecology and the Accumulation of Capital*. London: Verso.

Morris, Craig. 2013. *El palacio, la plaza y la fiesta en el imperio inca*. Lima: Fondo Editorial, PUCP.

Morton, Gregory Duff. 2015. "Managing Transience: Bolsa Família and Its Subjects in an MST Landless Settlement." *Journal of Peasant Studies* 42 (6): 1283–1305.

Mosse, David. 2005. *Cultivating Development: An Ethnography of Aid Policy and Practice*. London: Pluto Press.

Mumford, Jeremy. 2012. *Vertical Empire: The General Resettlement of Indians in the Colonial Andes*. Durham, NC: Duke University Press.

Murphy, Michelle. 2015. "Unsettling Care: Troubling Transnational Itineraries of Care in Feminist Health Practices." *Social Studies of Science* 45 (5): 717–37.

———. 2017. *The Economization of Life*. Durham, NC: Duke University Press.

Murra, John. 1972. "El control vertical de un máximo de pisos ecológicos en las sociedades andinas." In *Formaciones económicas y políticas del mundo andino*, ed. John Murra, 59–115. Lima: Instituto de Estudios Peruanos.

Nash, June. 1993. *We Eat the Mines and the Mines Eat Us: Dependency and Exploitation in Bolivian Tin Mines*. New York: Columbia University Press.

Navaro-Yashin, Yael. 2002. *Faces of the State: Secularism and Public Life in Turkey*. Princeton, NJ: Princeton University Press.

———. 2012. *The Make-Believe Space: Affective Geography in a Postwar Polity*. Durham, NC: Duke University Press.

Newell, Peter. 2005. "Citizenship, Accountability, and Community: The Limits of the CSR Agenda." *International Affairs* 81 (3): 541–57.

Neyra, Gonzalo. 2017. *Descentralización y desarrollo regional: Balance de investigación en políticas públicas 2011–2016 y agenda de investigación 2017–2021*. Lima: Consorcio de Investigación Económica y Social.

Nixon, Rob. 2011. *Slow Violence and the Environmentalism of the Poor*. Cambridge, MA: Harvard University Press.

Noriega, Carlos. 2020. "Victor Zamora: 'lo ocurrido en esta pandemia expresa el fracaso del modelo neoliberal.'" *Quehacer* 6 (segunda etapa). http://revistaquehacer.pe/n6.

Oakdale, Suzanne. 2008. "The Commensality of 'Contact,' 'Pacification,' and Inter-Ethnic Relations in the Amazon: Kayabi Autobiographical Perspectives." *Journal of the Royal Anthropological Institute* 14 (4): 791–807.

Ocsa, Zacarías. 2013. *La guerra del agua*. Arequipa, Peru: Comercial Cueva Impresores EIRL.

Orellana Lopez, Aldo, and Philippa de Boissiére. 2014. "Glencore Xstrata and Corporate Power in Peru." *The Ecologist*. December 27. http://www.theecologist.org/News/news _analysis/2686355/glencore_xstrata_and_corporate_power_in_peru.html.

Orlove, Ben. 2002. *Lines in the Water: Nature and Culture at Lake Titicaca*. Berkeley: University of California Press.

Paerregaard, Karsten. 1994. "Why Fight over Water? Power, Conflict, and Irrigation in an Andean Village." In *Irrigation at High Altitudes: The Social Organization of Water Control Systems in the Andes*, ed. William P. Mitchell and David Guillet, 189–202. Washington, DC: Society for Latin American Anthropology and the American Anthropological Association.

———. 2017. "Ayni Unbounded: Cooperation, Inequality, and Migration in the Peruvian Andes." *Journal of Latin American and Caribbean Anthropology* 22 (3): 459–74.

Pajuelo Teves, Ramón. 2019. *Trayectorias comunales: Cambios y continuidades en comunidades campesinas e indígenas del sur andino*. Lima: Grupo Propuesta Ciudadana.

Paulson, Susan. 2006. "Body, Nation, and Consubstantiation in Bolivian Ritual Meals." *American Ethnologist* 33 (4): 650–64.

———. 2015. *Masculinities and Femininities in Latin America's Uneven Development*. London: Routledge.

———. 2017. "Degrowth: Culture, Power, and Change." *Journal of Political Ecology* 24: 425–48.

———. 2020. "Degrowth and Feminisms Ally to Forge Care-Full Paths Beyond Pandemic." *Interface* 12 (1): 232–46.

Peebles, Gustav. 2010. "The Anthropology of Credit and Debt." *Annual Review of Anthropology* 39: 225–40.

Peluso, Daniela. 2015. "Circulating Between Rural and Urban Communities: Multisited Dwellings in Amazonian Frontiers." *Journal of Latin American and Caribbean Anthropology* 20 (1): 57–79.

Perez, Francisco L. 1992. "The Ecological Impact of Cattle on Caulescent Andean Rosettes in a High Venezuelan Paramo." *Mountain Research and Development* 12 (1): 29–46.

Perreault, Tom. 2015. "Performing Participation: Mining, Power, and the Limits of Consultation in Bolivia." *Journal of Latin American and Caribbean Anthropology* 20 (3): 433–51.

Pine, Joseph, II, and James Gilmore. 2011. *The Experience Economy*. Cambridge, MA: Harvard Business Review Press.

Portocarrero, Gonzalo. 2007. *Racismo y mestizaje y otros ensayos*. Lima: Fondo Editorial del Congreso del Perú.

Postero, Nancy Grey. 2007. *Now We Are Citizens: Indigenous Politics in Postmulticultural Bolivia*. Stanford, CA: Stanford University Press.

Povinelli, Elizabeth A. 2002. *The Cunning of Recognition: Indigenous Alterities and the Making of Australian Multiculturalism*. Durham, NC: Duke University Press.

———. 2011. *Economies of Abandonment: Social Belonging and Endurance in Late Liberalism*. Durham, NC: Duke University Press.

PromPerú. 2017. "Peru, the Richest Country in the World." https://perutherichestcountry .peru.travel/en.

———. 2019. "Business." https://peru.info/en-us/business.

Puig de la Bellacasa, María. 2017. *Matters of Care: Speculative Ethics in More Than Human Worlds*. Minneapolis: University of Minnesota Press.

Quijano, Anibal. 2000. "Coloniality of Power, Eurocentrism, and Latin America," trans. Michael Ennis. *Nepantla* 1 (3): 533–80.

Radcliffe, Sarah. 2015. *Dilemmas of Difference: Indigenous Women and the Limits of Postcolonial Development Policy*. Durham, NC: Duke University Press.

Rafael, Vicente. 1988. *Contracting Colonialism: Translation and Christian Conversion in Tagalog Society Under Early Spanish Rule*. Ithaca, NY: Cornell University Press.

Ramos, Alcida Rita. 1994. "The Hyperreal Indian." *Critique of Anthropology* 14 (2): 153–71.

Rasmussen, Mattias Borg. 2016. "Tactics of the Governed: Figures of Abandonment in Andean Peru." *Journal of Latin American Studies* 49: 327–53.

Real Academia Española. 2019. "Cultura." https://dle.rae.es/cultura.

Riles, Annelise, ed. 2006. *Documents: Artifacts of Modern Knowledge*. Ann Arbor: University of Michigan Press.

Rivera Cusicanqui, Silvia. 2008. "Colonialism and Ethnic Resistance in Bolivia: A View from the Coca Markets." In *Empire and Dissent: The United States and Latin America*, ed. Fred Rosen, 137–61. Durham, NC: Duke University Press.

Robinson, Cedric J. 1983. *Black Marxism: The Making of the Black Radical Tradition*. Chapel Hill: University of North Carolina Press.

Robinson, David J. 2006. *Collaguas III: Yanque Collaguas-sociedad, economía y población, 1604–1617*. Lima: Fondo Editorial, PUCP.

Rofel, Lisa, and Sylvia J. Yanagisako. 2019. *Fabricating Transnational Capitalism: A Collaborative Ethnography of Italian-Chinese Global Fashion*. Durham, NC: Duke University Press.

Rojas-Downing, M. Melissa, A. Pouyan Nejadhashemi, Timothy Harrigan, and Sean A. Woznicki. 2017. "Climate Change and Livestock: Impacts, Adaptation, and Mitigation." *Climate Risk Management* 16: 145–63.

Rojas-Perez, Isaias. 2017. *Mourning Remains: State Atrocity, Exhumations, and Governing the Disappeared in Peru's Postwar Andes*. Stanford, CA: Stanford University Press.

Rondón, Martha B. 2020. "Covid-19: La mayoría quedará obsesiva, desconfiada y exhausta." *Quehacer* 6 (segunda etapa). http://revistaquehacer.pe/n6.

Ross, Michael L. 2001. "Does Oil Hinder Democracy?" *World Politics* 53 (3): 325–61.

Roy, Ananya. 2010. *Poverty Capital: Microfinance and the Making of Development*. London: Routledge.

Sahlins, Marshall. 2017. *Stone Age Economics*. London: Routledge.

Salas Carreño, Guillermo. 2014. "The Glacier, the Rock, the Image: Emotional Experience and Semiotic Diversity at the Quyllurit'i Pilgrimage (Cuzco, Peru)." *Signs and Society* 2 (suppl. 1): S188–S214.

———. 2020. "Indexicality and the Indigenization of Politics: Dancer-Pilgrims Protesting Mining Concessions in the Andes." *Journal of Latin American and Caribbean Anthropology* 25 (1): 7–27.

Salas Carreño, Guillermo, and Alejandro Diez Hurtado. 2018. "Estado, concesiones mineras y comuneros: Los múltiples conflictos alrededor de la minería en las inmediaciones del santuario de qoyllurit'i (Cusco, Perú)." *Colombia Internacional* 93: 65–91.

Salazar Parreñas, Juno. 2018. *Decolonizing Extinction: The Work of Care in Orangutan Rehabilitation*. Durham, NC: Duke University Press.

Salomon, Frank, and Mercedes Niño-Murcia. 2011. *The Lettered Mountain: A Peruvian Village's Way with Writing*. Durham, NC: Duke University Press.

Sánchez Dávila, Mario. 2019. "Grabando el prestigio social: Autoridades locales y uso político de la internet y el celular en la comunidad de Yanque (Caylloma, Arequipa)." *Anthropologica* 37 (42): 223–43.

Sassen, Saskia. 2014. *Expulsions: Brutality and Complexity in the Global Economy*. Cambridge, MA: Harvard University Press.

Sax, Mareika. 2018. "Southern Sacrifice and Northern Sorcery: Mountain Spirits and Encantos in the Peruvian Andes." In *Non-Humans in Amerindian South America: Ethnographies of Indigenous Cosmologies, Rituals, and Songs*, ed. Juan Javier Rivera Andía, 97–125. Oxford, UK: Berghahn Books.

Schuller, Mark. 2009. "Gluing Globalization: NGOs as Intermediaries in Haiti." *PoLAR: Political and Legal Anthropology Review* 32 (1): 84–104.

———. 2012. *Killing with Kindness: Haiti, International Aid, and NGOs*. New Brunswick, NJ: Rutgers University Press.

Schuster, Caroline. 2015. *Social Collateral: Women and Microfinance in Paraguay's Smuggling Economy*. Berkeley: University of California Press.

Schwittay, Anke. 2011. "The Financial Inclusion Assemblage: Subjects, Technics, Rationalities." *Critique of Anthropology* 31 (4): 381–401.

———. 2015. *New Media and International Development: Representation and Affect in Microfinance*. London: Routledge.

Scott, James. 1990. *Domination and the Arts of Resistance: Hidden Transcripts*. New Haven, CT: Yale University Press.

———. 1998. *Seeing Like a State: How Certain Schemes to Improve the Human Condition Have Failed*. New Haven, CT: Yale University Press.

Searle, Llerena Guiu. 2016. *Landscapes of Accumulation: Real Estate and the Neoliberal Imagination in Contemporary India*. Chicago: University of Chicago Press.

Sedgwick, Eve Kosofsky. 1990. *Epistemology of the Closet*. Berkeley: University of California Press.

Seemann, Miriam. 2016. *Water Security, Justice, and the Politics of Water Rights in Peru and Bolivia*. London: Palgrave Macmillan.

Seligmann, Linda J. 2004. *Peruvian Street Lives: Culture, Power, and Economy Among Market Women of Cuzco*. Champaign-Urbana: University of Illinois Press.

Sharma, Aradhana. 2008. *Logics of Empowerment: Development, Gender, and Governance in Neoliberal India*. Minneapolis: University of Minnesota Press.

Shepherd, Chris. 2004. "Agricultural Hybridity and the 'Pathology' of Traditional Ways: The Translation of Desire and Need in Postcolonial Development." *Journal of Latin American Anthropology* 9 (2): 235–66.

Sierra Sur. 2011. "Visión y misión." http://www.sierrasur.gob.pe/inicio/index.php?option=com_content&view=article&id=22&Itemid=34.

———. 2014a. "2013 Informe Anual." Oficina Local de Ichupampa.

———. 2014b. "Bases de concurso de resultados de iniciativas rurales en territorios." Oficina Local de Ichupampa.

Silverman, Helaine. 2015. "Branding Peru: Cultural Heritage and Popular Culture in the Marketing Strategy of PromPerú." In *Encounters with Popular Pasts: Cultural Heritage and Popular Culture*, ed. Mike Robinson and Helaine Silverman, 131–48. New York: Springer.

Silverstein, Michael. 1998. "The Uses and Utility of Ideology: A Commentary." In *Language Ideologies: Practice and Theory*, ed. B. B. Schieffelin and K. A. Woolard, 123–45. New York: Oxford University Press.

Simpson, Audra. 2014. *Mohawk Interruptus: Political Life Across the Borders of Settler States*. Durham, NC: Duke University Press.

Smith, Linda Tuhiwai. 2012. *Decolonizing Methodologies: Research and Indigenous Peoples*, 2nd ed. London: Zed Books.

Smith, Monica, ed. 2017. *Abundance: The Archaeology of Plenitude*. Boulder: University of Colorado Press.

Smith, Neil. 2010. *Uneven Development: Nature, Capital, and the Production of Space*. Athens: University of Georgia Press.

SNMPE (Sociedad Nacional de Minería, Petróleo y Energía). 2018. "Quienes somos?" https://www.snmpe.org.pe/.

Starn, Orin. 1991. "Missing the Revolution: Anthropologists and the War in Peru." *Cultural Anthropology* 6 (1): 63–91.

———. 1999. *Nightwatch: The Politics of Protest in the Andes*. Durham, NC: Duke University Press.

Stensrud, Astrid B. 2016. "Climate Change, Water Practices, and Relational Worlds in the Andes." *Ethnos* 81 (1): 75–98.

———. 2018. "Water as Resource and Being: Water Extractivism and Life Projects in Peru." In *Indigenous Life Projects and Extractivism: Ethnographies from South America*, ed. Cecile Vindal Ødegaard and Juan Javier Rivera Andía, 143–64. London: Palgrave Macmillan.

Stoler, Ann. 2004. "Affective States." In *A Companion to the Anthropology of Politics*, ed. David Nugent and Joan Vincent, 4–20. Oxford, UK: Blackwell.

Stout, Noelle. 2016. "Petitioning a Giant: Debt, Reciprocity, and Mortgage Modification in the Sacramento Valley." *American Ethnologist* 43 (1): 158–71.

Taj, Mitra. 2015. "Peru Gov't Says Applying Indigenous Rights Law in Mining Sector." *Reuters*, November 12. https://www.reuters.com/article/peru-mining-idAFL1N1353B320151112.

TallBear, Kim. 2019. "Caretaking Relations, not American Dreaming." *Kalfou* 6 (1): 24–41.

Tanaka, Martín. 2002. "Lima: Centralized Authority vs. the Struggle for Autonomy." In *Capital City Politics in Latin America: Democratization and Empowerment*, ed. David J. Myers and Henry A. Dietz, 193–226. Boulder, CO: Lynne Rienner.

Thomas, Deborah A. 2019. *Political Life in the Wake of the Plantation: Sovereignty, Witnessing, Repair*. Durham, NC: Duke University Press.

Todd, Zoe. 2018. "Refracting the State Through Human-Fish Relations: Fishing, Indigenous Legal Orders, and Colonialism in North/Western Canada." *Decolonization: Indigeneity, Education, and Society* 7 (1): 60–75.

Toledo, Francisco de. 1986 [1570]. *Disposiciones gubernativas para el virreinato del Perú, 1569–1574*," ed. Guillermo Lohmann Villena. Madrid: Consejo Superior de Investigaciones Científicas.

Trawick, Paul. 2001. "The Moral Economy of Water: Equity and Antiquity in the Andean Commons." *American Anthropologist* 103 (2): 361–79.

Treacy, John M. 1994. "Teaching Water: Hydraulic Management and Terracing in Coporaque, the Colca Valley, Peru." In *Irrigation at High Altitudes: The Social Organization of Water Control Systems in the Andes*, ed. William P. Mitchell and David Guillet, 99–114. Washington, DC: Society for Latin American Anthropology and the American Anthropological Association.

Tsing, Anna Lowenhaupt. 2000. "Inside the Economy of Appearances." *Public Culture* 12 (1): 115–44.

————. 2009. "Supply Chains and the Human Condition." *Rethinking Marxism* 21 (2): 148–76.

————. 2015a. *The Mushroom at the End of the World: On the Possibility of Life in Capitalist Ruins*. Princeton, NJ: Princeton University Press.

————. 2015b. "Salvage Accumulation, or the Structural Effects of Capitalist Generativity." Blog post, *Theorizing the Contemporary, Fieldsights*, March 30. https://culanth.org/fieldsights/salvage-accumulation-or-the-structural-effects-of-capitalist-generativity.

Tubb, Daniel. 2020. *Shifting Livelihoods: Gold Mining and Subsistence in the Chocó, Colombia*. Seattle: University of Washington Press.

UGEL (Unidad de Gestión Educativa Local-Caylloma). 2019. "Invitación a II.EE para visitar la 'Casa Abierta Chivay—2019' en el marco de la campaña minería de todos promovida por la Sociedad Nacional de Minería." Letter. https://ugelcaylloma.blogspot.com/2019/06/invitacion-iiee-para-visitar-la-casa.html.

UNESCO. 2015. "Wititi Dance of the Colca Valley." Intangible Cultural Heritage. https://ich.unesco.org/en/RL/wititi-dance-of-the-colca-valley-01056.

————. 2017. "Colca y volcanes de Andagua (Peru)." http://www.unesco.org/new/en/natural-sciences/environment/earth-sciences/unesco-global-geoparks/list-of-unesco-global-geoparks/peru/colca-y-volcanes-de-andagua/.

Urry, John. 1990. *The Tourist Gaze: Leisure and Travel in Contemporary Societies*. Thousand Oaks, CA: SAGE.

Valderrama Fernandez, Ricardo, and Carmen Escalante Gutierrez. 1987. "Distribución, manejo y uso del agua de riego en Yanque (Valle del Colca.)." In *Seminario sobre tecnologías tradicionales: Primera reunión de manejo de suelos y agua en la sociedad andina (Cieneguilla)*. Lima: Asociación Peruana para el Fomento de las Ciencias Sociales.

————. 1988. *Del tata mallku a la mama pacha: Riego, sociedad y ritos en los andes peruanos*. Lima: Desco. (Gerardo Huaracha Archive)

VanValkenburgh, Parker. 2017. "Unsettling Time: Persistence and Memory in Spanish Colonial Peru." *Journal of Archeological Method and Theory* 24: 117–48.

Vich, Víctor. 2007. "Magical, Mystical: 'The Royal Tour' of Alejandro Toledo." *Journal of Latin American Cultural Studies* 16 (1): 1–10.

Vilaça, Aparecida. 2010. *Strange Enemies: Indigenous Agency and Scenes of Encounters in Amazonia*. Durham, NC: Duke University Press.

Walsh-Dilley, Marygold. 2017. "Theorizing Reciprocity: Andean Cooperation and the Reproduction of Community in Highland Bolivia." *Journal of Latin American and Caribbean Anthropology* 22 (3): 514–35.

Warner, Michael. 2005. *Publics and Counterpublics*. New York: Zone Books.

Watts, Michael. 2004. "Resource Curse? Governmentality, Oil, and Power in the Niger Delta, Nigeria." *Geopolitics* 9 (1): 50–80.

Watts, Michael, and Nancy Peluso. 2014. "Resource Violence." In *Critical Environmental Politics*, ed. Carl Death, 184–97. London: Routledge.

Weismantel, Mary. 2001. *Cholas and Pishtacos: Stories of Race and Sex in the Andes*. Chicago: University of Chicago Press.

Weiss, Joseph. 2018. *Shaping the Future on Haida Gwaii: Life Beyond Settler Colonialism.* Vancouver: University of British Columbia Press.

Welker, Marina. 2012. "The Green Revolution's Ghost: Unruly Subjects of Participatory Development in Rural Indonesia." *American Ethnologist* 39 (2): 389–406.

———. 2014. *Enacting the Corporation: An American Mining Firm in Post-Authoritarian Indonesia.* Berkeley: University of California Press.

Wenzel, Jennifer. 2020. *The Disposition of Nature: Environmental Crisis and World Literature.* New York: Fordham University Press.

Wernke, Steven. 2007. "Negotiating Community and Landscape in the Peruvian Andes: A Transconquest View." *American Anthropologist* 109 (1): 130–52.

———. 2010. "A Reduced Landscape: Toward a Multi-Causal Understanding of Historic Period Agricultural Deintensification in Highland Peru." *Journal of Latin American Geography* 9 (3): 51–83.

———. 2013. *Negotiated Settlements: Andean Communities and Landscapes Under Inka and Spanish Colonialism.* Gainesville: University Press of Florida. (Gerardo Huaracha Archive)

West, Paige. 2016. *Dispossession and the Environment: Rhetoric and Inequality in Papua New Guinea.* New York: Columbia University Press.

Whyte, Kyle Powys. 2016. "Indigeneity." In *Keywords for Environmental Studies*, ed. Jodi Adamson, William A. Gleason, and David Pellow, 143–44. New York: NYU Press.

Williams, Raymond. 1977. *Marxism and Literature.* Oxford, UK: Oxford University Press.

Wilson, Shawn. 2008. *Research Is Ceremony: Indigenous Research Methods.* New York: Columbia University Press.

Wilson, Thomas. 2017. "Glencore Will Double Dividend, Restart Zinc as Metals Rally." *Bloomberg,* December 12. https://www.bloomberg.com/news/articles/2017-12-12/glencore-to-restart-some-zinc-mines-with-prices-near-decade-high.

World Bank. 2013. "OP 4.12—Involuntary Resettlement." World Bank Policy Paper. https://ppfdocuments.azureedge.net/1572.pdf.

Yanagisako, Sylvia. 2002. *Producing Culture and Capital: Family Firms in Italy.* Princeton, NJ: Princeton University Press.

Yashar, Deborah. 2005. *Contesting Citizenship in Latin America: The Rise of Indigenous Movements and the Postliberal Challenge.* Cambridge, UK: Cambridge University Press.

Zaloom, Caitlin. 2006. *Out of the Pits: Traders and Technology from Chicago to London.* Chicago: University of Chicago Press.

# Index

Note: Page numbers in *italic* type indicate illustrations.

CPSIA information can be obtained
at www.ICGtesting.com
Printed in the USA
JSHW041145100122
21886JS00002B/2

9 781503 630949